A Tale of Two Villains

Themes and Symbolism in Dracula

and the Harry Potter Saga

Calvin H. Cherry

A Tale of Two Villains

Themes and Symbolism in Dracula

and The Harry Potter Saga

GAUDIUM

Gaudium Publishing

Las Vegas ◊ Chicago ◊ Palm Beach

Published in the United States of America by
Histria Books
7181 N. Hualapai Way, Ste. 130-86
Las Vegas, NV 89166 U.S.A
HistriaBooks.com

Gaudium Publishing is an imprint of Histria Books. Titles published under the imprints of Histria Books are distributed worldwide.

This work is not associated with or endorsed by J.K. Rowling or Warner Brothers Pictures.

Library of Congress Control Number: 2022941220

ISBN 978-1-59211-167-1 (hardcover)
ISBN 978-1-59211-374-3 (softbound)
ISBN 978-1-59211-231-9 (eBook)

Contents

For my late grandfather, Lex Cherry, who was my
Van Helsing and my Albus Dumbledore

Introduction

Count Dracula. This name is known worldwide in every media format: literature, film, television, video games, comic books, food, and more. Indeed, just as author John Edgar Browning cleverly proves in his 2010 publication *Dracula in Visual Media*, the name has become part of our popular culture. Likewise, Bram Stoker, the remarkable man responsible for bringing the now immortal vampire to life, shows no sign of being staked anytime soon. Incredibly, his novel, *Dracula,* has never been out of print since its publication in 1897 and remains the biggest selling novel in the world next to that of the Holy Bible. Furthermore, the fan base is staggering and ranges from literary professors and academic scholars to children who love monsters to adults and individuals living as modern-day vampires. Having been portrayed more than any other character in modern film for 120 years, the King Vampire is the ultimate villain we love to hate.

Lord Voldemort. This name is also commonplace around the globe, and this monster has claimed his own stake in modern culture. From seven brilliant best-selling novels to eight blockbuster movies, since the Slytherin half-blood dark wizard came to life in 1997 (here it is interesting to note exactly 100 years after the publication of Dracula), as of 2020, the Harry Potter Saga has sucked in over 25 billion dollars and shows no sign of being buried. As I write, over 500 million copies of the Harry Potter books have been sold worldwide and translated into 80 languages. It is the best-selling series of all time, and from clothing to role-playing board and video games to amusement parks and food and beverage, the success of the Harry Potter saga has made the talented J.K. Rowling the first billionaire author. The unique fandom is made up of all ages of individuals who adore to loathe 'He-Who-Must-Not-Be-Named.'

And then there are those who are inspired by both. I am one of those, and this is why…

Part One

Characters

Chapter One

Count Dracula and Lord Voldemort

Throughout recorded history, society has demonstrated a fascination with heroes and villains. Indeed, it seems that in the womb, we are programmed to root for the good guy and dream of having their superhero traits. As a child, I gravitated toward the darker hero, Batman, wishing that I had his 'toys' — as Jack Nicholson amusingly called them in the 1988 film adaptation — which enabled him to fly. On the other hand, most of us have, at one time or another, fought a love-hate relationship with the rogue the hero was chasing. For me, this was the Joker. While Batman was cool and protected Gotham like a dark knight, I found the Prince of Crime far more interesting and colorful (quite literally and figuratively speaking) as so with the Prince of Darkness, Dracula.

While there is no doubt that Harry Potter is a hero that is almost impossible not to adore, the storyline would lack the adventure, crisis, and mystery we love if it was not for Lord Voldemort. While overlooking the blatantly obvious fact that both Dracula and Voldemort are pure evil incarnate, I think there are many interesting similarities worth bringing to the table as we psychoanalyze each protagonist. Let's start with the brute in the novel Dracula himself — a vampire, centuries old, with unique strengths, powers, and intellect. Right away, Professor Van Helsing tells the small group of intrepid hunters that Dracula is exceptionally physically strong, as in Chapter 19 when he recounts, "Remember he has the strength of twenty men." He describes himself to Jonathan Harker as a ruthless soldier and defender of his country, while his enemies refer to him as proud, 'clever as a fox,' and a threatening force not to be reckoned with. The Count uses these traits to his advantage while fighting fearlessly to enforce his dark vision on mankind.

In comparison, Lord Voldemort has the same character makeup. As a young student and man, he is an exceptionally brilliant and potent wizard. In fact, J.K. Rowling refers to him as one of the most powerful wizards to ever exist. However, as with Voivode Dracula, Voldemort begins using his strengths for evil, thus morphing into a monster. Using the whirling Pensieve in *The Order of the Phoenix*, Professor Dumbledore shows Harry Potter that he first met Tom Riddle at the orphanage where he was already using his newfound magical abilities to control and punish other children.

Even as a small boy, this control of his powers labels him as a prodigy. Indeed, the insightful professor likewise reveals to Harry that he finds the troubled lad so proficient in dark magic that he enters magical realms far unknown and beyond any wizard in history. In doing so, Voldemort discovers the ability to fly without a broom and cast new and powerful deadly curses at the sacrifice of his humanity.

Along with great physical strength, Count Dracula also has a unique ability to control others and read their thoughts. The numerous sleepwalking ventures of Lucy Westenra are a testament to his mind control, as Dracula time and time again visits her in the night, commands her to open the bedroom window, and unaware, trek up and down rough and dangerous terrain while barefoot, asleep, and half-naked. This unique gift is used for evil, ultimately leading to Lucy's demise. Furthermore, two-thirds into Stoker's novel, Van Helsing warns his younger colleague, Dr. Seward, and new friend Jonathan Harker that he is afraid that Mina Harker will put the team of vampire killers into mortal danger, exposing her thoughts and dreams to the monster's mind control. However, the reverse is revealed when Mina pleads to Van Helsing in Chapter 26 to be hypnotized at dusk and dawn to pry into the vampire's mind and obtain intelligence on his planned escape and whereabouts.

Similarly, we learn that Lord Voldemort is also an accomplished 'Legilimens,' thus able to see into almost anyone's mind. Indeed, the dark wizard uses this skill numerous times on Harry Potter and others to seek out information that will help him carry out his villainous scheme. For example, in *Harry Potter and the Chamber of Secrets*, Voldemort manipulates Ginny Weasley, first-year Hogwarts student and sister of Ronald Weasley, to open and begin using Tom Riddle's diary. Ginny finds and opens the long-rumored but undiscovered Chamber of Secrets, home to a basilisk that petrifies Argus Filch's cat, Mrs. Norris, and she writes several warnings in blood on the castle walls — all while in a sleepwalking trance. Like Lucy, Ginny wakes up with muddy feet, discovers traces of blood on her clothes, and experiences vague and troubled thoughts of nocturnal creeping.

It would be difficult to overlook how both monsters find their strength of influence early on in their dubious careers and thus use them at the expense of those around them. For example, as a curious Hogwarts student, Tom Riddle exerts his charisma and wiles to camouflage his shady and devious nature from all his teachers, excluding Albus Dumbledore. From getting Hagrid expelled to obtaining out-of-bounds dark magic facts from Professor Slughorn, time and time again, J.K. Rowling shows how Voldemort capitalizes exploiting his deceptive charm to take advantage of the weak and innocent. Despite his malice and viciousness, Voldemort's magnetism permits him to recruit a loyal following while promising benefits he seldom delivers. Consequently, the dark wizard becomes so powerful that his Death Eaters remain faithful primarily out of consternation, fearing they will be tormented or exterminated for the slightest slip-up. Like a roach motel, you can check in to the Dark Lord's service; however, there is no leaving it behind.

Count Dracula's characteristics are no different; however, in fact, we see his evil influence as early as Chapter Three in Stoker's novel when the vampire takes advantage of Jonathan Harker's desire to be promoted and convinces him to stay in the castle for a month. "– write to our friend and to any other; and say, if it will please you, that you shall stay with me until a month from now...." And when Harker questions why so long, Dracula responds, "I desire it much; nay, I will take no refusal." With this, Harker is held captive, pumped for information, and eventually abandoned to the three 'weird sisters' that are chomping at the bit for his jugular. Renfield, the other incarcerated soul, is promised countless lives for his service to the Count. Once more, Dracula takes advantage of the inmate's fragile mind to gain access to Dr. Seward's lunatic asylum and, ultimately, Mina Harker. The cunning vampire, however, lies to his loyal follower — leaving him also abandoned and to die after punishing him with a massive head injury and broken back.

As great authority is linked paradoxically with responsibility, excessive toughness is often associated with frailty. Thus, even though Count Dracula and Lord Voldemort emanate great strength, they also display parallel patterns with their weaknesses. There is a wonderful scene at Castle Dracula where Jonathan Harker recoils as he looks upon the bloodsucker in his full revelation, realizing that he is actually helping unleash this evil monster upon the city of London. Grabbing a nearby shovel and raising it above the creature's coffin to strike, Harker compares Dracula to a bloated leech. The fact is that the vampire needs others to survive. He needs a new life. He needs to regain power. And like a blood-thirsty leech, he must attach himself to individuals to control and manipulate them in order to help carry out his affairs. And those that he cannot use for his bidding simply become prey.

True fans of the Harry Potter series will likely balk at any comparison of Lord Voldemort to a leech. After all, the wizard is not undead by definition — at least, according to the vampiric lore we all are familiar with; therefore, no bloodsucking...no leech. However, I strongly suspect Professor Quirrell would disagree in Book One. On the author's Pottermore website, J.K. Rowling describes how the Dark Lord used the professor in *Harry Potter and the Philosopher's Stone*:

"While Quirrell did not lose his soul, he became completely subjugated by Voldemort, who caused a frightful mutation of Quirrell's body: now Voldemort looked out of the back of Quirrell's head and directed his movements, even forcing him to attempt murder. Quirrell tried to put up a feeble resistance on occasion, but Voldemort was far too strong for him."

Indeed, attaching himself to the nervous wizard, he sucks Quirrell's life source to live and grow until Voldemort is strong enough to rise again.

I believe both villains' main motivations are three-fold and appear in their respective texts in a particular order: to be reborn, to create an army, and to regain power. One can look at these goals as weaknesses, for without them, Dracula will waste away in his castle on the hill, and Voldemort will remain an embryo. It is clear at the beginning of Stoker's novel that Dracula's main desire is to move from Transylvania to London. He needs to be closer to modern society — new blood leads to a restored youth, yet as a vampire, his devices are limited: there are certain travel restrictions, and he must rest on his native Transylvanian soil. Dracula is determined to solve these dilemmas by buying an old property in London and filling it with Transylvanian dirt. The great population of the city will be the feast he lacks in the Carpathians, thus enabling him to grow stronger while converting the weak and turning the strong. However, doing so underestimates Van Helsing's knowledge and determination to chase the vampire back to Transylvania before ridding the world of him.

By the same token, Voldemort must also be carried across lands unnoticed and in secrecy and fed until he is strong enough to become more of a talking face on the back of another's head; in addition, others must sacrifice their lives or become members of his alliance to accomplish this malevolent strategy. His weakness of having to rely on others becomes his downfall when he is outsmarted by Harry Potter, the very same boy who brought him down the first time.

Still, if heroes were the only ones with supernatural powers, how dull such epic adventures would be for readers. Thank goodness Bram Stoker and J.K. Rowling were not stingy in dishing out their dosage of counter-hero powers when developing Count Dracula and Lord Voldemort's characters. In addition to the abilities previously discussed, Dracula can shapeshift into different forms, control the elements, and materialize at will. For instance, Dracula appears in Renfield's cell in the form of mist and brings fog around the harbor — an act which stalls the departure of the ship, Czarina Catherine, until the Count can get his earth-filled boxes onboard. And as the three weird sisters are about to attack Jonathan Harker, the vampire emerges out of nowhere 'lapped in a storm of fury.'

Comparably, throughout the Harry Potter series, we find Lord Voldemort appearing and disappearing out of a black fog. Likewise, the dark wizard has an impressive ability to create and manipulate fire, as demonstrated in the Battle of the Department of Mysteries and his duel with Dumbledore. In the same battle, Voldemort uses the ability of apparition frequently to silently appear and reappear at will to change his position and avoid spells cast by the headmaster of Hogwarts.

I find it also interesting how both authors capitalize on the adage 'appearance is everything' to exemplify the macabre facets of their narratives. For indeed, Bram Stoker immediately sets out to paint a bizarre, unsettling picture of a vampire so revolting that it almost compels guest Jonathan Harker to vomit;

"his face was a strong — a very strong — aquiline, with high bridge of the thin nose and peculiarly arched nostrils; with lofty domed forehead,"

Jonathan describes in his journal.

"The mouth…was fixed and rather cruel-looking, with peculiarly sharp white teeth; these protruded over the lips, whose remarkable ruddiness showed astonishing vitality in a man of his years. For the rest, his ears were pale and at the tops extremely pointed; the chin was broad and strong, and the cheeks firm though thin. The general effect was one of extraordinary pallor."

The Count's physical characteristics and appearance are further described by countless others as being a tall, pale, thin man clad all in black, with livid eyes which glowed red in color. In comparison, J.K. Rowling describes He-Who-Must-Not-be-Named in this way:

"tall and skeletally thin," with a face "whiter than a skull, with wide, livid scarlet eyes…, his hands were like large, pale spiders; his long white fingers caressed his own chest, his arms, his face; the red eyes, like a cat's, gleamed still more brightly through the darkness."

As Stoker's book progresses and Dracula devours more victims, his appearance begins to grow younger. We see this play out brilliantly on a busy street in London's West End when Jonathan collapses into his wife's arms while realizing Piccadilly's new voyeur is none other than the Count himself. Not only did he realize that his nightmares were real, but he testified to Mina that the monster's youth had been completely restored. Both Count Dracula and Lord Voldemort are born human and grow into respectable young men with great intellect and leadership abilities, but they also choose a life path of corruption, thus turning themselves into heinous monstrosities. The fascinating difference between their 'rebirths' is that while Dracula grows younger as he continues to feed, in contrast, Lord Voldemort is reborn in the literal sense, regaining his body in the physical form. This transformation finally occurs in *Harry Potter and the Goblet of Fire*:

> "It was as though Wormtail had flipped over a stone, and revealed something ugly, slimy and blind — but worse, a hundred times worse. The thing Wormtail had been carrying had the shape of a crouched human child, except that Harry had never seen anything less like a child. It was hairless and scaly looking, a dark, raw, reddish black. Its arms and legs were thin and feeble, and its face — no child alive ever had a face like that — was flat and snake-like, with gleaming red eyes."

Despite these different methods of recapturing youth, the end result is symbolically the same: restored youth equals returned power. However, this newfound sway is carried out by terror instead of assurance — a theme that steadily builds throughout both works. As previously discussed, both Count Dracula and Lord Voldemort used fear to control their followers. Although most believe it is how the characters choose to respond to this horror that ultimately decides the path of either life or death — silence becomes synonymous with fear in both hair-raising plots.

In Stoker's novel, one by one, each character experiences macabre sights and sounds which ultimately drive him to his journals in a vague fear that spirals into unbridled terror. For example, Jonathan Harker begins to question his sanity, while Mina rationally invents excuses for Lucy's odd behavior. Dr. Seward looks to his intellect for answers, while Lucy insists on keeping her ill health private out of her Victorian lady-like trait of not wanting to cause trouble for others. It is worth mentioning that secrecy does kill, for it is not until one-third into the novel before diaries are shared for analysis and answers. And more importantly, it is critical to point out that the word 'vampire' is not even mentioned in *Dracula* until a staggering halfway through the book! Ultimately, it is the sole, open-minded Van Helsing who ever-so-slowly brings Dr. Seward around to this conclusion, only to be rebutted by his former pupil in utter disbelief. Regardless of whether it is skepticism, pride, or selflessness, it is clear that when fear drives us to silence, we will be awakened by screams in time.

This same concept holds true in the Harry Potter novels. Without a doubt, Cornelius Fudge's rejection of Harry's testimony and denial of Voldemort's rise — coupled with his refusal of Dumbledore's advice — results in social division, confusion, and eventually, death. Disbelief brings discord, and failure to take Professor Moody's 'constant vigilance' mantra to heart delivers danger. One only needs to look at the character of bullying Slytherin pupil Draco Malfoy for proof. Throughout the series, he's callous and unpleasant, and in time we learn of an internal struggle taking place within his mind and soul: his heart does not fully belong to the Dark Lord. Draco keeps this dilemma secret from audiences and lets his jealousy and prejudice overcome his very being. By the time Draco realizes Harry's accounts of the return of Voldemort are true — and not a narcissistic fabrication to bolster his own ego — his silence, prompted by fear, puts his own morality in jeopardy. Indeed, by Book Seven, Malfoy's father Lucius is being punished by Voldemort, and Draco's mother fears for her son's life. However, as all three of them silently disagree with the Dark Lord's plan, Draco reluctantly becomes a Death Eater alongside his parents, and their plight becomes dire when 'He-Who-Must-Not-be-Named' chooses Draco to murder the beloved head-master. It is positively evident that, like Dracula, the Dark Wizard massages the hushed fear of the weak to drive his devious agenda.

Fear. It is a powerful word and an unpleasant emotion that can transport us to a crossroads of ethical ambiguity. Do I choose the righteous road or the dark path? Im-agine, for example, a terminally ill individual reaching out to everyone they might have hurt to make amends and give their inheritance away to people in need. Yet another sick person could choose to abandon their moral compass, living their last days outside of the law. Indeed, fearing what we know is often at the root of many psychological behaviors; however, on the other hand, one could argue that perhaps we are more afraid of what we don't know. After all, is it not our human instinct to naturally shy away from the unknown, the unexplained, or the unseen?

In each of their masterpieces, Stoker and Rowling capitalize upon this the powerful use of 'absence' to invoke fear. Consider the fact that Dracula is referenced throughout the novel, but the physical presence of the character himself is limited to only a few pages. The dramatic effect the writer creates by hiding the central character in the shadows for most of the novel is one of mystery, doom, and terror. Stoker's stylistic choice here is strategic and adds a foreboding atmosphere of the supernatural, making readers uneasy and horrified.

Undeniably, J.K. Rowling employs the same technique throughout the entire Harry Potter series. To illustrate this point (not including when the Dark Lord kills Harry's parents), we can only count six occurrences when Harry comes face to face with Lord Voldemort! This number is staggeringly diminutive, considering all seven books total 4,224 pages! At the end of *The Philosopher's Stone*, Harry first encounters Voldemort in the back of Professor Quirrell's head. Then, in *The Chamber of Secrets*, he comes face to face with Voldemort in the form of Tom Riddle. At the end of the third task in Book Four, Harry battles Voldemort as he is reborn, and as *The Order of the Phoenix* concludes, Harry watches Professor Dumbledore fight the Dark Lord in the Ministry of Magic. Finally, in Book Seven, *The Deathly Hallows*, Harry encounters

Voldemort on two occasions: at the beginning of the book, as he and Hagrid flee the Dursleys on a motorcycle to go into hiding, and at the end in the final fight at Hogwarts. An even more startling find is that Harry does not encounter Voldemort in Books 3 and 6 at all — *The Prisoner of Azkaban* and *The Half-Blood Prince*. Indeed, these few reserved pages in the entire seven-book series testify that, in this case, absence makes the heart grow colder.

Chapter Two

Jonathan Harker and Harry Potter

Imagine if personal advertisements existed in Britain in the late 1800s. Now ponder for a minute how such an announcement might have read for Bram Stoker's character Jonathan Harker in his novel *Dracula*. It would read like the following: "Inquiring the availability of a young, innately honorable and well-respected English gentleman — soft-spoken yet valiant; professional and exceptionally astute; loyal and full of aspirations and vigor."

Now flash forward exactly one hundred years and think about how a similar entry in the classifieds would read for J.K. Rowling's 'Boy who lived.' "ISO brave, noble, SWM — daring but humble. British replies only." Both descriptions beg the question: Are the two really that much different? If Jonathan Harker had put on the Hogwarts sorting hat when he was eleven, he would have ended up in the Gryffindor house, sitting right next to Harry Potter, Ron Weasley, and Hermione Granger. In fact, this author boldly argues that Harker is Harry's brother from another 'muggle' mother, for both their epic adventures start with an unforeseen voyage.

At the opening of *Dracula*, Jonathan Harker is en route to Count Dracula's castle in Transylvania. As the story unfolds, readers learn that it is actually Harker's boss, Peter Hawkins, who was initially expected to make the trip; however, Hawkins suddenly becomes ill, and Harker is sent as a last-minute replacement. Many literary critics note that Jonathan is ill-prepared and inexperienced to take on such a challenging assignment from the demanding Count. He is also preoccupied with other business. The young solicitor — a lad who just previously passed the bar exam — is in the midst of trying to find his place in life with his recently engaged fiancée, Wilhelmina Murray.

Comparably, the beginning of *Harry Potter and the Philosopher's Stone* finds an eleven-year-old Harry Potter traveling to Hogwarts Castle. Rowling establishes this supernatural setting as a second home and an escape from Harry's domestic dwelling of unsolicited horror. Just as Jonathan Harker does not expect such an opportunity to come his way, so is Potter taken aback by the arrival of an 'owl post.' Harry is especially disadvantaged on his archetypal journey of starting school because he does not even know he is a wizard. In fact, he is a step below being green or ill-equipped: Potter does not even know who he is or anything about his noble lineage. His aunt and uncle have lied to him for the first decade of his life.

However, Harry Potter is not the only young hero to endure deception. At the beginning of Chapter Two of *Dracula*, Jonathan Harker arrives at the Count's castle only to realize the place is a prison. In the last sentence of this segment of the novel, the solicitor exclaims, "The castle is a veritable prison, and I am a prisoner!" Quickly, the vampire begins to fabricate and explain away deceptive reasons for Harker's unwanted entrapment, although Dracula's motives are clearly communicated in Chapter Four when he insists that his guest be on his way. He falsely states, "Not an hour shall you wait in my house against your will [...] Come!" Nonetheless, the angry howling pack of hungry wolves waiting on the other side of the front door tells the grim reality.

Sadly, 'The Boy Who Lived' does not fare much better under Rowling's control. *The Philosopher's Stone* opens with eleven-year-old Harry living in the 'cupboard under the stairs,' where his closest companions are darkness and spiders. The Dursleys' mistreatment of Harry keeps him confined there most of the time, and the family goes to great lengths to cut him off from the world. They place steel bars on the windows and confiscate Harry's mail, making the fledgling sorcerer believe he is a nobody whose worthless parents died in a car crash. In sum, Harry is bullied.

The Merriam-Webster Dictionary defines the word 'bully' as "one who is habitually cruel, insulting, or threatening to others who are weaker, smaller, or in some way vulnerable." Without a doubt, Bram Stoker's Count Dracula is also a bully with a capital B. From his callousness in leaving Jonathan Harker in the castle to die to donning his victim's garb in an attempt to frame him for his own heinous crimes, the Count will do anything to vanquish his challenger. Stoker wonderfully piles on the vampire's dirty deeds at Castle Dracula so that readers gradually distrust the Count and, in turn, feel sorry for Harker and root for revenge.

Facing up to one bully is bad enough for Jonathan Harker as an adult. However, young Harry Potter has four to deal with — and sometimes all at once: Aunt Petunia, Uncle Vernon, Cousin Dudley, and Aunt Marge. Like her predecessor, J.K. Rowling creates a cast of antagonists so unlikeable that readers cannot help but fall in love with the young wizard straight away and quickly want to come to his aid. For example, take this sad — but slightly humorous — scene at the beginning of Book Four: *The Goblet of Fire*:

"Uncle Vernon rounded on Harry. "And you?"

"I'll be in my bedroom, making no noise and pretending I'm not there," said Harry tonelessly.

"Exactly," said Uncle Vernon nastily.

Such aggression does not last long, though, for Harry's presence becomes quickly known by everyone, and the Dursley dinner engagement is cut short as a result! Indeed, Harry gets to retaliate by sidesplittingly hysterical means, and the bullying subsides for a moment.

Despite being held captive by an oppressor, being brave, is quite a task. However, Jonathan Harker eventually finds out the truth, and this provides just the amount of nerve to step out on a ledge (both figuratively and literally!) and escape Dracula's Castle and the three predators the Count left waiting to devour him. Equally, Harry Potter learns the facts from half-giant Hagrid, and this confidence delivers the courage he needs to leave the three oppressors back at Number 4, Privet Drive.

Even though the protagonists gain freedom, the past still haunts them. Indeed, in Chapter 8 of Stoker's novel, Sister Agatha explains in a letter addressed to Mina that Jonathan Harker suffers from a "fearful shock" and "in his delirium, his ravings have been dreadful; of wolves and poison and blood; of ghosts and demons." Similarly, Harry Potter begins to hear his mother's death scream; he sits in front of the Mirror of Erised to visit with his parents, and eventually, the nightmares of Voldemort, his plans, and his murders begin to affect the young wizard profoundly. In *The Philosopher's Stone*, Professor Dumbledore warns Harry before taking the Mirror of Erised away, "It does not do to dwell on dreams and forget to live, remember that."

In *Dracula* and the Harry Potter series, both heroes must take a 'time out' to recover from their ordeals and even go so far as to question their own sanity as a result of their encounters with the fantastic. For example, after Jonathan Harker escapes Castle Dracula, he is found wandering around Buda-Pest, raving wildly, and is admitted into the Hospital of St. Joseph and St. Mary, a sanatorium, where he remains for several weeks until his 'brain fever' subsides. However, it is not until Professor Van Helsing's meeting with him and Mina that the attorney truly feels validated: "I was ill, I have had a shock; but you have cured me already," Harker states to Van Helsing in Chapter 14. "I was in doubt, and then everything took a hue of unreality, and I did not know what to trust, even the evidence of my own senses." Even Mina writes in her diary that she would not have believed her husband's written account of his adventure in Transylvania if it were not for Van Helsing testifying to its validity.

The ability to share outlandish claims to those closest to you without the fear of rejection is a privilege Harry Potter also experiences. In *The Chamber of Secrets*, the innocent but overtly wise Hermione Granger provides audiences with one of the most notable quotes in the entire Harry Potter series. Harry is hearing the castle walls call his name — to which she cleverly replies: "Hearing voices no one else can hear isn't a good sign, even in the wizarding world." Unbeknownst to Harry, he has the dubious gift of being parseltongue or able to communicate with snakes. This causes Harry to question not only the soundness of his own morality but also the very thing that he perceived as defining who and what he was. He seems to contend with varying voices of different persuasions, making him question himself and his own history. Still, voices are not the extent of his troubles. There are occasions in the last few books of the series where Harry begins to not only tap into the same sensory experiences as Voldemort but to feel them as well, thus, beginning to question his sudden bursts of controlled anger and violence toward Dumbledore and others that he loves. Once He-Who-Must-Not-be-Named rises at the end of *The Goblet of Fire*, only the headmaster believes Harry's story. Danger abounds, and as a result, Harry is continuously in the hospital wing due to injuries or severe emotional upset. Indeed, Harry would have benefitted from a conversation with Jonathan Harker about 'brain fever' and vice versa.

Another common link between the two heroes centers on how they face their first encounter with the enemy alone. In *Dracula*, Harker ventures down to the crypt at the end of Chapter Four unaided.

"There was no lethal weapon at hand, but I seized a shovel which the workmen had been using to fill the cases, and lifting it high struck, with the edge downward, at the hateful face. But as I did so, the head turned, and the eyes fell full upon me, with all their blaze of basilisk horror."

However, this daringly brave attempt to rid the world of the evil Count is prematurely unsuccessful. The shovel signals to the vampire that the young attorney means business, and it will not be the last time the two battle.

Essentially, the same concept is played out at the end of *Harry Potter and the Philosopher's Stone*. Harry makes his way down to the bowels of the castle and finds himself facing Lord Voldemort without a weapon.

"He saw his reflection, pale and scared-looking at first. But a moment later, the reflection smiled at him. It put its hand into its pocket and pulled out a blood-red stone. It winked and put the Stone back in its pocket — and as it did so, Harry felt something heavy drop into his real pocket. Somehow — incredibly — he'd got the Stone."

The stone fails to be the means to the Dark Lord's end, but as with Harker, this audacious effort confronting He-Who-Must-Not-be-Named is proof that the eleven-year-old will not avoid the prophecy. This, too, will not be the last time the wizards clash.

The adage that there is power in numbers is true in literature, especially when battling monsters. Indeed, Harker and Potter are not left alone for future combat. They have help from others. In Chapter 18 of *Dracula*, Professor Van Helsing requests a meeting to discuss the Count. Mina Harker's journal of September 30 reads:

> "The Professor stood up and, after laying his golden crucifix on the table, held out his hand on either side. I took his right hand, and Lord Godalming his left; Jonathan held my right with his left and stretched across to Mr. Morris. So, as we all took hands, our solemn compact was made."

The intrepid group then spends the remainder of the novel closing in on the vampire, and each character plays an important role in the beast's demise.

The same holds true for Harry Potter. In *The Order of the Phoenix*, Harry, Hermione, and Ron hold a secret meeting at the Hog's Head pub where twenty-eight members sign a membership list forming 'Dumbledore's Army,' or D.A. for short. Harry encourages them by saying, "Every great wizard in history has started out as nothing more than what we are now: students. If they can do it, why not us?" Just as Van Helsing is the teacher of Dracula's hunters, Hermione persuades Harry to give practical defense lessons to the members of their secret organization when she says, "Harry, don't you see? This… this is exactly why we need you… We need to know what it's really like… facing him… facing V-Voldemort."

Even though Jonathan Harker and Harry Potter have the support and aid of others to fight the evil in their respective worlds, each man has to sacrifice along the way. Jonathan Harker experiences time away from his fiancée — not only when he is being held prisoner in Castle Dracula, but often during the outings initiated by Van Helsing. Harker suffers a mental breakdown, and by the conclusion of the novel, the stress of the quest takes its toll on his physical state as well. If one were to track all the deviations that take place in Jonathan's character from Chapter One through the end of the novel, the sacrifices are staggering: Harker gradually becomes increasingly similar to the one he is hunting. His eagerness to kill, his greying hair, and his fondness for his knife — coupled with his fixation on keeping it sharpened — makes him a kindred spirit of his undead tormentor. Harker's preoccupation with Dracula parallels the vampire's own obsession with Harker's wife, Mina. Jonathan's strength and hatred surge by the novel's end as he morphs from a discreet, professional, peaceful gentleman to the polar opposite. Stoker skillfully shows glimpses of this in the descriptions of the Count and the attorney in the conflict in London as the group is sanitizing the vampire's lairs.

The premature graying of Jonathan's hair is only one element in this pattern of sacrificing his lighter character to that of the darker Count. His warrior-like change is evident in the final battle as the group races from the sun:

> "[...] as Jonathan, with desperate energy, attacked one end of the chest, attempting to prize off the lid with his great Kukri knife, he [Morris] attacked the other frantically with his bowie," described Mina in her journal. "But on the instant, came the sweep and flash of Jonathan's great knife. I shrieked as I saw it shear through the throat...."

This is an indication of the attorney's corruption through his interaction with Dracula, the three women, and even Mina after she is infected by the vampire. Though Mina develops and maintains mental connections with the Count, Jonathan develops and maintains physical connections. Harker's recent bond of marriage to Mina is what keeps him from being completely overtaken by the vampire's influences — love is the one sacrifice Jonathan refuses to surrender.

Along with incredible bravery and supportive friends, the two tales also have counsellorship in common. Most of us are drawn to larger-than-life ventures where some mentoring is taking place. Think of Luke Skywalker consulting with Obi-Wan Kanobi in *Star Wars — A New Hope*; or Hobbit Bilbo Baggins taking advice from the wise wizard Gandalf the White. Both Dracula and the Harry Potter series have this formula in common, and the use of it makes the stories more enjoyable.

Indeed, Jonathan Harker not only looks to Professor Abraham Van Helsing for confirmation that his horrors in Transylvania are real, but he requires his expert knowledge to identify what killed Lucy Westenra, to keep his wife Mina safe, and to utilize his abilities to lead the effort to trap and ultimately kill Dracula. Nevertheless, Jonathan Harker has complete confidence in his elder as reflected in his diary of September 26 —

"Look here, sir," I said, "does what you have to do concern the Count?"

"It does," he said solemnly.

"Then I am with you heart and soul."

When one is in the dark, having a trusted guru to assist in the transition to light can be a game-changer. Fortunately, Harry Potter has a similar kind of experience: he retains the great ear, sound advice, and humble service of the most respected, wise, and powerful wizard of the day to fall back on in times of trouble at Hogwarts. From a look in the Pensieve to show an important but tampered memory of Professor Slughorn to taking Harry to a hidden lake in a reclusive cave to search for a Horcrux, the headmaster's counsel is always encouraging and sound — although sometimes slightly enigmatic with a dash of humor (i.e., the room of requirement turning into a room of chamber pots when the headmaster has to go to the bathroom). Harry's devotion to his ultimate teacher is illustrated movingly in *The Order of the Phoenix* when the young wizard is telling his elder that Rufus Scrimgeour, the new Minister of Magic, is prowling for information. Naturally, Harry refuses to tell him anything.

"He accused me of being Dumbledore's man through and through."

"How very rude of him."

"I told him I was."

Dumbledore opened his mouth to speak and then closed it again. Fawkes, the Phoenix, let out a low, soft, musical cry. To Harry's intense embarrassment, he suddenly realized that Dumbledore's bright blue eyes looked rather watery and stared hastily at his own knee. When Dumbledore spoke, however, his voice was quite steady.

"I am very touched, Harry."

Love has, is, and always will be, the ultimate, powerful emotion, gift, blessing, and purpose. Jonathan Harker and Harry Potter are driven by love to act. Their motivation is to step out of their comfort zone and boldly act when danger closes in on them.

Harker, the young attorney, loves God, his wife Mina, and his employer Peter Hawkins dearly, and many of his diary entries at Castle Dracula communicate this sentiment. For example, when Harker discovers a possible escape route from the castle, he writes on June 25 —

"God help me in my task! Good-bye, Mina, if I fail; good-bye, my faithful friend and second father; good-bye, all, and last of all Mina!"

And on October 5, as the group is planning their hunt for the Count, it is the thought of bringing happiness back into Mina's life that keeps him focused and on task. He pens, "How strange it all is. I sat watching Mina's happy sleep and came as near to being happy myself as I suppose I shall ever be."

Equally, Harry's utmost strength is his inordinate capability to love, regardless of his neglect as a child and mistreatment by others. Harry, time and time again, demonstrates an incredible capacity to be fiercely devoted to and defensive of his loved ones. Hermione refers to it as a 'saving-people-thing,' while his friends think him naive for allowing Wormtail to live after discovering it was he who ratted his parents out to the Dark Lord and not Sirius Black. Indeed, the love that was passed down from his mother protected Harry and allowed him to overcome Voldemort.

"Your mother died to save you. If there is one thing Voldemort cannot understand, it is love," Albus Dumbledore explains to Harry Potter at the end of *The*

Philosopher's Stone: "He didn't realize that love as powerful as your mother's for you leaves its own mark. Not a scar, no visible sign… to have been loved so deeply, even though the person who loved us is gone, will give us some protection forever. It is in your very skin. Quirrell, full of hatred, greed, and ambition, sharing his soul with Voldemort, could not touch you for this reason. It was agony to touch a person marked by something so good."

Just as love and loss are often paired in life, both heroes share in experiencing the death of others as they pursue the greater good. Though the loss of Peter Hawkins is never tied back to the Count, this death kicks off the sequence of other fatalities that are contributed to the vampire: Mrs. Westenra, Lucy Westenra, and Quincey Morris. Mina is almost taken from him too, but the transition to vampire reverses itself once Harker practically decapitates Dracula at the conclusion of the novel.

Harry Potter's loss of friends and family is a more extensive list because they span seven books. One fan counted up 76 deaths across the series. The most significant for Harry include the following: his parents, James and Lily Potter, Godfather Sirius Black, friend and fellow student Cedric Diggory; mentor, headmaster and friend, Albus Dumbledore, Harry's pet snowy owl, Hedwig, friend, teacher, and Order member Alastor 'Mad-Eye' Moody; friend and house-elf Dobby, Ron's brother Fred Wesley, friend, teacher and Order member Remus Lupin; and teacher Professor Severus Snape.

Harker's character plans to get ahead by doing the right thing. Readers of Bram Stoker's *Dracula* admire Johnathan because he is brave and becomes a hero in the end. While he might appear to others as reserved and very ordinary on the outside, on the inside, however, he is quite the contrary. Upon learning of Harker's trip to the Count's tomb—not once but twice even—Van Helsing tells the solicitor's newlywed Mina,

"He is a noble fellow, and let me tell you from experience of men, that one who would do as he did in going down that wall and to that room—ay, and going a second time—is not one to be injured in permanence by a shock. His brain and his heart are all right; this I swear before I have even seen him; so be at rest."

Ultimately, Harry Potter is also a male figure trying to find his place in life while pursuing the right thing. J.K. Rowling's character grows up in the series, causing readers to feel like the 'Boy who Lived' is family. Harry is admired because the underdog is victorious in his own right, and he possesses something unique. Albus Dumbledore describes it best in *The Order of the Phoenix* when he addresses Harry by saying:

"There is a room in the Department of Mysteries that is kept locked at all times. It contains a force that is at once more wonderful and more terrible than death, than human intelligence, than the forces of nature. It is also, perhaps, the most mysterious of the many subjects for study that reside there. It is the power held within that room that you possess in such quantities and which Voldemort has not at all."

Both protagonists prove that in the end, love always wins.

Chapter Three

Professor Abraham Van Helsing and

Professor Albus Percival Wulfric Brian Dumbledore

Let's begin with the obvious: both of these guys are aged professors. Their higher learning level might be considered a little 'over the top' for the laymen of the world. Case in point: Van Helsing is introduced to the readers of *Dracula* by Dr. John (Jack) Seward via a letter. The response Seward receives reads as such: LETTER FROM ABRAHAM VAN HELSING, M.D., D.Ph., D.Lit., Etc., Etc. It seems that even Van Helsing himself is too busy to list his extensive list of degrees and reduces them to a few etceteras to hurry up with the meat of his correspondence. Aside from holding advanced degrees in medicine, philosophy, and literature, our vampire hunter also holds a law certificate. At the beginning of Chapter 13, Dr. Seward's diary goes into a conversation he and the professor had while deciding what to do with Lucy Westenra's private papers: "Van Helsing and I took it upon ourselves to examine papers, etc. He insisted upon looking at Lucy's papers himself. I asked him why, for I feared that he, being a foreigner, might not quite be aware of English legal requirements, and so might in ignorance make some unnecessary trouble. He answered me:

"I know, I know. You forget that I am a lawyer as well as a doctor."

It is slightly amusing that even the doctor's 'favorite pupil' overlooks the varying magnitude of his mentor's education.

Dumbledore's obituary begins as a resume: Professor Albus Percival Wulfric Brian Dumbledore, O.M. (First Class), Grand Sorc., D. Wiz., X.J. (sorc.), S. of Mag. Q. (c. Summer, 1881 — June 30 1997) was the Transfiguration Professor, and later headmaster of Hogwarts School of Witchcraft and Wizardry. Professor Dumbledore also served as Supreme Mugwump of the International Confederation of Wizards (?–1995) and Chief Warlock of the Wizengamot (?-1995; 1996-1997). Careful readers should stop and ponder an important circumstance here, for while both these men were so incredibly loved and admired by others, they were alone. We know that Van Helsing had a son that died suddenly at a young age, and unable to cope with this loss, his wife went insane and was admitted into a mental institution. Even though the professor remained married to her under the rules of the Catholic church, he dedicated his time to his many books, a wide range of studies and interests, and his oath as a doctor to make others well. In one of the most moving speeches in *Dracula*, he explains to Arthur Holmwood (then Lord Godalming):

> "My Lord Godalming, I too, have a duty to do, a duty to others, a duty to you, a duty to the dead; and, by God, I shall do it! [...] Just think. For why should I give myself so much of labour and so much of sorrow? I have come here from my own land to do what I can of good; at the first to please my friend John, and then to help a sweet young lady, whom, too, I came to love. For her—I am ashamed to say so much, but I say it in kindness—I gave what you gave: the blood of my veins; I gave it, I, who was not, like you, her lover, but only her physician and her friend. I gave to her my nights and days—before death, after death; and if my death can do her good even now when she is the dead undead, she shall have it freely."

In early interviews, J.K. Rowling described her beloved Albus Dumbledore in similar terms. She notes that he is "the epitome of goodness" who leads a "celibate and bookish life." Indeed, his office at Hogwarts is full of books on vast subjects. He never marries, and he spends the majority of his one-hundred-plus years providing service to others. We learn that he turns down several offers over the years to become Minister of Magic mainly because he feels his greatest talents are in leading the school and shaping young minds. In the advanced stages of the Potter series, he tells Harry, "I had proven, as a very young man, that power was my weakness and temptation. I was safer at Hogwarts. I think I was a good teacher."

"You were the best!" responded Harry.

Dumbledore was not the only bookworm and teacher in literature. Regardless of the topic of conversation, Abraham Van Helsing seems to know the answer.

From ancient superstition and foreign languages to the science of blood transfusions to religious studies to the art of growing garlic, he is the subject matter expert on practically everything. In Chapter 14 of *Dracula*, Van Helsing is having a conversation with Dr. Seward, which jumps topics — from corporeal transference, materialization, and astral bodies to hypnotism, stories of men and women who cannot die, and countless examples of nature's eccentricities. Seward becomes so overwhelmed by the information that he stops the professor by saying,

> "Professor, let me be your pet student again. Tell me the thesis so that I may apply your knowledge as you go on. At present, I am going in my mind from

point to point as a madman, and not a sane one, follows an idea. I feel like a novice lumbering through a bog in a mist jumping from one tussock to another in the mere blind effort to move on without knowing where I am going."

To which Van Helsing replied, "That is a good image," he said. "Well, I shall tell you. My thesis is this: I want you to believe."

Professor Dumbledore possesses a wide range of knowledge; in fact, his head is so overloaded with thoughts on such a wide diversity of topics that he often has to suck them out through his temple and place them in a Pensieve for future reference and study. Throughout the series, we learn of his wide-ranging passions ranging from occlumency, alchemy, and sherbet lemons to dragons, the Deathly Hallows, and raspberry marmalade.

Many intellectual giants are often labeled as being eccentric, and the byproduct of this trait is usually a taste of offbeat humor. However, these characters never let their incredible wisdom and dire duties get in the way of their quirkiness and quick wit.

Because Van Helsing and Dumbledore are kindred spirits, their words often intersect. For example, when Van Helsing is taking several pages to explain to Dr. Seward that Miss Lucy made the bite marks found on the 'Bloofer Lady's' victims, his response is, "Dr. Van Helsing, are you mad?" And one must not forget that upon seeing Albus Dumbledore for the first time in *The Philosopher's Stone*, the conversation between Harry and Percy Weasley happens like this:

Albus Dumbledore: "Welcome! Welcome to a new year at Hogwarts! Before we begin our banquet, I would like to say a few words. And here they are: Nitwit! Blubber! Oddment! Tweak! Thank you!"

Harry Potter: "Is he — a bit mad?"

Percy Weasley: "Mad? He's a genius! Best wizard in the world! But he is a bit mad, yes."

The two professors' similar personalities can also be reflected in their quirky satire and candor. For example, after spending half the book slowly and carefully explaining that vampires *do* exist and that Miss Lucy became one, Dr. Seward struggles with his answer by saying,

"Do not press me too hard all at once. [...] How will you do this bloody work?"

To which the professor abruptly replies: "I shall cut off her head and fill her mouth with garlic, and I shall drive a stake through her body."

A similar, yet much less horrific reaction occurs between Harry and Dumbledore in *The Philosopher's Stone* when the professor finds the young wizard sitting in front of the Mirror of Erised.

"Sir, Professor Dumbledore? Can I ask you something?"

'Obviously, you have just done so' Dumbledore smiled. 'You can ask me one more thing, however.'

'What do you see when you look in the mirror?'

'I? I see myself holding a pair of thick woolen socks.'

Harry stared.

'One can never have enough socks,' said Dumbledore. 'Another Christmas has come and gone, and I didn't get a single pair. People will insist on giving me books."

Another example of Dumbledore's oddness occurs when he shows up at a reception wearing a flowered patch bonnet, and he reads muggle magazines because he is "fond of knitting patterns." Perhaps the most treasured Dumbledore-ism is offered when the professor is talking to Harry about his scar. He explains, "scars can come in handy. I have one myself above my left knee that is a perfect map of the London Underground."

Though Van Helsing does not wear a lady's hat, his behavior is certainly bizarre in certain situations. For example, when the group of men is at Lucy's tomb, Dr. Seward describes the professor's actions in his diary in Chapter 16:

"He crumbled the wafer up fine and worked it into the mass between his hands. This he then took, and rolling it into thin strips, began to lay them into the crevices between the door and its setting in the tomb. I was somewhat puzzled at this and, being close, asked him what it was that he was doing. Arthur and Quincey drew near also, as they too were curious. He answered:

"I am closing the tomb, so that the undead may not enter."

"And is that stuff you have put there going to do it?" asked Quincey. "Great Scott! Is this a game?"

"It is."

"What is that which you are using?" This time the question was by Arthur. Van Helsing reverently lifted his hat as he answered: "The Host. I brought it from Amsterdam. I have an Indulgence."

Part of Stoker's and Rowling's genius lies in the fact that they allow their mentor archetypes to scatter clues about shrouded truth and explanations throughout their narratives. Even the most skilled readers will often overlook these thematic bread-crumbs and find themselves rereading to connect the dots.

A great example of this is the professor's very first visit with Lucy. In Dr. Seward's diary dated September 3, Van Helsing tells his former pupil,

> "I have asked her to send me her maid, that I may ask just one or two questions, that so I may not chance to miss nothing. I know well what she will say. And yet there is a cause; there is always a cause for everything."

We do not know exactly what questions Van Helsing is going to ask Lucy's servant; however, after revisiting this section several times, it becomes evident that the professor knows straight away the reason for the loss of blood. Another example of the professor's gift of intuitiveness is his eccentric behavior displayed after Lucy's funeral. On the carriage drive back with Dr. Seward, Van Helsing 'gave way to a regular fit of hysterics' by laughing uncontrollably and then unexpectedly switched to crying — and then laughing and crying together 'as a woman does,' described Seward, who considered his friend's actions were an inappropriate 'joke.'

> "Friend John, forgive me if I pain, I showed not my feelings to others when it would wound, but only to you, my old friend, whom I can trust. If you could have looked into my heart then when I want to laugh; if you could have done so when the laugh arrived; if you could do so now, when King Laugh has packed up his crown and all that is to him—for he go far, far away from me, and for a long, long time—maybe you would perhaps pity me the most of all."

> "I [Dr. Seward] was touched by the tenderness of his tone and asked why.'

> "Because I know!"

Professor Dumbledore and Van Helsing have to spoon-feed the individuals they interact with and reveal supernatural facts because the truth is too fantastical for their counterparts to swallow at once. Indeed, both men drop hints for audiences and characters alike to foreshadow upcoming plot twists and gradually expose the thematic boon.

In *The Philosopher's Stone*, Harry has only experienced death with the passing of his parents. Of course, he is too young to remember these events; however, recurring dreams and visions eventually begin to torment him, bringing to life Voldemort's vicious attack on his family. At the beginning of the series, Harry is only eleven; yet the undertaking he is about to embark upon in the next seven years is more than what one hundred adults could face in a combined lifetime — even in the magical world! From the outset, Dumbledore knew this unreservedly.

In Book One, Dumbledore makes this wise and intuitive remark to Harry when he is in the hospital wing: "To the well-organized mind, death is but the next great adventure." Undeniably, the passing of Nicolas Flamel is imminent as he surrenders his own immortality — he, by allowing the stone to be destroyed, is thus thwarting Voldemort from regaining power. Here the great wizard is preparing Harry for the great losses and self-sacrifice he will experience in *The Deathly Hallows*. Indeed, Flamel becomes a martyr by making the altruistic choice to ransom himself for the good of Hogwarts and of the world. This decision instructs Harry, for prophecy foretells that the young wizard must one day act in a similar manner. Dumbledore's and Flamel's insights were surely lacking in Voldemort, who clung abnormally to life, negating acceptance of the normal mortal adventure of death. Proving that a healthy acceptance of death is a characteristic of a 'well-organized mind,' Dumbledore implies that the Dark Lord's frantic hunt for immortality is not well ordered at all but instead deranged. Harry will need comfort and reassurance to get through his remaining years of school. The headmaster sees the long and winding road before him, so it is no surprise that Dumbledore's words always echo in his protégé's head: "Death is a beginning rather than an end." Indeed, just as Jesus Christ sacrificed himself for the salvation of humankind, Dumbledore is encouragingly sharing wisdom in preparation for Harry to follow suit.

Another hidden example of the great wizard being the first to see things takes place in the same conversation.

"Harry nodded, but stopped quickly, because it made his head hurt. Then he said, 'Sir, there are some other things I'd like to know, if you can tell me... things I want to know the truth about...'

'The truth.' Dumbledore sighed. 'It is a beautiful and terrible thing and should therefore be treated with great caution. However, I shall answer your questions unless I have a very good reason not to, in which case I beg you'll forgive me. I shall not, of course, lie.'

'Well ... Voldemort said that he only killed my mother because she tried to stop him from killing me. But why would he want to kill me in the first place?'

Dumbledore sighed very deeply this time.

'Alas, the first thing you ask me, I cannot tell you. Not today. Not now. You will know, one day ... put it from your mind for now, Harry. When you are older ... I know you hate to hear this ... when you are ready, you will know.'"

Just as Van Helsing has to slowly and methodically dish out the truth in small bits and pieces along the way, the headmaster is in the same position. Like his literary twin, he thoughtfully and lovingly waits for the right moment to arrive.

Ironically, however, as these good qualities elevate Professors Van Helsing and Dumbledore to hero status, they also reduce them to objects of scorn in their enemies' eyes.

Consider the scene in *Dracula* where the Count stumbles upon his home in Piccadilly. He realizes that his 'earth boxes' have been sanitized and crashes through the window after grabbing a handful of money. Van Helsing is the first to speak: "We have learnt something—much! Notwithstanding his brave words, he fears us; he fears time, he fears want! For if not, why did he hurry so? His very tone betrays him, or my ears deceive. Why take that money?"

Another example occurs in Chapter 16 when Van Helsing has Lucy trapped between her coffin, which contains a 'sacred wafer,' and the professor's cross. Dr. Seward describes the scene in his diary dated September 29:

"Within a foot or two of the door, however, she stopped as if arrested by some irresistible force. Then she turned, and her face was shown in the clear burst of moonlight and by the lamp, which had now no quiver from Van Helsing's iron nerve [...] And so for full half a minute, which seemed an eternity, she remained between the lifted crucifix and the sacred closing of her means of entry."

Just as the undead fear Van Helsing, dark wizards fear Dumbledore. In fact, Rowling directly vows throughout the series that the only wizard Voldemort truly fears is the headmaster of Hogwarts. She even titles Chapter 36 of *Harry Potter and the Order of the Phoenix*, 'The Only One He Ever Feared.' In this action-packed sequence, Voldemort is disappointed that the Death Eaters have again failed him. Upon learning of Dumbledore's presence, they have abandoned the Ministry of Magic. Because of their 'scared straight' paralysis, Voldemort must take matters into his own hands, show up himself, and eventually fire a killing curse at Harry. The professor enters the atrium and manipulates the then-headless wizard from the Fountain of Magical Brethren to block the spell, protecting Harry while the stone figure of the witch statue pins Bellatrix to the floor. In the meantime, Dumbledore and Voldemort duel while Harry is restricted to the role of bystander. Voldemort hurls a killing curse directly at Dumbledore, but Fawkes flies between them, tackles the curse head-on, and falls to the floor. Realizing he is no match for the older wizard, The Dark Lord vanishes before entering Harry's mind. Utilizing Harry's voice, He-Who-Must-Not-Be-Named demands that

Dumbledore kill him by killing Harry. Upon hearing his own voice, Harry is then filled with thoughts of Sirius. If Dumbledore kills him [Harry], he will be able to see Sirius again. Learning that Harry is willing to die to rejoin Sirius, The Dark Lord suddenly exits Harry's body. The lesson is obvious: Voldemort fears death even more than Albus Dumbledore.

Finally, one cannot read either *Dracula* or the Harry Potter books without recognizing that Professors Abraham Van Helsing and Albus Dumbledore are exceptionally brilliant leaders. Many studies have attempted to enumerate the traits of a leader, and their final lists vary greatly. However, all agree that humbleness and selflessness are key. In addition, leaders must own a calm and encouraging demeanor. They must appear trustworthy and be driven by a desire to mentor their juniors.

In comparing Stoker's Van Helsing to this list, he achieves high marks. Indeed, he dedicates his life to the service of teaching and helping others in need. As reflected earlier in this chapter, Van Helsing is willing to die to save Miss Lucy. He often gives speeches of encouragement to others individually and in front of the courageous group. For example, in Chapter 16, Van Helsing says to Godalming,

"My friend Arthur, you have had a sore trial, but after, when you look back, you will see how it was necessary. You are now in the bitter waters, my child. By this time tomorrow, you will, please God, have passed them, and have drunk of the sweet waters. So do not mourn over-much. Till then I shall not ask you to forgive me."

And above all, the professor does all of these things from a didactic perspective, leaving the pupil with the opportunity to agree or disagree with his methods and motives. This plays out wonderfully as Van Helsing tries to prove to everyone that Lucy is, indeed, the 'Bloofer Lady' luring the children away from Hampstead Heath, leaving them lost, pallid, and muddled with tiny bite marks on their necks. In Chapter 16, the professor is in the churchyard with his old pupil and colleague when they stumble upon a young child. From Dr. Seward's diary: — I heard the rustle of actual movement where I had first seen the white figure, and coming over, found the Professor holding in his arms a tiny child. When he saw me, he held it out to me and said—

"Are you satisfied now?"

"No," I said, in a way that I felt was aggressive.

"Do you not see the child?"

"Yes, it is a child, but who brought it here? And is it wounded?" I asked.

Thankfully, they saved the child before the vampire Lucy was able to feed on it; therefore, Seward was still not convinced. Consequently, Van Helsing remained calm and accepted his nonbelief for two days later when the entire group visited Lucy's tomb. In this pivotal scene, Seward, Godalming, and Morris all see the 'turned' Lucy with their own eyes and cannot deny the horrible truth. Dr. Seward wrote, "Van Helsing broke the silence by asking Arthur:

"Answer me, oh my friend! Am I to proceed in my work?"

Arthur threw himself on his knees, and hid his face in his hands, as he answered:

"Do as you will, friend; do as you will. There can be no horror like this ever anymore! And he groaned in spirit." Indeed, not only does he win the group's belief in vampires, but he gains Arthur's acceptance and his willingness to be the one to put his Un-Dead wife to eternal peace.

Seward's diary continues with Van Helsing asking: "So that, my friend, it will be a blessed hand for her that shall strike the blow that sets her free. To this I am willing; but is there none amongst us who has a better right?" To which Arthur answers, "My true friend, from the bottom of my broken heart I thank you. Tell me what I am to do, and I shall not falter!"

Likewise, Professor Dumbledore devotes the majority of his extended life to serving others. Indeed, he obliges Hogwarts and the wizarding community with such prodigious guidance that he is offered the position of Minister of Magic several times. He carries an aura of tranquility and remains composed while in the midst of atrocious storms of disorder. Even during the darkest of days, he seldom displays extreme emotions of rage or panic; instead, he speaks to others with cunningness and refined words of wisdom, all of which align him with the superior aspects of civilization — i.e., love, hope, and companionship.

Undeniably, an entire book could be written about Dumbledore's quotes alone, but the single gem which stands out and justifies his superior status is located in *The Philosopher's Stone*. He pontificates, "It is our choices that show what we truly are far more than our abilities." Albus then lives by this advice so as to set an example for others and counsels those around him to do the same.

During the Civil War, it is said that Abraham Lincoln once gave a particular order to be carried out, and a congressman named Lovejoy gave it to Secretary of War Edwin M. Stanton. To which an irate Stanton replied,

"He is a damned fool."

"Do you mean to say the president is a damned fool?' asked Lovejoy in amazement.

'Yes, sir, if he gave you such an order as that.'

The bewildered congressman from Illinois betook himself at once to the president and related the result of his conference.

'Did Stanton say I was a damned fool?' Asked Lincoln at the close of the recital.

'He did, sir, and repeated it.'

After a moment's pause, and looking up, the president said:

'If Stanton said I was a damned fool, then I must be one, for he is nearly always right and generally says what he means. I will step over and see him.'"

A good leader must be modest enough to admit when he is wrong, and Albus Dumbledore confides in a then sixteen-year-old Harry Potter that he let his guard down, put the safety of Harry and others in jeopardy, and let his weakness — that is, the gain of power by acquiring the Deathly Hallows — get in the way of his better judgment. In Book Six, the ailing headmaster tells Harry:

"I cared about you too much. I cared more for your happiness than your knowing the truth, more for your peace of mind than my plan, more for your life than the lives that might be lost if the plan failed. In other words, I acted exactly as Voldemort expects we fools who love to act." Perhaps Elphias Doge sums up the great wizard's leadership qualities best in his obituary given at the beginning of *The Deathly Hallows*:

"Albus Dumbledore was never proud or vain; he could find something to value in anyone, however apparently insignificant or wretched, and I believe that his early losses endowed him with great humanity and sympathy. I shall miss his friendship more than I can say, but my loss is as nothing compared to the wizarding world's. That he was the most inspiring and the best loved of all Hogwarts headmasters cannot be in question."

One can conclude that Professors Van Helsing and Dumbledore are undoubtedly living, breathing representations of all that is pure. Whether it be the combined knowledge of science and superstition to solve a mystery or the deep capacity for affection, they each delivered what is required in their respective worlds. If the current requirement for a given scenario is a moral inspiration to bolster others or, rather, a fierce leader of 'indomitable resolution, self-command, and toleration,' they each acquiesce. Perhaps Van Helsing's supreme prerogative to legend status is that it is through him that Stoker passes to the readers the particulars of vampire folklore: what predisposes one to become undead, what the powers and restrictions of vampires are, and how to abolish the monsters. His 'briefing' to the small group of hunters in Chapter 18 reads like a Cliff Notes introduction to vampirism. In the same manner, Harry Potter would not have been able to gain the knowledge of student Tom Riddle, the transformation, rise, and fall of He-Who-Must-Not-Be-Named, or the regaining of power and ultimate destruction of Lord Voldemort without the countless conversations, memory shares, and knowledge that Professor Dumbledore eloquently passed down to him.

Besides being gifted with a superior intellect, both characters are emotionally intelligent; their knowledge of a person's true personality ventures beyond simply being a good judge of character. This is never more apparent than in their complex insights into the monsters they hunted, which they piece together with their respective mentees. And just like a Horcrux, their wise and kind souls will live on as two of the greatest dispositions literature has been given the gift of admiring.

Chapter Four

R.M. Renfield and Peter 'Wormtail' Pettigrew

Renfield and Pettigrew. Anyone who is remotely familiar with *Dracula* and the Harry Potter series immediately visualizes two crazed men up to no good, two rotten souls that smile in devious amusement. It's easy to snub these characters off under the notion that their place in their respective tales is not significant enough to take up much page space. However, deeper critical analysis suggests that the men's intelligence runs deeper than their external ravings and disheveled appearances, and their characters' development interweaves an important thematic thread in Stoker's and Rowling's narratives.

Dr. Seward, the operator of the lunatic asylum where R.M. Renfield is a patient, introduces this foolish character in *Dracula*. Seward describes him to the world as a man with "sanguine temperament; great physical strength, morbidly excitable; and periods of gloom, ending in some fixed idea I cannot make out." No doubt the man has issues, although his background and physical appearance are greatly left to readers' imaginations. His erratic behavior of sometimes brooding in the corner of his cell, gnawing at his fingers, frothing at the mouth, or outwardly expressing fits of 'religious mania' brings to mind the modern slang term 'hot mess.' Most *Dracula* films that include Renfield portray him as a wild-eyed, unkempt man with a high-pitched voice.

Peter Pettigrew is introduced to Harry Potter readers as 'Wormtail' by his colleagues Remus Lupin ('Moony') and Sirius Black ('Padfoot'). Our first impression of Peter is a man who is trapped, nervous, afraid, and pleading for his life and liberty. In fact, this scene is very reminiscent of Renfield's plea for freedom to Dr. Seward at the end of Chapter 18 of *Dracula* as Van Helsing, Lord Godalming, and Quincey Morris look on. Pettigrew is depicted in the saga as a short man with grubby skin and small watery eyes. He has a pointed nose, a squeaky voice, and wild-growing hair with a bald patch on top. Though we do not get such descriptions of Renfield, Hollywood has often brought him to life on the big screen with striking similarities.

Though Wormtail is not labeled as insane, and he is not a prisoner of Azkaban or a patient of St. Mungo's Hospital for Magical Maladies and Injuries, this does not deem him a creature of sane mind and body. Clinicians often define insanity as repeatedly engaging in the same actions yet expecting a different result. It is clear that Peter Pettigrew passes information to He-Who-Must-Not-Be-Named, resulting in the death of Harry's parents. When Voldemort loses power, Pettigrew kills thirteen muggles, framing Sirius Black for their deaths, who in turn fakes his death and retreats into hiding for ten years. What does Peter do ten years later? He begins to pass information to He-Who-Must-Not-Be-Named, which results in the deaths of too many individuals to mention. He fakes his death in Ron's room to run and hide from Sirius Black. Remember that definition from earlier? Though 'inmate' in Renfield's world translates to a physical cell, this is not the only way to be incarcerated. Indeed, Pettigrew has been trapped in animagus form for over ten years because of his choices. Confined and isolated in close quarters, his decisions weighed heavily on his heart and mind, making him a prisoner of his past.

Every leader needs a loyal follower. It probably goes without saying that usually, good leaders have a legion of faithful disciples. Likewise, it is fair to say that not everyone is cut out to lead, as with the paradigm of Renfield and Pettigrew. In the case of Renfield, he is the perfect target for Dracula to hone in on because of his selfish nature. Dr. Seward explains in his diary, "I presume that the sanguine temperament itself and the disturbing influence end in a mentally-accomplished finish, a possibly dangerous man, probably dangerous if unselfish. In selfish men, caution is as secure an armor for their foes as for themselves. What I think of on this point is, when self is the fixed point, the centripetal force is balanced with the centrifugal. When duty, a cause, etc., is the fixed point, the latter force is paramount, and only accident or a series of accidents can balance it." Countless times in *Dracula*, the self-centered patient calls for everything from extra sugar, a full-grown cat, or an army of rats and his release into society. Naturally, this character flaw causes him to align himself with whatever available means of power that promises to acquiesce to his demands. Renfield naïvely believes the Count's promises, and his gullible nature works to his disadvantage, allowing him to be easily influenced and manipulated.

In comparison, He-Who-Must-Not-Be-Named capitalizes upon the same weaknesses in Pettigrew, using him as a spy in exchange for what one might describe as 'low fortunes.' Voldemort refers to his service in terms of, "Your devotion is nothing more than cowardice. You would not be here if you had anywhere else to go." Likewise, when Wormtail proudly boasts to the Dark Lord that he returns as a faithful servant, his cold response is, "Out of fear. Not loyalty." Rather, it is Pettigrew's desire to save his own life which leads him to betray his friends, murder innocent people, and go into exile for twelve years.

Peter: "You don't understand! He [Voldemort] would have killed me, Sirius!"

Sirius Black: "THEN YOU SHOULD HAVE DIED! DIED RATHER THAN BETRAY YOUR FRIENDS, AS WE WOULD HAVE DONE FOR YOU!"

— Pettigrew and Sirius arguing over the former's betrayal of the Potters

One of the most distinctive and unique parallels between these peculiar characters is their fixation with the animal world. In *Dracula*, Renfield plans to literally consume as many lives as he can by eating them raw. He believes this digestive regimen will gradually increase his size and standing on the food chain. In Chapter 6, our frenetic patient passionately asks Dr. Seward for a kitten under the guise of feeding his flock of sparrows to it; thus, by eating the kitten, he is connected to all of the lives of the birds and spiders, and the flies which they fed on respectively. After realizing this macabre behavior, the doctor refers to Renfield in his diary as a 'zoophagous maniac' or a 'life-eating maniac' and eventually asks his patient in Chapter 20 if he would like to 'breakfast on an elephant.'

By contrast, Wormtail does not consume animals; he quite literally becomes them. In *The Prisoner of Azkaban*, audiences learn that Wormtail is an Animagus — that is to say, he has been Ron Weasley's pet rat Scabbers for the past two years and his brother Percy's before that. Acting as a rat, Pettigrew follows other animagus wizards (such as Moony, Padfoot, and Prongs) in the forms of wolves, dogs, and stags and is also pursued by Crookshanks, Hermione's pet cat. Upon realizing that Ron's rat is, indeed, Wormtail, Pettigrew is trapped and forced into human form. Sirius commented, "If you made a better rat than a human, Peter, that's not much to boast about." One can only imagine what would have occurred if Scabbers happened to be one of the rats that Dracula promised Renfield!

Despite Renfield's and Wormtail's eccentricities and lapses, in reality, both of these supporting characters are actually well aware of what is going on in their respective worlds — sometimes even more so than the primary characters. One of the most amusing scenes in *Dracula* occurs in Chapter 18 when Mina Harker visits Renfield's cell. Upon hearing he will have a guest, Renfield decides to 'tidy up' his room simply by swallowing all of the spiders and flies on hand. But then moments later, he converses with Mina intellectually with the utmost level of courtesy, lucidity, and respect. Dr. Seward recalled,

"I positively opened my eyes at this new development. Here was my own pet lunatic — the most pronounced of his type that I had ever met with — talking elemental philosophy and with the manner of a polished gentleman.... I hardly knew what to either think or say; it was hard to imagine that I had seen him eat up his spiders and flies not five minutes before."

In this conversation, Renfield recommends that Mrs. Harker not remain at Carfax because he knows Dracula will call on her. Unfortunately, Mina does not heed his warning. Indeed, in Chapter 18, Renfield claims to be cured and ready to be released — right then and there on the spot — almost convincing Van Helsing, Lord Godalming, and Quincey Morris with a sheer force of logical reasoning and sharp cross-examination and debate skills. However, again his counsel is not taken, and sickness and death follow. Dr. Seward is the last of the party to leave his patient's cell at the end of the chapter. Upon doing so, Renfield says to him in a quiet, well-bred voice, "You will, I trust, Dr. Seward, do me the justice to bear in mind, later on, that I did what I could to convince you tonight."

Like the 'zoophagous maniac,' Pettigrew's intelligence is dismissed by all, largely because of his eccentric nature, follower mentality, selfish choices, and desire to ride on the coattails of whoever has the most power at the time. J.K. Rowling once described Peter Pettigrew in this way: "It turned out that he was a better wizard than they knew." Despite Professor McGonagall maintaining that Peter Pettigrew is less gifted than his friends and Voldemort's classification of him as a poor wizard, he exhibits an unforeseen degree of magical competency when hard-pressed. Aside from being a skilled animagus and co-creator of the impressively smart Marauder's Map in *The Deathly Hallows*, Pettigrew (Wormtail) showcases his intellect to the extent that one can argue that he is not any less functioning than the other Marauders (Mooney, Padfoot, and Prongs) and probably more knowledgeable of the Dark Arts than all of them.

With his wand positioned behind his back, Pettigrew uses a powerful blasting curse that kills twelve Muggles in 1981. Fourteen years later, he uses a non-allegiant wand to perform the killing curse to end Cedric Diggory's life. And to top it off, he conjures up the ultimate Dark Magic rudimentary body and regeneration potions, enabling Voldemort to regain a temporary and then permanent form.

Professor McGonagall once described Peter Pettigrew's dueling skills as "hopeless," yet Pettigrew overtakes Sirius Black in 1981 and overpowers Bertha Jorkins in 1994, forcing her to disclose facts to assist in Lord Voldemort's rebirth. Moreover, in *The Goblet of Fire*, Pettigrew (Wormtail) manages to aid in the incarceration of an exceptionally fierce Auror, Mad-Eye Moody, in an enchanted trunk. In this same book, Pettigrew demonstrates 'conjuration,' an advanced type of transfiguration, when he invokes ropes that bind Harry Potter to Tom Riddle Senior's grave. In addition, he exhibits wand versatility by levitating Harry and lighting a fire with the Dark Lord's wand — an instrument for which Wormtail has not won allegiance.

Hogwarts School of Witchcraft and Wizardry taught its students that nonverbal magic requires a resilient will. Once again, Pettigrew, notwithstanding his gutless persona, attests to such aptitude. Indeed, during his escape in Book Three, Pettigrew nonverbally stuns Ron and Crookshanks before absconding. In Book Seven, he bolts and unbolts the cell door at Malfoy Manor without uttering a solitary word.

Finally, any analysis of Pettigrew's character would be remiss if it did not address his deductive skills. Upon realizing Voldemort's initial defeat at the Potter residence, Pettigrew seizes the Dark Lord's dropped wand and hides it instead of leaving it for the Ministry of Magic to claim and inspect. Pettigrew uses detective-like skills to find the hidden location of He-Who-Must-Not-Be-Named's fragmented soul — a daunting task that other, more gifted Death Eaters miscarry. Pettigrew's intelligence is also demonstrated by the fact that he strategically delays the precise moment to turn Harry over, thwarting other Death Eaters from claiming him as a conspirator.

Another trait these two characters share is that they are both accomplished escape artists. Thrice to be exact. In *Dracula*, Renfield frees himself on 19 August and is recaptured on the grounds of Carfax, where Dr. Seward discovers him "pressed close against the old iron-bound oak door of the chapel." As the attendants are closing in on him, the doctor hears him say, "I am here to do Your bidding, Master. I am Your slave, and You will reward me, for I shall be faithful..." Dr. Seward describes a second 'night adventure' in his diary dated 23 August—where he described:

> "Again he went into the grounds of the deserted house, and we found him in the same place, pressed against the old chapel door. When he saw me, he became furious, and had not the attendants seized him in time, he would have tried to kill me."

The third occurrence takes place on the 20th of September and is reported in a letter by Patrick Hennessey to Dr. Seward:

> "...With regard to patient, Renfield, there is more to say. He has had another outbreak, which might have had a dreadful ending, but which, as it fortunately happened, was unattended with any unhappy results [—] This time, he had broken out through the window of his room and was running down the avenue."

We can surmise that the first escape is to pledge his allegiance to the Count. With the second attempt, he realizes his Master is not answering, and this final attempt is to rate, curse, bully and beat a small group of men bringing large wooden (earth) boxes to Carfax in protest of not being heard.

Pettigrew's first escape is in 1981, when the remaining Death Eaters are being rounded up after Voldemort's fall from power. When Sirius Black closes in on him, Pettigrew shrieks in front of everyone, claiming that Sirius has betrayed the Potters. Before Black has the chance to draw his wand, Pettigrew casts the blasting curse, thus creating a massive crater in the street and killing twelve Muggles in the process. Cutting off his own finger to leave behind, he fakes his own death by fleeing in the form of a rat and is veiled for fourteen years. As a result, Sirius is detained for being a Death Eater, murdering Pettigrew and the Muggles, and betraying the Potters. Sadly, he is imprisoned in Azkaban and deprived of a trial. Surviving Muggles who observe the stand-down have their recollections erased and are given an explanation by the Muggle-Worthy Excuse Committee that a 'gas leak' is the cause. Wormtail is unfairly awarded the Order of Merlin, First Class, for his bravery with Sirius, which along with the recovered finger, are subsequently given to his oblivious mother. Remus, the other remaining Marauder, understands Sirius betrays them and kills Pettigrew. Due to elapsed time and fallacies, many believe that Black draws his wand first and kills before Pettigrew has a chance to defend himself. For a mediocre wizard, that getaway is well-organized and executed from every possible angle.

In *The Prisoner of Azkaban*, Pettigrew, in the form of Scabbers, fakes his demise a second time when he feels his cover as a rat is about to be blown. After biting himself and leaving droplets of blood about — thus causing Ron to believe that Crookshanks has eaten the rat — Pettigrew leaves the castle. This escape almost ruins Ron's relationship with Hermione until they reconcile, and she happens upon Scabbers (Pettigrew) hiding in a milk jug in Hagrid's hut.

Escape number three occurs at the end of Book Three. Intending to kill their childhood colleague, Remus and Sirius force Pettigrew out of his animagus form; however, Harry intercedes after Pettigrew petitions that James, Harry's father, would have let him live. This supplication, along with Harry's belief that his father would not want his best friends to become killers, leads him to spare Wormtail's life. Even though Harry intends to hand Pettigrew over to the Dementors and use him to clear Sirius' name, this merciful act creates a life debt between Harry and Pettigrew. Finally, this decision does not go as planned: Remus forgets to take his wolfsbane potion, and when the full moon rises, he transforms into a werewolf, forcing Sirius to take on his animagus form of a dog to protect Harry, Ron, and Hermione. During the chaos, Pettigrew takes advantage of the distraction. After cursing Ron with Remus' wand, he morphs back into a rat and flees for the final time.

Probably, the most interesting parallel between these two characters — aside from all their oddities, disorders, and psychoses — is the fact that they share a common weakness. In the end, this 'chink in their armor' brings about their untimely deaths. Oddly enough, this flaw has nothing to do with intelligence, power, knowledge, skills, or abilities. It centers on love.

No doubt, R. M. Renfield is a complex, troubled man chiefly caught up in his bizarre world of heavy drinking and soul forfeiting. Yet a certain young lady — Wilhelmina Harker — piques his interest when they are introduced, and this encounter shifts his own self-centered priorities in favor of her safety.

In Chapter 18, when Mina shows interest in meeting Renfield, his immediate response to Dr. Seward is the question, "Why?" This puzzling interest in why a lady would care to see him sparks the desire to 'tidy up' and completely change his demeanor from one of a 'zoophagous' patient to that of a 'polished gentleman.' During the conversation, he asks her to no longer stay with Dr. Seward; and at the conclusion of the scene, Renfield tells Mina as she leaves, "Goodbye, my dear. I pray to God I may never see your sweet face again. May He bless and keep you!"

This strange farewell is fully understood in Chapter 21 when Renfield explains to the men,

"When Mrs. Harker came in to see me this afternoon, she wasn't the same. It was like tea after the teapot has been watered...."

"I didn't know that she was here till she spoke, and she didn't look the same. I don't care for the pale people. I like them with lots of blood in them, and hers all seemed to have run out. I didn't think of it at the time, but when she went away, I began to think, and it made me mad to know that He had been taking the life out of her."

Renfield further goes on to tell the others that he is determined to be ready for the Count, and when he last entered his cell, "...He didn't even smell the same as he went by me. I couldn't hold him. I thought that, somehow, Mrs. Harker had come into the room." The lunatic wrestles with Dracula for a spell until the vampire picks him up and throws him to the floor, breaking his back and finally beating his head against the floor so severely it leaves him with a brain hemorrhage and paralysis on the right side of his body. Renfield's last words are sobering:

"There was a red cloud before me, and a noise like thunder, and the mist seemed to steal away under the door."

Sadly, the brave patient's attempt to save Mrs. Harker fails, for as Renfield takes his last breath, the Count is in Mina's room, forcing her to feed on his blood and beginning her transformation into being one of his undead wives.

Pettigrew is equally a rambling bedlam of mischief, but his selfish waywardness is temporarily interrupted in Book Three when Sirius Black and Remus Lupin have their wands at the ready to finally avenge the trail of carnage the 'rat' causes, including the death of Harry's parents and Black's imprisonment. Upon realizing he is about to be killed, he begins begging everyone for his life. When rounding on Harry, he cries,

"Harry... you look just like your father... just like him [...] James wouldn't have wanted me killed... James would have understood, Harry... he would have shown me mercy..."

Remus Lupin: "You should have realized, if Voldemort didn't kill you, we would. Goodbye, Peter."

Harry Potter: "NO! You can't kill him. You can't."

Sirius Black: "Harry, this piece of vermin is the reason you have no parents. This cringing bit of filth would have seen you die, too, without turning a hair. You heard him. His own stinking skin meant more to him than your whole family."

Harry Potter: "I know. We'll take him up to the castle. We'll hand him over to the Dementors... He can go to Azkaban... but don't kill him."

Peter Pettigrew: "Harry! You — thank you — it's more than I deserve — thank you —"

Harry's compassionate act of saving Peter's life creates a 'life debt' between him and Wormtail. A life debt, in the 'wizarding world,' is a magical oath formed between a wizard or witch and the individual whose life they rescue. The one who owes the debt [Pettigrew] to the savior [Harry] will one day be obligated to repay the deed by doing something favorable to the said savior. In Rowling's novel, however, there is something deeper taking place here. It is a fact that while Pettigrew is in school at Hogwarts, he admires James Potter. Minerva McGonagall refers to it as 'hero-worship,' while Sirius Black recalls how Pettigrew would practically wet himself from excitement while observing James. It is made clear in the series that Pettigrew 'trails' after Harry's father, and they created the Marauder's Map together. Moreover, they become Animagus together. One would obviously conclude from these observations that they were very close friends. Peter holds a special affection for James.

When Remus confronts Pettigrew about killing Harry's parents, he exclaims, "I didn't mean to! The Dark Lord... You've no idea of the weapons he possesses!" Is this remorse? Dumbledore and Harry feel this too. In a conversation between Harry and the headmaster, Harry tells Dumbledore at the end of Book Three, "And you [Dumbledore] understood Wormtail too... you knew there was a bit of regret there, somewhere...."

Because Harry reminds Pettigrew so much of his father, the affection Pettigrew feels for James transfers to his son. Pettigrew consciously demonstrates appreciation toward the boy as he advocates that the Dark Lord should use another wizard's blood for the rebirth ritual. When Voldemort questions his follower, Pettigrew hurriedly implies that Harry means nothing to him, a response that is a ruse. The evidence mounts even more in the Little Hangleton graveyard scene in *The Goblet of Fire*. Pettigrew straps Potter to Tom Riddle Senior's grave, striking and cutting him yet never making eye contact with him.

Finally, in *The Deathly Hallows*, Pettigrew's life debt is ultimately repaid when The Boy Who Lived is captured and held prisoner at Malfoy Manor. However, when the silver hand — the same one Voldemort magically attaches to Pettigrew's arm — realizes its owner is setting Harry free, it turns on Pettigrew, thus strangling him to death. Whether one calls it a life debt, guilty conscience, genuine affection, or a good deed, it goes without saying: Pettigrew denounces the 'Dark Side' and finds his way back as a 'Jedi Knight.'

In conclusion, it is frustrating to hear readers of *Dracula* or the Harry Potter saga suggest that Renfield or Pettigrew are unnecessary characters, expendable, and secondary rubbish. On the contrary, they provide a level of balance where it is required, a degree of comic relief where it is needed, and equality of hope when obscurity closes in. Years ago, the late Alfred Hitchcock talked about the role of dramatic irony in his works. Specifically, he discussed how he approached directing his films with the concept of the viewer knowing that a ticking bomb was placed under a chair unbeknownst to any of the actors. Indeed, readers of Stoker's and J.K. Rowling's respective masterpieces know about the 'bomb' through Renfield and Pettigrew. As the other 'smarter' characters in these books are busy asking questions, the 'crazy ones' have the answers. And in some situations, they are Hitchcock's 'bomb.' Stoker minimizes Dracula's presence to only a few pages in his masterpiece, and Rowling does the same with Voldemort to build suspense. Each writer keeps their respective audiences informed of the monsters' business through their faithful followers, only to be unfollowed, sacrificing their own lives for love. In the end, virtue prevails.

Chapter Five

Wilhelmina Murray Harker

and Hermione Jean Granger

Given that society is still dominated heavily by men, it is refreshing to discover literature where females 'take charge' and give the leading male characters a hearty lesson in
'the way things should be done.' In the late 1800s, the term 'new woman' was used to
describe how the female sex was eager to step out of traditional 'behind the scenes'
roles in books. In the late 1900s, singers Helen Reddy and the Eurythmics and Aretha
Franklin sang about females being "strong and roaring" and "coming out of the
kitchen and doing it for themselves." Movies such as the *Alien* franchise proved that
actress Sigourney Weaver could fight and win a battle that her male counterparts could
not, and the latest *Star Wars* films have opened the Jedi Knight job requirement to
include women. Bram Stoker was part of this movement in 1897 when he wrote Wilhelmina Murray Harker into his novel *Dracula*. Following suit, exactly one hundred
years later, J.K. Rowling introduced Hermione Granger to the world, and in both
instances, the universe applauded and fell in love with them.

There are obvious connections between these two female characters: they are both
single at the beginning of their respective stories and then marry one of the leading
male characters; they are part of a small group that joins in the witch hunt and destruction of a monster at large, and they have children at the end of their fight as they
try to put the ghosts of the past behind them and claim peace in their new 'evil free'
lives. However, the ladies are of such dire importance to their respective narratives that
it leads one to imagine, 'What would Dracula and the Harry Potter series be like if
Mina Harker and Hermione Granger did not exist?'

First and foremost, the pair brought the structure, organization, and analytical
skills required to pick up on unique plot clues that were otherwise hidden amongst a
vast forest of camouflaged trees.

What is this 'New Woman' anyhow? It was a feminist belief that arose in the late
nineteenth century and had a deep influence on women's rights completely into the

twentieth century. The term was utilized to portray the rise in the number of suffragette, educated, self-sufficient career women in Europe and the United States — a group that tested the boundaries set by a male-dominated society. The New Woman springs fully armed from Bram Stoker's brain in the creation of Mina Murray Harker. In fact, in *Dracula*, the author flagrantly references this term in its pages, with Mina openly discussing the changing roles of women. Mina Harker is introduced as a schoolteacher and embodies several characteristics of the New Woman, but to the amazement of her masculine protagonists, she employs manly skills such as typing and deductive reasoning. She and her friend Lucy Westenra wonder if the New Woman can marry several men at once to avoid turning down multiple proposals. If Mina did not adopt this radical belief, one would assume her skills of short-hand, memorization, interviewing, writing, and inferential analysis would not have been there to benefit the group. If it were not for Mina, the group would not have had all of their diaries, letters, and newspaper clippings typed out in chronological order — a feat that enables them to discover that the man who Jonathan Harker visits in Transylvania is the same man who moves into Carfax Abby next door to Doctor Seward's asylum. If it were not for Mina's request to be hypnotized, the protagonists would have been unaided in determining the Count's itinerary for escape. Most importantly, the vampire hunters would not have been able to reach Dracula in time without Mina's clever attention to detail, for she brilliantly discovers Dracula's ploy to throw the group off his trail. In Chapter 26, she writes: "I do believe that under God's providence, I have made a discovery. I shall get the maps and look over them. I am more than ever sure that I am right. My new conclusion is ready, so I shall get our party together and read it. They can judge it. It is well to be accurate, and every minute is precious."

Mina Harker's Memorandum
(Entered In Her Journal)

Ground of inquiry. — Count Dracula's problem is to get back to his own place.

(a) He must be brought back by someone. This is evident. For had he power to move himself as he wished he could go either as man, or wolf, or bat, or in some other way. He evidently fears discovery or interference, in the state of helplessness in which he must be, confined as he is between dawn and sunset in his wooden box.

(b) How is he to be taken? — Here a process of exclusions may help us. By road, by rail, by water?

1. By Road. — There are endless difficulties, especially in leaving the city.

(x) There are people. And people are curious and investigate. A hint, a surmise, a doubt as to what might be in the box, would destroy him.

(y) There are, or there may be, customs and octroi officers to pass.

(z) His pursuers might follow. This is his highest fear. And in order to prevent his being betrayed he has repelled, so far as he can, even his victim, me!

2. By Rail. — There is no one in charge of the box. It would have to take its chance of being delayed, and delay would be fatal, with enemies on the track. True, he might escape at night. But what would he be, if left in a strange place with no refuge that he could fly to? This is not what he intends, and he does not mean to risk it.

3. By Water. — Here is the safest way, in one respect, but with most danger in another. On the water he is powerless except at night. Even then he can only summon fog and storm and snow and his wolves. But were he wrecked, the living water would engulf him, helpless, and he would indeed be lost. He could have the vessel drive to land, but if it were unfriendly land, wherein he was not free to move, his position would still be desperate.

We know from the record that he was on the water, so what we have to do is to ascertain what water.

The first thing is to realize exactly what he has done as yet. We may, then, get a light on what his task is to be.

Firstly. — We must differentiate between what he did in London as part of his general plan of action, when he was pressed for moments and had to arrange as best he could.

Secondly, we must see, as well as we can surmise it from the facts we know of, what he has done here.

As to the first, he evidently intended to arrive at Galatz, and sent invoice to Varna to deceive us lest we should ascertain his means of exit from England. His immediate and sole purpose then was to escape. The proof of this, is the letter of instructions sent to Immanuel Hildesheim to clear and take away the box before sunrise. There is also the instruction to Petrof Skinsky. These we must only guess at, but there must have been some letter or message, since Skinsky came to Hildesheim.

That, so far, his plans were successful we know. The Czarina Catherine made a phenomenally quick journey. So much so that Captain Donelson's suspicions were aroused. But his superstition united with his canniness played the Count's game for him, and he ran with his favoring wind through fogs and all till he brought up blindfold at Galatz. That the Count's arrangements were well made, has been proved. Hildesheim cleared the box, took it off, and gave it to Skinsky. Skinsky took it, and here we lose the trail. We only know that the box is somewhere on the water, moving along. The customs and the octroi, if there be any, have been avoided.

Now we come to what the Count must have done after his arrival, on land, at Galatz.

The box was given to Skinsky before sunrise. At sunrise the Count could appear in his own form. Here, we ask why Skinsky was chosen at all to aid in the work? In my husband's diary, Skinsky is mentioned as dealing with the Slovaks who trade down the river to the port. And the man's remark, that the murder was the work of a Slovak, showed the general feeling against his class. The Count wanted isolation.

My surmise is this, that in London the Count decided to get back to his castle by water, as the most safe and secret way. He was brought from the castle by Szgany, and probably they delivered their cargo to Slovaks who took the boxes to Varna, for there they were shipped to London. Thus the Count had knowledge of the persons who could arrange this service. When the box was on land, before sunrise or after sunset, he came out from his box, met Skinsky and instructed him what to do as to arranging the carriage of the box up some river. When this was done, and he knew that all was in train, he blotted out his traces, as he thought, by murdering his agent.

I have examined the map and find that the river most suitable for the Slovaks to have ascended is either the Pruth or the Sereth. I read in the typescript that in my trance I heard cows low and water swirling level with my ears and the creaking of wood. The Count in his box, then, was on a river in an open boat, propelled probably either by oars or poles, for the banks are near and it is working against stream. There would be no such if floating down stream.

Of course, it may not be either the Sereth or the Pruth, but we may possibly investigate further. Now of these two, the Pruth is the more easily navigated, but the Sereth is, at Fundu, joined by the Bistritza which runs up round the Borgo Pass. The loop it makes is manifestly as close to Dracula's castle as can be got by water."

Thus, Mina's profession as a teacher is not limited to the schoolhouse, for the group of men need her help if they are to succeed in their quest. Van Helsing says it best when he tells Dr. Seward,

"Ah, that wonderful Madam Mina! She has a man's brain — a brain that a man should have were he much gifted — and a woman's heart. The good God fashioned her for a purpose, believe me, when He made that so good combination. Friend John, up to now fortune has made that woman of help to us" — Van Helsing (Stoker 251)

Though Hermione Granger is not a teacher by profession, she is an exceptional student at Hogwarts. In *The Prisoner of Azkaban*, Professor Lupin muses, "You're the cleverest witch of your age I've ever met, Hermione." Due to her many visits to the school library and ample time spent reading and studying, she could have very easily joined the faculty. Like Mina Harker, Hermione has a 'man's brain,' and she pushes the envelope when it comes to women's rights. According to J.K. Rowling, "She [Hermione] is very brave because she fights for what she believes in." Rowling also states that her feminist conscience is saved by Hermione, "who's the brightest character" and is a "very strong female character [...] logical, upright and good." Indeed, from finding out about Nicholas Flamel in *The Philosophers Stone* all the way to disguising Harry from enemies by using a stinging jinx in *The Deathly Hallows*, there are at least nineteen times in the complete series where Hermione saves the day. J.K. Rowling describes Granger's character as, "[...] her cleverness is inspirational, and she is extremely good at spells and has a great work ethic". Even Hagrid makes a point to praise the second-year witch in *The Chamber of Secrets* when he says to Harry and Ron, "An' they haven't invented a spell our Hermione can' do." Furthermore, her loyalty is demonstrated beautifully throughout the Harry Potter series. "These are the reasons why her character means so much to me," Rowling stated. Much like Mina Harker memorizes the train schedules, Hermione admits to memorizing her textbooks by heart before ever setting foot onto the Hogwarts campus. In *The Goblet of Fire*, Hermione asks Ron Weasley: "Aren't you ever going to read *Hogwarts, A History?*"

"What's the point?" replies Ron. "You know it by heart; we can just ask you."

This encyclopedic knowledge not only helps Harry and Ron through school but it aids them time and again in their pursuit to locate and eradicate Lord Voldemort. For example, in Book Two, it is Granger's sense of susceptibility and subjection that drives her to ascertain the nature of the Chamber of Secrets. She formulates the strategy to use a polyjuice potion so that she, Harry, and Ron can infiltrate the Slytherin common room; however, both Ron and Harry are atypically intimidated by the plan: "Well, if you two are going to chicken out, fine, I don't want to break rules, you know. I think threatening Muggle-borns is far worse than brewing up a difficult potion. But if you don't want to find out if it's Malfoy, I'll go straight to Madam Pince now and hand the book back in —" Enough said. They change their minds instantly. Just like Mina Harker, Hermione displays a brilliant talent for collecting information from her research and cleverly presenting it to others. She devises logical, carefully crafted courses of action for each epic quest and corners the market on specialized skill sets. Indubitably, Hermione makes herself indispensable to her partners. Her constant guidance, inspiration, knowledge, ideas, and answers prevent Harry and Ron from suffering many well-deserved timeouts and punishments in Dumbledore's office. Heed Slughorn's assessment in *The Half-Blood Prince*: "One of my best friends is Muggle-born, and she is the best in our year."

One of the qualities Mina Harker and Hermione Granger share that makes them so endearing is their nurturing, motherly-like stance. Indeed, their raw femininity keeps the machismo of several male characters in check, preventing them from losing focus, acting over-aggressively, and getting frustrated to the point of giving up.

Much like a lioness protecting her cubs, Wilhelmina Harker steps into this matriarch role several times in Bram Stoker's *Dracula* when the leading men get shaken up and need comfort. From keeping her husband Jonathan from collapsing after encountering the Count on the street in Piccadilly Circus to holding Arthur Holmwood as he breaks down and cries on her shoulder after Lucy dies, Mina is a constant balm of protection and inspiration that the men are drawn to, binding all the characters together for a common purpose. For example, in Chapter 17, Mina writes,

> "We women have something of the mother in us that makes us rise above smaller matters when the mother-spirit is invoked; I felt this big, sorrowing man's head resting on me, as though it were that of the baby that someday may lie on my bosom, and I stroked his hair as though he were my own child."

Indeed, Mina is like everyone's 'mother magnet'— for not less than five minutes after she allows Arthur to cry on her shoulder, Quincey Morris walks up to her and does the same.

Similarly, Hermione Granger provides a motherly safety net, consolation, and encouragement to Harry and Ron in times when life in the wizarding world gets to be too much. From comforting Harry upon the death of his godfather, Sirius Black, to reassuring Ron when he thought he was not cut out for playing Quidditch, Hermione is always offering maternal advice and love. One of the most touching examples of this enduring quality emerges in *The Deathly Hallows* in the scene where Harry and Hermione visit the graves of Harry's parents. Hermione consoles Harry without saying a word:

> "Hermione had taken his hand again and was gripping it tightly. He could not look at her but returned the pressure, now taking deep, sharp gulps of the night air, trying to steady himself, trying to regain control. He should have brought something to give them, and he had not thought of it, and every plant in the graveyard was leafless and frozen. But Hermione raised her wand, moved it in a circle through the air, and a wreath of Christmas roses blossomed before them. Harry caught it and laid it on his parent's grave. As soon as he stood up, he wanted to leave: he did not think he could stand another moment there. He put his arm around Hermione's shoulders, and she put hers around his waist, and they turned in silence and walked away through the snow, past Dumbledore's mother and sister, back toward the dark church and the out-of-sight kissing gate."

Finally, the characters of Mina Harker and Hermione Granger both take on a level of compassion, balancing out the empathy their male companions lack. In *Dracula*, Mina Harker takes an interest in Renfield in a 'human way,' yet her male counterparts approach the patient with a judgmental, medical, or informational purpose to track down the vampire. As the men consult about their plans to destroy the Count and project a growing hatred and vengeance that makes them monsters, Mina interjects with an insightful speech:

> "[…] I want you to bear something in mind through all this dreadful time. I know that you must fight—that you must destroy even as you destroyed the false Lucy so that the true Lucy might live hereafter; but it is not a work of hate. That poor soul who has wrought all this misery is the saddest case of all. Just think what his joy will be when he, too, is destroyed in his worse part that his better part may have spiritual immortality. You must be pitiful to him, too, though it may not hold your hands from his destruction."

Without Mina's soothing touch to counterbalance their anger and remind the men of their humanness, five more fiends might have been added to the grisly ranks of Dracula's army.

In the same vein, throughout the Harry Potter saga, Hermione is often diffusing moments when Harry or Ron's temper is about to get them in trouble. Many times, Harry's fury over Voldemort's malicious attacks unnerves the young wizard, and in doing so, the rage backfires — breaking his resistance and allowing the Dark Lord to enter his thoughts. Like a responsible parent, Hermione scolds Harry numerous times by making pleas for cooler heads: "Harry, he has overpowered the Ministry, the newspapers, and half the wizarding community! Don't let him enter your mind, too!"

As Mina shows empathy for those less fortunate, Hermione stands up for bullied students, Mudbloods, and house-elves. In *The Goblet of Fire*, Hermione initiates a campaign for the better treatment of house-elves by making an observation at the Quidditch World Cup: "You know, house-elves get a very raw deal! It's slavery, that's what it is! That Mr. Crouch made her [Winky] go up to the top of the stadium, and she was terrified, and he's got her bewitched so she can't even run when they start trampling tents! Why doesn't anyone do something about it?" Once she and her friends return to Hogwarts, she creates an organization called S.P.E.W and begins to hand out badges to promote her agenda.

"Spew?" said Harry, picking up a badge and looking at it. "What's this about?"

"Not spew," said Hermione impatiently, "It's S-P-E-W. Stands for the Society for the Promotion of Elfish Welfare." If it were not for Hermione's progressive voice throughout the series, one would have to wonder if those she defends would have had the courage to stand up, unite, and fight when their help is needed.

In closing, without the characters of Mina Harker and Hermione Granger, the book *Dracula* and the Harry Potter saga would have lacked the level of intellect, organization, benevolence, and harmony required for our hearty bands of male monster hunters to succeed. Indeed, these strong female characters represent the 'New Woman' perfectly, and their bravery and loyalty to their respective groups help bind the main characters together for a shared goal. Furthermore, as a result of their resilient, instrumental virtues, their male counterparts' work becomes less complicated.

Chapter Six

The Weird Sisters

and The Weird Sisters

William Shakespeare's renowned play *Macbeth* has long been labeled as his darkest tragedy. Lord Macbeth, the Thane of Glamis, is the central character and nominal chief hero turned main rival (c. 1603–1607) of Malcolm. The role was based on the historical King Macbeth of Scotland and stemmed considerably from the narrative in *Holinshed's Chronicles* (1587), a history of Britain. The play was written for King James I of England and King James V of Scotland. A Scottish gallant and bold military man, Macbeth, after a mystical prophecy and under the influence of his wife, commits regicide against the king of Scotland. Going forward, he lives in constant distress and worries over his actions, robbing his soul of relaxation and trust for his noblemen. He rules with a reign of terror until overcome by his ex-supporter, Macduff. Finally, the throne is restored to the murdered King Duncan's son, Malcolm, the rightful heir.

As a Trinity graduate and admirer of the theater, Bram Stoker was intimately knowledgeable of Shakespeare's work. In fact, he served as acting manager of the famous Lyceum Theatre and the right-hand man of the most famous actor of his time, Sir Henry Irving. The writer witnessed Irving perform the play on multiple occasions, and its recurring themes and dark images were essential key elements in the development of Dracula. Indeed, entire essays have been devoted to this very topic alone, but a few points bear witnessing. Both Dracula and Macbeth rest their action on the grounds of forsaken, gloomy castles to which unwary foreigners are lured. Both include scenes of sleepwalking, and the protagonists, driven by control and motivation, receive a sense of immortality from their pledge to the supernatural, yet perish confined in their castles with their throats slashed. Evil, it seems, is viewed as a communicable plague that must be destroyed by teamwork, and the image of blood is central to both. Still, the most striking similarity between these texts is the three witches. Shakespeare's original text reads, "The weyward Sisters, hand in hand, Posters of the Sea and Land..."

The trio of enchantresses — complete with their filthy "Double double toil and trouble" symbols and mystic activities — help create an ominous tone for the play. Scholars have suggested that the concept of the Three Witches was influenced by the Old Norse skaldic poem Darraðarljóð (found in chapter 157 of Njáls saga), in which twelve Valkyries weave and choose who is to be slain at the Battle of Clontarf (outside of Dublin) in 1014. (Is it just a coincidence that Bram Stoker was born in Clontarf?) Macbeth's three "weyward Sisters" are resurrected to tantalize Jonathan Harker in *Dracula*. Indeed, in his journal dated 16 May, at the end of Chapter 3, he writes:

"I was not alone. The room was the same, unchanged in any way since I came into it. I could see along the floor, in the brilliant moonlight, my own footsteps marked where I had disturbed the long accumulation of dust. In the moonlight opposite me were three young women, ladies by their dress and manner. I thought at the time that I must be dreaming when I saw them, they threw no shadow on the floor. They came close to me, and looked at me for some time, and then whispered together. Two were dark, and had high aquiline noses, like the Count, and great dark, piercing eyes, that seemed to be almost red when contrasted with the pale-yellow moon. The other was fair, as fair as can be, with great masses of golden hair and eyes like pale sapphires. I seemed somehow to know her face, and to know it in connection with some dreamy fear, but I could not recollect at the moment how or where. All three had brilliant white teeth that shone like pearls against the ruby of their voluptuous lips. There was something about them that made me uneasy, some longing and at the same time some deadly fear. I felt in my heart a wicked, burning desire that they would kiss me with those red lips. It is not good to note this down, lest someday it should meet Mina's eyes and cause her pain, but it is the truth. They whispered together, and then they all three laughed, such a silvery, musical laugh, but as hard as though the sound never could have come through the softness of human lips. It was like the intolerable, tingling sweetness of waterglasses when played on by a cunning hand. The fair girl shook her head coquettishly, and the other two urged her on. One said, "Go on! You are first, and we shall follow. Yours is the right to begin." The other added, "He is young and strong. There are kisses for us all." I lay quiet, looking out from under my eyelashes in an agony of delightful anticipation. The fair girl advanced and bent over me till I could feel the movement of her breath upon me. Sweet it was in one sense, honey-sweet, and sent the same tingling through the nerves as her voice, but with a bitter underlying the sweet, a bitter offensiveness, as one smells in blood. I was afraid to raise my eyelids but looked out and saw perfectly under the lashes. The girl went on her knees, and bent over me, simply gloating. There was a deliberate voluptuousness which was both thrilling and repulsive, and as she arched her neck she actually licked her lips like an animal, till I could see in the moonlight the moisture shining on the scarlet lips and on the red tongue as it lapped the white sharp teeth. Lower and lower went her head as the lips went below the range of my mouth and chin and seemed to fasten on my throat. Then she paused, and I could hear the churning sound of her tongue as it licked her teeth and lips, and I could feel the hot breath on my neck. Then the skin of my throat began to tingle as one's flesh does when the hand that is to tickle it approaches nearer, nearer. I could feel the soft, shivering touch of the lips on the super sensitive skin of my throat, and the hard dents of two sharp teeth, just touching and pausing there. I closed my eyes in languorous ecstasy and waited, waited with beating heart."

In Chapter 4, Harker recollects, "[–] for nothing can be more dreadful than those awful women, who were—who are—waiting to suck my blood." Further along in the same chapter, the prisoner writes on 29 June — "[–] I dared not wait to see him [Dracula] return, for I feared to see those weird sisters."

It is interesting and noteworthy to point out that in the original Folio Edition (1623) of Macbeth, Shakespeare uses the adjective 'Weyward Sisters.' This early 'old English' edition is what Stoker was likely familiar with, as the modern translation did not emerge until after *Dracula* was published. How remarkable it is to stress that the translation to modern English changed 'weyward' to 'weird' AFTER the publication of Bram's masterpiece! Indeed, the heavy-laden cross-impact influences of *Dracula* in today's literature and society as a whole is undeniably awe-inspiring!

The three vampire women who dwell in the 'out-of-bounds' secluded region of Castle Dracula are of vast import to the tale. The representation of them is a nightmarishly far-reaching contradiction of Victorian womanhood. Furthermore, Harker's responses after his happenstance with the 'weird sisters' express late-nineteenth-century angst surrounding the feminization of males — in that the concept of a man being seduced by women would be a stark reversal of ideals.

Exactly a century after Bram introduced his vampiric 'weird sisters.' J.K. Rowling presents her variation to the wizarding world as a very popular progressive band featured on the Wizarding Wireless Network. Headmaster Albus Dumbledore books them to perform at Hogwarts at the 1994 Yule Ball in Book 4: *The Goblet of Fire*. J.K. Rowling has stated Macbeth is "quite possibly her favorite Shakespeare play," while the Spanish edition of the book refers to the band by the name las Brujas de Macbeth

(Macbeth's Witches). It is also worth mentioning a second reference to Macbeth was made in the year three film, *The Prisoner of Azkaban* when the Frog Choir sings *Double Double Toil and Trouble.*

Indeed, it might not appear like there is ample opportunity for a vogue musical group amongst all the sorcery, Quidditch, and additional 'wizarding world' conjured things (ones that Muggles cannot comprehend) at the school of Hogwarts. However, in walk the Weird Sisters in the fourth year of the saga-turned-film franchise — a remarkable star-studded Britpop band featuring Pulp's Jarvis Cocker on lead vocals and members of Radiohead, All Seeing I, and Add N to (X). They show up to musically (and literally) teach the students and teachers alike how to "Do the Hippogriff."

In spite of their name, all eight known members of the Weird Sisters are male. Aside from their most popular track, *Do the Hippogriff,* which they perform at the Yule Ball, their other hits, *Magic Works* and *This is the Night,* are also debuted. The former song's last verse actually repeats the lyrics "a creature of the night" twice. The Weird Sisters' tracks could be classified as grunge, and their look is ultra-glam rock. Undeniably, all members of the band are described as being "extremely hairy," and all wear "black robes" that have been artfully torn. In fact, one could make the argument that the band is made up of a group of vampires, for not only are they clad all in black, but they each have dark hair, pale faces, black eye makeup, and red lipstick. To make it even more convincing, the stage is covered in a mysterious fog-like mist as they perform and hypnotize everyone on the dance floor. Just as Jonathan Harker gets carried away by a silvery, musical laugh, Professor Flitwick is lost in a mosh pit by a hot alt-rock lark. Are they good enough to become one of the greatest bands ever? *Rolling Stone* magazine ranks Harry Potter's Weird Sisters as number twenty-two of the twenty-five greatest cinematic bands of all time. So, it appeared they were in it for the long haul. Who knows, in fifty years, they may grow to be as famous as J.K. Rowling herself.

Part Two

Locations

Chapter Seven

The United Kingdom

The setting, or place and time, of a book, stages the story, immersing readers into the author's world, creating a mood and atmosphere that matches the parameters for the characters' lives and actions. The place can evolve and change as the story progresses as a clever tool to show the passage of time, thus, making the story feel more real. Stoker and Rowling decided to set their respective works in the United Kingdom (save for the Transylvanian opening and closing of *Dracula*), which makes valuable and perfect sense. After all, both master writers were born and raised in the U.K (Stoker, Dublin and Rowling, Yate) and drew inspiration from the rich history, customs, and culture that blended wonderfully into their magical and fantastical tales.

If one were to stand today on the tarmac outside the Royal Hotel on Whitby's West Cliff and look out across the harbor village as the sun sinks low, one could visualize the early chapters of *Dracula*. Indeed, across the bay, in the silhouette of the half-ruined abbey, sits St Mary's Churchyard, where Lucy Westenra is bitten by the newly-arrived vampire. Below is Tate Hill Pier and its infamous sands, where the Russian ship, the Demeter, transporting the Count runs aground — its crew missing, and the dead skipper lashed to the wheel. Finally, the 199 steps, celebrated locally as the 'church stairs,' rise to the East Cliff, where Dracula, in the guise of a black dog, disappears after arriving in Whitby. Aside from a few modern alterations, today's picturesque view would be the same that Bram Stoker himself would have drawn inspiration from in his 1897 novel. This peaceful view quickly becomes synonymous with the horror of *Dracula*.

Undeniably, it was at the end of July 1890 that the blaze of Stoker's classic was sparked. The moonlighting writer, whose day job was business manager of the actor Sir Henry Irving, had just withstood a slightly disastrous tour of Scotland with his theatrical company. Consequently, Irving felt they should all take a month's holiday before regrouping for the next performance, and he suggested Stoker visit Whitby on the North Yorkshire coast, where the actor had once operated a circus. Taking his boss's advice, Stoker took rooms at a guesthouse at 6 Royal Crescent, where his wife Florence and son Noel would join him in August. Bram was alone for a week and a half, roaming the fishing port and talking to the locals, formulating ideas that would appear in his famous work. Little has changed in the streets around Royal Crescent since, such as the whalebone arch framing the cold grey North Sea. It has been said that when the writer took up residency in Royal Crescent that his landlady would put him out in the morning so she could clean the room. Stoker would go to the reading room of the Royal Hotel and look out at the same scene you can see now, which was instrumental in the creation of *Dracula*. Bram would go around, saturating himself in the ambiance. From talking to the old salts on the harbor to mooching around the churchyard up on the East Cliff, Stoker amassed an indulgence of local myths and lore noticeable to anyone acquainted with the *Dracula* story. For example, in the novel, the Count's arrival was based on a real 1885 event when a ship, the Dmitry, was beached on Tate Hill Sands. The vampire running ashore as a black dog was more than likely based on a legend Bram would have overheard about a dark hound brought over by the Vikings. Finally, the black coach that takes Jonathan Harker to Castle Dracula was taken from a local story about the lord of Mulgrave Castle, who used a black coach that clattered down the path when he was on his way to court Elizabeth Cholmeley.

Such research, background, and details are essential in story writing. In fact, literary professors suggest that a location is critical to the creation of a novel because the setting itself becomes an essential character in the tale — complete with a past, present, and future. Critic and author Aliya Whiteley comments, "the best creepy stories take place against the creepy backdrop of the British countryside." With British gothic authors like Horace Walpole, the Bronte sisters, Montague Summers, Algernon Blackwood, and Clive Barker in the mix, one would have to agree. Now close your eyes for a minute and picture a remote village — full of mysterious folklore and black moors. Next, imagine moist westerly winds and unsettling storms engulfing the setting. Finally, place an ancient church, crumbling graveyard, and a ruined abbey amidst the haunting imagery. Welcome to Whitby!

In 1990, exactly one hundred years since Stoker's *Dracula* flame was ignited, J.K. Rowling first conceptualized the Harry Potter saga while delayed for hours on a crowded train traveling from Manchester to London's King's Cross. It just "fell into my head," she explained. "I had been writing almost continuously since the age of six, but I had never been so excited about an idea before. I simply sat and thought for four hours, and all the details bubbled up in my brain, and this scrawny, black-haired, be-spectacled boy who did not know he was a wizard became more and more real to me." Similarly, as Stoker wrote in Whitby and Cruden Bay, where those influences, sights, and sounds mingled their way into *Dracula*, Rowling took her ideas to Edinburgh, where she wrote at the Nicholson's and Elephant's House cafes. In November 2006, Rowling locked herself in the Balmoral Hotel in Edinburgh to write the critical final chapters of *The Deathly Hallows.* Her research and sightings around the city found their respective places into her wizarding world in the most interesting of ways.

Edinburgh, Scotland, is famous for its towering castle, annual international arts festival, delightful scones, and Victoria Street — a curving, cobblestoned stone road bursting with charming shops, stale pubs, and buildings with colorfully painted exteriors. This narrow, wavy street with stony high-rise structures and pointed gables causes Diagon Alley to come to mind instantaneously. Indeed, it was here that Rowling was inspired to create the enchanted shopping street. In fact, Aha Ha Ha Jokes & Novelties, located at the bottom of the street, has placed a sign in its window warning tourists not to mistake their shop for a real-life take on Weasleys' Wizard Wheezes. Likewise, an RBS bank and stationery store are located in the same positions on Victoria Street as Gringotts Bank, while Flourish and Blotts are on Diagon Alley. To see the actual Diagon Alley set used in the Harry Potter films, one would need to visit Leavesden Film Studios, which is located about 20 miles north of London.

Located behind Victoria is the café, The Elephant House, that Rowling haunted while writing the Harry Potter series. The author usually wrote in the back room, sitting by a window overlooking George Heriot's School, a former hospital built in the Scottish Renaissance style in 1628. This building aided as her graphic muse for the Hogwarts School of Witchcraft and Wizardry.

As Stoker did at Whitby, Rowling would frequently take mental breaks from writing, and stroll along the alleys of Edinburgh's Old Town. Like Bram, having a touch of a morbid streak, Rowling would often meander through Greyfriars Kirkyard, a cemetery dating back to the late 16th Century. There the author toured the gravestones of many of Scotland's supreme philosophers, novelists, soldiers, and nobles. Some of those buried there — including the grave of Thomas Riddell and the renowned unmarked tomb of William McGonagall — aided Rowling with names for some of her most adored and abhorred characters.

Rowling has said, "I've taken horrible liberties with folklore and mythology, and I'm quite unashamed about that because British folklore and British mythology is a totally bastard mythology. You know, we've been invaded by people, we've appropriated their gods, we've taken their mythical creatures, and we've soldered them all together to make, what I would say, is one of the richest folklores in the world because it's so varied. So, I feel no compunction about borrowing from that freely but adding a few things of my own."

Once more, shut your eyes for a minute and picture a port city — one full of mystifying folklore. Now, envision cold, northern windstorms overwhelming the setting. Then place an ancient dominating castle on a massive rock in the center of the town. Finally, visualize a medieval street that sweeps to an old village, where its southern edge is adjacent to a haunting church and 16th-century graveyard. No, we are not in Whitby this time…we have taken the Hogwarts Express to Edinburgh!

Just as the ideas for Harry Potter were mentally written while waiting on a delayed train, so did Jonathan Harker make entries in his diary while waiting on a delayed train, writing "[—] I had to sit in the carriage for more than an hour before we began to move. It seems to me that the further East you go the more unpunctual are the trains. What ought they to be in China?"

To make matters more interesting, it is a known fact that J.K. Rowling's parents, like Harry, Ron, and Hermione, met on a train while traveling from Kings Cross Station, London, to Arbroath in Scotland.

Like her famous orphaned young wizard, Joanne Rowling was brought up in suburban British neighborhoods, much like the Dursleys in her books, in the south of England, outside Bristol. Her home even had a cupboard under the stairs, but at the impressionable age of nine, Rowling's family moved to the country, near the Forest of Dean — a location that undoubtedly extended a wide range of creative juices: ghostly beings, mysterious creatures, and supernatural intrigue. Rowling said in a November 2006 interview with James Runcie, which has been obtained by ABC News. "The advantage of a forest is it can be so many things: it can be a place of enchantment, you never imagine a crowd in a forest; it's a solitary place. But there's just something, is it because it used to be a place of shelter and safety to us, I suppose, so I think, I, I am very drawn to them, even though they can be spooky." Bram Stoker concurred with Rowling because Transylvania literally means 'land beyond the forest.' Jonathan Harker writes, "I read that every known superstition in the world is gathered into the horseshoe of the Carpathians, as if it were the center of some sort of imaginative whirlpool; if so, my stay may be very interesting."

London, and various areas around England, were the central locations of *Dracula* and the Harry Potter series. In 1897, the year that *Dracula* was published, London was the center of the British Empire, which contained a vast percentage of the world's population. It was the capital city and one of the largest metropolitan areas on the globe. Its overcrowded, labyrinth-like thoroughfares made it an awe-inspiring place of potential danger. After all, it was home to the infamous Jack the Ripper, who terrorized London in late 1888. London was the perfect city for a vampire to run amuck, and

Stoker capitalized on this. But he was not alone; London inspired many writers of darker fiction at the time: *The Picture of Dorian Gray* by Oscar Wilde, *Dr. Jekyll and Mr. Hyde* by Robert Louis Stevenson, The Sherlock Holmes series by Arthur Conan Doyle, and the works of Charles Dickens.

Victorian London was a hectic, hustling, dirty place, infamous for its dense smog and stench. The vile combination of sewage, coal fires, and unwashed bodies added to the city's reputation for having a horrendous odor. The rich and the poor had to contend with the pungent air around the city. Even the royal family was not immune to the squalor and, at one time, was forced to cancel a water excursion due to raw sewage being dumped into the Thames. London streets were filled with manure from horses. Illness was rampant as buildings became covered in layers of soot from coal fires, thus causing the air to be heavy and sometimes unbreathable from smoke. Stoker cunningly used the powerful sense of smell by seizing the authentic, deplorable conditions of his Victorian London and spewed them on the pages of *Dracula*. Because the king vampire's character was symbolic of an evil disease, the London hideouts of the Count were infested with the repulsive smells that followed. Jonathan Harker regurgitates this imagery grotesquely from his journal in Chapter 19:

> "With a little trouble we found the key on the bunch and opened the door. We were prepared for some unpleasantness, for as we were opening the door a faint, malodorous air seemed to exhale through the gaps, but none of us ever expected such an odour as we encountered. None of the others had met the Count at all at close quarters, and when I had seen him he was either in the fasting stage of his existence in his rooms or, when he was gloated with fresh blood, in a ruined building open to the air; but here the place was small and close, and the long disuse had made the air stagnant and foul. There was an earthy smell, as of some dry miasma, which came through the fouler air. But as to the odour itself, how shall I describe it? It was not alone that it was composed of all the ills of mortality and with the pungent, acrid smell of blood, but it seemed as though corruption had become itself corrupt. Faugh! it sickens me to think of it. Every breath exhaled by that monster seemed to have clung to the place and intensified its loathsomeness."

Victorian London not only suffered from unpleasant smells — the population of the city skyrocketed in the 18th century, leading to a severe contrast between the fertile modern building developments in prosperous areas and the overcrowded shantytowns. Living circumstances for the poor were abysmal, and the streets were bursting with beggars, desperate children, and sellers of everything from flowers and trinkets to shoddy meat. The conditions led to pick-pocketing and other petty crimes. The wealthier residents of the city, much like the characters in *Dracula*, owned large residences, complete with running water, servants, and even electricity. A household would be managed by a sizable staff, including a maid, cook, butler, coachman, gardener, courier, porter, usher, chasseur, and footman. Merchants would bring groceries to the servant's entrance of the mansion, where the cook or housekeeper would make the purchase. Well-to-do Victorian mistresses and gentlemen were not to be bothered with any of the mundane, dirty, or menial tasks about the household. During Stoker's time, the rich and the poor were often at odds with one another. Much of the immigration that overpopulated the city only contributed to the rise of 'unfortunates.' London society feared foreigners, for many of these 'strangers from a strange land' were symbolic of corruption. This real-life stance is reinvented perfectly when Dracula refers to himself as a "stranger in a strange land" and proceeds to bring his vampiric pestilence to Victorian England at a time when the Black Death was still feared, the cholera epidemic was fresh in thought, and the consumption (tuberculosis) panic had many believing in the undead.

"But a stranger in a strange land, he is no one. Men know him not, and to know not is to care not for." Dracula to Jonathan Harker

As described in *Dracula*, wealthy Victorians would travel about London in horse-drawn carriages, and public cabs were available for hire if needed. Theatres, opera houses, and concert halls offered diverse entertainments. And as Mina Murray often describes, brass bands could be heard playing on bandstands in the parks. The Royal Albert Hall provided an impressive stage for concerts as of 1871, and the Great Exhibition of 1851 led to the founding of the Science Museum and the Victoria & Albert Museum. The British Museum was likewise an admired attraction, which Van Helsing (and Stoker) visited during his research on Dracula.

Like Whitby, Stoker references many actual locations in *Dracula* that can still be visited today. For example, the Zoological Gardens that house the escaped wolf 'Berserker' are located in Regent's Park, London. Opened in 1828, it is the world's oldest scientific zoo. In literature, a zoo can be a metaphor for modern society, the "wild at large," and how — even as hard as man may try — its primitive nature cannot remain imprisoned. In Chapter 11 of the novel, an unnamed journalist for the *Pall Mall Gazette* interviews the amusing zookeeper, Thomas Bilder, who speaks with a cockney accent. Bram Stoker's wit shines in these pages as the reporter asks Bilder how he accounts for the wolf's escape. To this question, Bilder replies, "Well then, Sir, I account for it this way. It seems to me that 'ere wolf escaped — simply because he wanted to get out."

Another location worth visiting in London is Hampstead Heath, located mostly in Camden. Going back to 1808, it is a large, ancient London park covering 790 acres of grassy public space, running from Hampstead to Highgate and one of the highest open spaces in London. In Chapter 13 of *Dracula*, Professor Van Helsing picks up a newspaper while boarding a train and reads:

"The Westminster Gazette, 25 September
Extra Special
The Hampstead Horror
Another Child Injured
The "Bloofer Lady"

We have just received intelligence that another child, missed last night, was only discovered late in the morning under a furze bush at the Shooter's Hill side of Hampstead Heath, which is perhaps, less frequented than the other parts. It has the same tiny wound in the throat as has been noticed in other cases. It was terribly weak and looked quite emaciated. It too, when partially restored, had the common story to tell of being lured away by the "bloofer lady."

At this point in the novel, the doctor realizes that Lucy Westenra is undead and needs to be stopped.

Highgate Cemetery, located at Swain's Lane, Highgate in London, was founded in 1839 in the north area of the city. It is designated Grade I on the Historic England Register of Parks and Gardens of Special Historic Interest in England. Divided into two parts, named the East and West cemetery, it is an immaculate spectacle of beautiful, gothic Victorian tombs and mausoleums. It was also the inspired location of Lucy Westenra's tomb and home of the Highgate Vampire, which was a media sensation in the 1970s. While surveying the graves for potential vampires, one could also pay their respects to writer Karl Marx and singer George Michael.

Toward the beginning of Chapter 15, after visiting one of the Bloofer Lady's young victims at the North Hospital, Professor Van Helsing and Dr. Seward have a late meal. As Dr. Seward's diary reads, "We dined at 'Jack Straws Castle' along with a little crowd of bicyclists and others who were genially noisy." Jack Straws Castle, located at 12 North End Way, Hampstead, was an iconic pub and trademark restaurant upstairs. Due to the property decline in the 2000s, it closed and has since been turned into a group of housing units with a small café. However, they kept the pub façade and name intact for horror enthusiasts.

The Spaniards Inn, located at Spaniards Road, Hampstead, is one of London's oldest pubs. Opened in 1585, it has rightfully earned a place in the history books in a literal sense. Charles Dickens immortalized the popular inn in *The Pickwick Papers*. Likewise, it is known that John Keats wrote *Ode to a Nightingale* there, in its beautiful garden, over a claret or two. In Chapter 15 of Bram Stoker's *Dracula*, Dr. Seward's diary mentions the location when he notes: "By good chance, we got a cab near the "Spaniards," and drove to town." Still thriving today with a few tales of its own to tell, the distinctive 16th-century inn is a romantic idyll in itself and a country pub in the city. It features a garden impressive enough to rival the vast Heath itself. There is a separate dining area that maintains roaring fires in the winter, and the inn is amply full of fascinating crannies in which to muse over the unmatched food and beverage menus.

Another popular spot in *Dracula* is Piccadilly. Not only did Jonathan Harker see the Count here — grown younger, staring at a beautiful girl in a big cart-wheel hat — but it was also the location of one of the vampire's lairs. Piccadilly, a thoroughfare in west-central London, begins at Piccadilly Circus and runs southwest approximately three-quarters of a mile to Hyde Park Corner. 138 Piccadilly, located opposite Green Park and the Hard Rock Cafe, is now known as the Eon House. It is believed this is the house that Stoker referenced as the Piccadilly location where Dracula hid a portion of his earth boxes. In literature, references to Piccadilly are synonymous with the mixing of different classes and cultures. While Stoker warns the world of the dangers of vampire migration in a city fueled by class and culture wars, Rowling, in the same way, explores human animosity between magic and non-magic folk and witches and wizards who follow a different path.

Though the Harry Potter saga was largely set in a magical United Kingdom, many locations were inspired by real places that were also used in the film series. Beginning in the fictional suburban London town of Little Whinging (where the gentle giant Hagrid landed his flying motorcycle), #4 Privet Drive becomes Harry's full-time non-enchanted residence until age 11. An infant Harry — a 'stranger in a strange land,' mind you — is left on the doorstep to be reared by an anti-magic aunt and uncle. In the first film, *Harry Potter and the Sorcerer's Stone* (2001), the Dursleys' home was shot in the town of Bracknell (pop. 50,000, 10 miles west of Heathrow) on a street of generic brick rowhouses called Picket Close. For the second film, *The Chamber of Secrets* (2002), Warner Brothers built a replica set of the house, which was also used for the subsequent six films. Many associate this house with Harry's home; however, further analysis proves quite the opposite. Harry never truly considered #4 Privet Drive home. The young wizard was a prisoner there. Just as Jonathan Harker looked for an opportunity to escape the prison of Castle Dracula in the opening of Stoker's novel, Rowling made it clear Harry could not wait to leave the Dursleys' abuse.

Fast forward ten years, and Harry first encounters his wizard powers when talking with a boa constrictor at the London Zoo's Reptile House in Regent's Park on Great Portland Street (the same zoo Berserker the wolf escaped from in *Dracula*). Harry soon gets invited to Hogwarts School of Witchcraft and Wizardry to learn the magical skills needed to confront his parents' murderer, Lord Voldemort. Along the Thames River, Big Ben and Parliament welcome Harry to the modern city of London that bustles with Muggles — quite oblivious to the parallel universe of wizards. There, Hagrid takes Harry shopping for school supplies. The wonderfully ornately decorated glassed-roof Leadenhall Market was used as Diagon Alley in the films. Located at Gracechurch St, London, the entrance to the wizard's pub, the Leaky Cauldron was in an optician's storefront at 42 Bull's Head Passage. In the Potter series, the pub is placed amongst the many stores of Charing Cross Road in London's West End, renowned for its assortment of bookshops and more general second-hand and antiquarian market, giving the street a fascinating appeal. This vicinity is used to hiding secrets, for a century earlier, a king vampire walked its streets and concealed his earth boxes amongst its naive citizens.

For Harry and Hagrid, the Leaky Cauldron's back wall parts and opens onto the mystic Diagon Alley, where they shop for wands, cauldrons, and wizard textbooks. Harry pays for them with gold Galleons from Gringotts, a wizarding bank run by goblins in a unique setting: the grand interior of the marble-floored and chandeliered Exhibition Hall of Australia House, opened by King George V in 1918 and home of the Australian Embassy located on the Strand in central London.

St. Pancras railway station, also known as London St Pancras and since 2007 as St Pancras International, is a central London railway terminus located on Euston Road in the London Borough of Camden. In the film adaptations of Rowling's work, this is where Harry catches the train to Hogwarts at King's Cross Station. In the first film, inside the glass-roofed train station, on a pedestrian sky bridge over the tracks, Hagrid gives Harry a train ticket. He proceeds to Platform 9¾, where he and his soon-to-become-best-mate Ron magically push their luggage carts through a brick pillar between the platforms, emerging into a hidden wizarding realm. One can visit King's Cross main concourse today and find a Platform 9 ¾ sign with a luggage cart that looks like it's disappearing into the wall next to a Harry Potter gift shop. During peak vacation seasons, it can take up to a 30-minute wait for a fun photo op next to the sign. It is worth mentioning that King's Cross station is one of the locations where

Dracula's 'earth boxes' are delivered, and the London railway is used repeatedly by Professor Van Helsing.

In the Potter saga, a red steam train known as the Hogwarts Express carries the young witches and wizards through the Scottish countryside to Hogwarts, where they spend the next seven years. The locomotive that transports the students to school each year was filmed along an actual steam-train line that ran between Fort William and Mallaig. The cinematic shots show the train chugging across the picturesque real-life Glenfinnan Viaduct — also the location where, in *The Goblet of Fire* (2005), the Dementors stopped to search the train and tormented Harry. Indeed, a locomotive bridge opposite Loch Shiel near Fort William was used in *The Chamber of Secrets* (2002) and popped up again when the Dementor boards the train in *The Prisoner of Azkaban* (2004). The steam engine used in filming is now on display at a Platform 9¾ exhibit at the Harry Potter Warner Bros. Studio Tour. Putting Hollywood props aside, it is worth noting that the allure of trains did not begin with Stoker nor end with Rowling. Literary critics have written for years that the use of trains in literature has been more than just a mode of transportation — that they can provide depth, mystery, murder, and adventure to a story. Indeed, each author uses locomotives as a place of bonding, sharing of information, and escape.

Like Stoker was influenced by England and Scotland in his literature, so was J.K. Rowling in hers. For the accompanying Harry Potter films, countless outdoor sequences — particularly scenes of the Hogwarts grounds — were also shot in rocky, overcast, enigmatic Scotland, much of it in the Fort William and Glencoe areas. In the third movie, *The Prisoner of Azkaban* (2004), Hogwarts Lake was shot using Loch Shiel, Loch Eilt, and Loch Morar near Fort William. Hagrid skips stones across the water at Loch Eilt, and Steal Falls, a waterfall at the base of Ben Nevis, was the locality for Harry's combat with a Hungarian Horntail dragon for the Triwizard Tournament in *The Goblet of Fire* (2005). Other scenes filmed in the Highlands included a bleak hillside with Hagrid's stone hut in Glencoe, which was also the main location for outdoor filming in *The Prisoner of Azkaban* (2004). Exterior scenes for *The Half-Blood Prince* (2009) were likewise filmed in Glencoe in addition to the tiny village of Glenfinnan.

Also, in *The Prisoner of Azkaban* (2004), Harry speeds through London's lamp-lit streets on a purple three-decker bus, which is also on display at the Warner Brothers studio tour. The bus discards him at The Leaky Cauldron pub, where its exterior this time was shot on jagged Stoney Street at the southeast edge of Borough Street Market, by The Market Porter pub, with trains rumbling overhead.

In *The Order of the Phoenix* (2007), the members take to the sky at dusk on broomsticks, swooping down on the famous Thames River and over London, passing many popular landmarks: the Tower Bridge, London Eye, Big Ben, and Buckingham Palace. The group arrives at 'Number Twelve Grimmauld Place,' Sirius Black's home, which was filmed at Lincoln's Inn Fields, a park-like square near Sir John Soane's Museum. In the dramatic finale to *The Half-Blood Prince* (2009), footage of the Millennium Bridge in London was used to represent Brockdale Bridge when it is attacked by Death Eaters and collapses into the Thames.

For *The Order of the Phoenix* (2007) and *The Deathly Hallows Part 1* (2010), the real government offices of Whitehall served as exteriors for the Ministry of Magic. The location is just off Trafalgar Square. The archway used in the films can be visited at the junction with Scotland Place. However, as this road was considered too short, filming was done on Great Scotland Yard, and the archway over the road was added in line with the first lamppost covering the doorway. In addition, a red telephone box (only a prop) was placed in front, just before the first window. It was along Scotland Place that Harry and Mr. Weasley walked as they made their way to the Ministry of Magic for Harry's hearing on charges of using magic in front of Muggles.

Just as the characters in *Dracula* find trouble in Piccadilly Circus, the same can be said for Harry Potter and his friends. In *The Deathly Hallows* (2010-2011), Harry, Ron, and Hermione battle Death Eaters in a Muggle café. In Part 1 of the film, this takes place at the Luchino located at Tottenham Court Road in West End's bustling Piccadilly Circus.

Ron Weasley: "Just as a matter of interest, why Tottenham Court Road?"

Hermione Granger: "I've no idea; it just popped into my head, but I'm sure we're safer out in the Muggle world; it's not where they'll expect us to be."

Ron Weasley: "True...but don't you feel a bit — exposed?"

Just as Dracula's Castle is a central and dominating structure in Bram Stoker's novel, Hogwarts, Harry's esteemed wizarding school, is the identifiable landmark in J.K. Rowling's series. For the films, Hogwarts Castle was an amalgamation of several locations — many of them real places in Oxford. For example, Christ Church, Oxford University, inspired two film sets recognizable to Potter enthusiasts. In *The Sorcerer's Stone*, the kids arrive at Hogwarts and climb a grand stone staircase — the exact one that, in reality, leads into Christ Church College's Great Hall. In truth, Christ Church's ostentatiously elevated-ceilinged dining hall (devoid of the floating candles and blazing braziers) was the model for the one seen throughout the films; however, the actual shooting occurred on a set at the Leavesden studios. In *The Sorcerer's Stone*

(2001), where Harry sneaks into the restricted book section of Hogwarts Library under a cloak of invisibility, the scene was filmed inside Oxford's Duke Humfrey's Library. Hermione reads about the Sorcerer's Stone there as well. At the end of *The Sorcerer's Stone* (2001), Harry awakens in the infirmary filmed in the large-windowed Divinity School on the ground floor of the Bodleian Library. This is the same location where Ron convalesces after being poisoned in *The Half-Blood Prince* (2009). And in *The Goblet of Fire* (2005), Mad-Eye Moody turns Draco Malfoy into a ferret in the New College cloister.

Once at Hogwarts, Harry is taught how to wave his wand by little Professor Flitwick in a wood-paneled classroom, filmed at Harrow School in Harrow on the Hill, eight miles northwest of London. In the same film, Harry walks with his snow-white owl, Hedwig, through a wintery ancient cloister courtyard filmed in the U.K.'s awe-inspiring Durham Cathedral. Another popular moment from the first book is when Harry learns to fly a broomstick on the emerald lawn of Hogwarts' grounds. This scene was filmed inside the walls of the breathtaking Alnwick Castle, located 30 miles from Newcastle. In *The Chamber of Secrets* (2002), Alnwick was also where the Weasleys' flying car crashed into the Whomping Willow.

As with Castle Dracula, there was a darker side of Hogwarts; many of these sequences were shot in the elaborate, fan-vaulted corridors of the Gloucester Cathedral cloisters, 50 miles north of Bath. For instance, in *The Sorcerer's Stone* (2001), when Harry and Ron leave their housemates to save Hermione, they look down an extended, shadowy Gloucester hallway and discover a creepy 20-foot-tall troll at the end. Another famous yet somewhat spooky location used in *The Sorcerer's Stone* (2001) was the halls of the 13th-century Lacock Abbey, 13 miles east of Bath. The abbey was chosen for the scene in which Harry officially joins Gryffindor's Quidditch team; likewise, Professor Snape's classroom was shot in one of the abbey's darker, neglected, flaking-plaster rooms — fitting perfectly with Snape's morose personality.

Finally, outdoor sequences from the first *Deathly Hallows* (2010) film, where Harry, Ron, and Hermione take sanctuary in the woods, were shot in the Swinley Forest area of Windsor's Great Park. In the second *Deathly Hallows* (2011), the crucial scene at Lily and James Potter's cottage (known as the De Vere house) in Godric's Hollow — when Harry becomes the 'Boy Who Lived' — was filmed in the feudal village of Lavenham, Suffolk, about 75 miles northeast of London. In the same film, Harry and Hagrid zip through Liverpool's Queensway Tunnel on Sirius Black's flying motorcycle as they escape a group of fervent Death Eaters. In both *Deathly Hallows* films (2010-2011), Shell Cottage, home of Bill Weasley and Fleur Delacour, is a hideaway for the central characters. The cottage provisionally sat on Freshwater West beach in the southwestern region of Pembrokeshire. Additionally, it's the same beach where Harry, Ron, and Hermione wash up after leaping off the back of a dragon in Part II and where they bury their dear friend, Dobby, the freed house-elf, after being stabbed by Bellatrix Lestrange at Malfoy Manor.

"Such a beautiful place it is, to be with friends. Dobby is happy to be with his friend, Harry Potter."

— Dobby's last words to Harry

To summarize, *Dracula* was described in a 26 June 1897 edition of Punch by a reviewer as 'the very weirdest of weird tales' as it presented a series of contrasts and clashes between old traditions and new ideas; scientific rationality was set against folklore and superstition; old Europe was set against modern London, and traditional notions of civilized restraint and duty were threatened at every turn by the spread of corruption and wanton depravity. The same could be stated for J.K. Rowling's Harry Potter series as Muggles and witches, and wizards collide with creatures of mythology and as Lord Voldemort's evil rationale perverts the Ministry of Magic, setting the United Kingdom of today against an older evil that must be traced back in ancient books of old magic.

Count Dracula's ventures into London, and his dark gift is his ability to move about unobserved through the packed streets while conveying the capacity to afflict all in his path with the stamp of vampirism, played upon late-Victorian fears of untrammeled immigration. One could look at Lord Voldemort in the same manner, converting fearful magical men and women into Death Eaters and killing all Muggles that cross his path.

In the late 1800s, immigration was feared as lending to a heightened rate of corruption and the upsurge of ghetto districts. In literature, dark alleyways and winding paths can be analyzed as archetypal passages into a character's mind. Indeed, *Dracula* alludes to several lairs in the megalopolis, one in Chicksand Street, Whitechapel — the area infamous for the Jack the Ripper massacres of 1888 — and one in Bermondsey, the locale of Jacob's Island — the slum rookery reinvigorated by Charles Dickens in *Oliver Twist*. In the Potter series, except for Hogwarts itself and Malfoy Manor, the rest of the wizarding world lives in modest to underprivileged areas while fearing attacks on Mudbloods, those born of only one wizarding parent, who are no longer welcome in the community per the 'new regime.'

Chapter Eight

Castles

Merriam-Webster's dictionary defines the word 'castle' as 1. A large fortified building or set of buildings; 2. A massive or imposing house; or 3. A retreat safe against intrusion or invasion. However, the perception of the word 'castle' carries, for many, deeper meaning or understanding. Indeed, some adventurers are so captivated by 'imposing safe retreats' that they make it their life's work to visit as many of these ancient structures as possible around Europe. As the Harry Potter series celebrated its 20th birthday in June 2017, hundreds of fans posted on social media their happy travels to the larger-than-life Hogwarts Castle's groundbreaking ride at Universal Studios or to the smaller scale model at Leavesden Studios, which was used for the many films. Stoker and Rowling knew that a building could influence one's feelings, behaviors, and aspirations, or, as daydreams are commonly referred to, 'castle(s) in the air.' Medieval architecture has historically been more closely connected to Gothic literature than any other type. In the 1700s, Gothic literature was born when Horace Walpole wrote *The Castle of Otranto* (1764), a dark tale whereby Walpole interjected into the modern novel elements of Ancient Romance. Known also as the first supernatural English novel, the text mixes aspects of realist fiction with the paranormal and fantastical, forming many of the plot strategies and character types that became the standard of the Gothic novel: hidden passageways, banging trapdoors, moving pictures, and self-closing doors. As the title boasts, the uncanny structure is the chief subject of the story, founding an eerie atmosphere at the beginning of the unsettling tale and building upon it until the climactic ending. Indeed, *Dracula* and the Harry Potter sagas begin and end in their respective castles, the edifices almost becoming living central characters themselves.

In Stoker's novel, Castle Dracula is the single most important location. The first and the last part of the story takes place in this unapproachable fortress — the location, which originally symbolized the vampire's power, becomes the blueprint of his extermination in the final pages. The actual locale of the Count's abode is undoubtedly the greatest mystery of the novel. The route descriptions in Stoker's narrative do not mention any recognizable landmarks but instead focus on hints and traces of a wild and snow-covered setting, disturbed by howling wolves and lit by ghostlike blue flames at night. Because of this conspicuous vagueness, Bran Castle has been nicknamed Dracula's Castle as it is the nearest domain to the Borgo Pass that fits Stoker's description. In Chapter 2, May 5, readers find this map: "...on the very edge of a terrific precipice ...with occasionally a deep rift where there is a chasm [with] silver threads where the rivers wind in deep gorges through the forests."

It is interesting to point out that Bram Stoker originally intended to have the castle destroyed at the end of the novel, similar to Hogwarts at the end of the Harry Potter saga. Indeed, three paragraphs from the original manuscript, in which the fortress is swallowed by a volcanic catastrophe, did not make the printed version. Explored reasoning has suggested that Stoker wanted to leave the option of a sequel open or that the alternate ending leaned too much on Edgar Allan Poe's *The Fall of the House of Usher*.

"As we looked there came a terrible convulsion of the earth so that we seemed to rock to and fro and fell to our knees. At the same moment, with a roar that seemed to shake the very heavens the whole castle and the rock and even the hill on which it stood seemed to rise into the air and scatter in fragments while a mighty cloud of black and yellow smoke volume on volume in rolling grandeur was shot upwards with inconceivable rapidity. Then there was a stillness in nature as the echoes of that thunderous report seemed to come as with the hollow boom of a thunder-clap — the long reverberating roll which seems as though the floors of heaven shook. Then down in a mighty ruin falling whence they rose came the fragments that had been tossed skywards in the cataclysm. From where we stood it seemed as though the one fierce volcano burst had satisfied the need of nature and that the castle and the structure of the hill had sunk again into the void. We were so appalled with the suddenness and the grandeur that we forgot to think of ourselves."

In his annotated *Dracula* edition, Leslie Klinger suggests that these lines were part of Count Dracula's efforts to 'cover up' the truth about the vampire's continuing activities but that Stoker sabotaged the Count's editorial intervention by deleting them.

Due to its unique role in one of the best-known horror classics of all time, Castle Dracula has lived on in numerous movies, such as *Blood of Dracula's Castle* (1969). In addition, there are copious video games: Dracula's Castle (Game Pac Adventure), Escape Dracula's Castle (Fun Flash Games), Restore Dracula's Castle, and Devil's Castle Dracula (Akumajō Dracula) — the latter best known to the west as Castlevania. And there is a Prosecco produced by a descendant of the Basarab dynasty bearing the name Castle of Dracula.

Similar to the Count's fictional abode, Hogwarts Castle has become a worldwide icon since J.K. Rowling published *The Philosopher's Stone* in 1997. From t-shirts and video games to Legos and theme parks, the fictitious school of witchcraft and wizardry has influenced pop culture in multi-facets. Indeed, Hogwarts was voted as the 36th best Scottish educational establishment in a 2008 online poll, outranking Edinburgh's Loretto School, a well-established academy that has taught many pupils that have gone on to become well-known actors, artists, athletes, and politicians. According to a director of the Independent Schools Network Rankings, Hogwarts was added to the school's listing 'for fun' and was then voted upon.

Hogwarts, an imaginary British school of magic for pupils aged eleven to eighteen, was the primary setting for the Harry Potter series. Like Jonathan Harker, Harry Potter walks into the castle spellbound and captivated in the beginning and then returns in the end to defeat evil. Rowling commented that she may have inadvertently taken the name from the hogwort plant (Croton capitatus), which she had seen at Kew Gardens, a botanical park in southwest London that houses the largest and most diverse botanical and mycological collections in the world. However, the names 'The Hogwarts' and 'Hoggwart' appeared in the 1954 Nigel Molesworth book *How To Be Topp* by Geoffrey Willans.

Like Castle Dracula, Rowling visualized Hogwarts as a colossal, irregular, quite frightening-looking fortress replete with a jumble of turrets and fortifications. Because it was built and protected by magic, it was not a structure that muggles (non-magical folk) could have resurrected or meant to see or visit. Indeed, Hogwarts is portrayed as having an indulgence of charms and spells on and around it that make it impossible for the Muggle world to detect. Non-magic beings cannot see the school; instead, they view only ruins and numerous cautions of peril.

In the Harry Potter series, Hogwarts is located somewhere in the highlands of Scotland near a loch. In the film *Prisoner of Azkaban* (2004), it was mentioned that Dufftown is near the school — a burgh in Moray, Scotland, in the ancient parish of Mortlach. The school's setting in the novels is depicted as having vast grounds with slanting lawns, flowerbeds, and vegetable gardens, a loch (referred to as the Black Lake), an enormous thick forest (named the Forbidden Forest), many greenhouses, and a Quidditch pitch. In addition to other outbuildings, there is also an owlery, which shelters all the resting birds owned by the school and students. Interestingly, various areas in the castle are predisposed to move around, such as the grand staircase. Witches and wizards cannot apparat (appear) or disapparate (disappear) on school grounds unless the headmaster lifts the enchantment — whether only in certain areas or for the whole campus –to make the castle less vulnerable.

Akin to Castle Dracula, electricity and electronic devices are absent at Hogwarts. In *The Goblet of Fire*, Hermione points out that because of the extreme levels of enchantment, "substitutes for magic [that] Muggles use" — such as computers, radar, and electricity — "go haywire" around Hogwarts. However, radios are an exception, for Rowling explains that they are powered by magic instead of electricity.

Like the Count's fortress is near water, Hogwarts rests on the shore of a loch referred to as the Black Lake and inhabited by merpeople, grindylows, and a giant squid. The magical creatures do not attack humans and even act as lifeguards when students swim in the loch. Indeed, both fictional castles are created with eccentricities, from forbidden areas with locked doors to ghostly apparitions deemed best to keep away from. Notwithstanding, the major difference between the two fortresses is that Hogwarts is a coeducational, secondary boarding school accepting children from ages eleven to eighteen. Castle Dracula is the Count's primary residence and houses young proteges — i.e., his three vampire brides. On the other hand, Rowling initially said there were about one thousand students at Hogwarts, which she referred to as a 'multifaith school.' In response to a query posed by an interviewer, "[D]o you think there are a lot of LGBT students in modern age Hogwarts?" "I like to imagine they formed an LGBT club," Rowling replied, "But of course." As Rowling fans visualize how that minority group might be run at Hogwarts Castle, Stoker scholars are at Dracula's Castle still dissecting Dracula's word's to the weird sisters when they were caught seducing Jonathan Harker: "How dare you touch him, any of you!.... This man belongs to me!" Indeed, the inter-workings of the word 'castle,' along with its myriad of mysteries, continue to influence readers' opinions, conduct, and hopes in a world where castles are being torn down instead of being built.

So why do so many of us go on searching for the fictional Dracula's Castle and Hogwarts School of Witchcraft and Wizardry? This retort may be unearthed in how our intellect perceives these enigmatic structures. Gothic scholar and researcher Nicolas Jay van der Ward suggests: "The Gothic castle is paradoxical in other ways. To confuse the audience into a 'push-pull' sensation, the Gothic (mode) evokes two specialized devices: the uncanny (familiar-alien) and the abject (what society 'throws off' from itself). So, when viewing the castle, not only is its ontological status liminal, its effect on the viewer is one of oscillation, stupor, and awe. The viewer could be drawn to something they know is dangerous; they could be repulsed by something that appears attractive. The outside of the castle can promise something 'grander' than its four walls. Once inside, the trespasser is doomed to experience Gothic feelings, confronting a dark side of themselves and of society at large."

Another answer to this question could come from redirecting oneself back to the introduction of this chapter and reconsidering why these medieval structures were built in the first place. During barbaric times of upset, those with the rare privilege of finding refuge in a castle regarded it as an escape from a corrupt society and into a false sense of peace and safety. But always remember, in literature, castles can serve as a democratic element that judges everyone.

Chapter Nine

Cemeteries

Ghostly cemeteries and spooky broken-down crypts have been an important element of Gothic literature for centuries. Classic literature by Charles Dickens, Mary Shelly, or Edgar Alan Poe often contains cemetery scenes and references to the burial process, and these postmortem traditions continue in the nimble hands of modern writers such as Anne Rice and Stephen King. Moreover, the dead were often buried on consecrated grounds or near a neglected chapel; a spiritual place that was once well treasured has, over time, physically decayed. The stories of Dracula and Harry Potter are no different — capitalizing on this simple formula, dating back to Horace Walpole's *The Castle of Otranto* (1754), which is considered to be the first Gothic horror novel ever published. Because both *Dracula* and the Harry Potter series contain important scenes that revolve around cemeteries, they elevate their respective tales to a darker and more threatening stage.

By Chapter Eight of *Dracula*, the Count has wreaked havoc on the derelict Russian schooner, The Demeter. Upon setting foot on Tate Hill Pier at Whitby, he turns into a wolf, leaves the ship behind, and absconds to one of his previously procured London flats. At this place in the story, Mina Murray begins journaling about her nocturnal adventures and Lucy Westenra's sleepwalking. Bram Stoker sets up a brilliant picturesque view of the bay via the entertaining yet morbidly eccentric Mr. Swales: its steep cliff, the 199 steps leading up to St. Mary's Church, and the many eroded tombstones and macabre inscriptions. However, with just a few sentences, the beautiful, relaxing, protected look-out of the vacationing women instantly shifts to a grizzly, traumatic, dangerous nightmare:

> "For a moment or two I could see nothing, as the shadow of a cloud obscured
> St. Mary's Church. Then as the cloud passed, I could see the ruins of the Abbey
> coming into view; and as the edge of a narrow band of light as sharp as a sword-
> cut moved along, the church and churchyard became gradually visible... It
> seemed to me as though something dark stood behind the seat where the white

figure shone and bent over it. What it was, whether man or beast, I could not tell."

This pivotal scene is the initial moment the readers get to witness the Count's feeding first-hand — and to a central character to boot. Lucy begins to have nightmares and vague awake moments where she speaks uncharacteristically, causing more worry to be placed on Mina's shoulders. As they return to the beautiful spot where they habitually walk during the day for fresh air and solitude, they are reminded of the horror at hand:

"This afternoon she made a funny remark. We were coming home for dinner and had come to the top of the steps up from the West Pier and stopped to look at the view, as we generally do. The setting sun, low down in the sky, was just dropping behind Kettleness; the red light was thrown over on the East Cliff and the old Abbey, and seemed to bathe everything in a beautiful rosy glow. We were silent for a while, and suddenly Lucy murmured as if to herself: —

"His red eyes again! They are just the same." It was such an odd expression, coming apropos of nothing, that it quite startled me. I slewed round a little, so as to see Lucy well without seeming to stare at her and saw that she was in a half-dreamy state, with an odd look on her face that I could not quite make out; so I said nothing but followed her eyes. She appeared to be looking over at our own seat, whereon was a dark figure seated alone. I was a little started myself, for it seemed for an instant as if the stranger had great eyes like burning flames; but a second look dispelled the illusion. The red sunlight was shining on the windows of St. Mary's Church behind our seat, and as the sun dipped there was just sufficient change in the refraction and reflection to make it appear as if the light moved. I called Lucy's attention to the peculiar effect, and she became herself with a start, but she looked sad all the same; it may have been that she was thinking of that terrible night up there."

Hereafter, the young women quickly learn the nightmare is real, the attacks are personal, and remaining at Whitby is life-threatening. Thus, they decide to leave their summer vacation early and return to London in desperation. Indeed, a battle between good and evil begins at the cemetery at St. Mary's: Dracula brings Lucy to her favorite seat to kill her; however, Mina saves her in the nick of time. Even 120 years later, readers of the novel still flock to Whitby daily to walk up those 199 steps, tour the ruined abbey, and locate their favorite bench amongst the many gravestones.

As Dracula springs into action in St. Mary's churchyard in Chapter 8, the Gothic development of the Harry Potter series also expands in Little Hangleton Graveyard in

The Goblet of Fire. Lucy is lured by Dracula into danger by a hypnotic sleepwalking adventure, so it should come as no surprise that Voldemort ensures the Goblet of Fire is turned into a port key to transport Harry to him. Just as Dracula needs Lucy's blood to become strong, the Dark Lord requires Harry's blood as the pivotal ingredient in a regeneration 'baptismal-like potion' that will cause He-Who-Must-Not-Be-Named to rise to full power in physical form.

> "Bone of the father, unknowingly given, you will renew your son! Flesh of the
> servant, willingly sacrificed, you will revive your master. Blood of the enemy,
> forcibly taken, you will resurrect your foe."

—Peter Pettigrew reciting the incantation for the potion's creation

Just as Lucy Westenra's blood is taken by force, the same is true for Harry Potter. However, the use of Harry's blood in the potion will come to be a grave error, for it thwarts the Dark Lord from killing Harry as the blood passes Lily Potter's protection to Voldemort, thus anchoring Harry to the living world through him. This mistake solidifies He-Who-Must-Not-Be-Named's downfall three years later. Out of his ignorance of the power of love, Voldemort assumes that Harry's blood will permit him to weaken Lily's protection, when in fact, the regeneration spell strengthens it. One could argue the same point with Dracula choosing to use Lucy's blood to grow stronger. It actually has the reverse effect because once the Count does so, he fails to realize the power of love that protects Lucy. Henceforth Dracula finds himself running from three strong male suitors, her 'new woman' best friend, and an eager professor bent on destroying him and his kind.

The Little Hangleton graveyard is where Lord Voldemort's (a.k.a. Tom Riddle) family is buried, a site close to their generational home. The area between the house and graveyard is where Lord Voldemort and Harry Potter duel for the first time immediately after the regeneration spell is complete. It is interesting to point out that just as Dracula means to kill Lucy Westenra in St. Mary's graveyard, the Dark Lord intends to murder Harry in a similar setting. However, just as Mina Harker surfaces to save Lucy, Harry's parents and other victims of He-Who-Must-Not-Be-Named appear in order to save the young wizard as the blasts of their wands meet. Due to their twin cores, a reverse spell called *Priori Incantatem* is forced to transpire, causing Voldemort's wand to spit out spectral figures of his last five victims in reverse order.

> "A jet of green light issued from Voldemort's wand just as a jet of red light
> blasted from Harry's — they met in midair — and suddenly, Harry's wand was
> vibrating as though an electric charge were surging through it; his hand seized
> up around it; he couldn't have released it if he'd wanted to — and a narrow

beam of light connected the two wands, neither red nor green, but bright, deep gold... he felt his feet lift from the ground. He and Voldemort were both being raised into the air, their wands still connected by that thread of shimmering golden light."

— When Harry's and Voldemort's twin wand cores connected

Finally, as fans of Dracula pay their respects to Lucy by sitting on her bench in the St. Mary's churchyard of Whitby, Potter followers show up at the Greyfriars Kirkyard in Edinburgh to place flowers or hate mail on Thomas Riddell's grave.

The second central cemetery utilized in Dracula is Highgate. Like St. Mary's at Whitby, Highgate is a real place in London, located near St. John's church in Hampstead. About halfway through the novel, several trips to Lucy's tomb become a crucial, fundamental part of the book when reality and acceptance set in; the word 'vampire' is spoken for the first time in the novel; Dr. Seward accepts Van Helsing's long-winded explanation that Miss Lucy (a.k.a. the Bloofer Lady) is the source of the attacks on children at Hampstead Heath; Lucy's fiancé, Arthur Holmwood (a.k.a. Lord Godalming) agrees to set his Undead beloved free himself with a stake in the heart; Quincey P. Morris accepts the professor's statement that it was not he — Van Helsing — who removed Lucy's body from her coffin; and all five men agree to hunt down and destroy the monster that turns Lucy Westenra into a vampire spawn. There is macabre irony in the circumstances here: just as Lucy previously goes to St. Mary's churchyard to pay her respects to the dead and is watched by Dracula, her friends go to her tomb to honor her 'true' death as she watches them from behind a yew tree.

Bram Stoker uses Lucy Westenra's tomb as a catalyst to pen a superb, definitive example of the most faithful Gothic literature ever recorded:

Chapter 15 — Dr. Seward's Diary — Cont. [...]"The tomb in the daytime, and when wreathed with fresh flowers, had looked grim and gruesome enough, but now, some days afterwards, when the flowers hung lank and dead, their whites turning to rust and their greens to browns, when the spider and the beetle had resumed their accustomed dominance, when the time-discoloured stone, and dust-encrusted mortar, and rusty, dank iron, and tarnished brass, and clouded silver-plating gave back the feeble glimmer of a candle, the effect was more miserable and sordid than could have been imagined. It conveyed irresistibly the idea that life, animal life, was not the only thing which could pass away."

J.K. Rowling replicates this kind of morose imagery in *The Deathly Hallows.* Like the graveyard of Little Hangleton, the second cemetery she writes of is an important turning point in the saga. Indeed, after six years of learning about his parents' true cause of death, Harry finally feels it is time to visit their graves. The graveyard at Godric's Hollow is not far from our hero's family home — just as the Riddle's graves were close to their residence — and seeing both allows Harry to make a brave step in reconciling his feelings and emotions about the past. The cemetery is also where Harry and Hermione encounter another symbol of the Deathly Hallows on Ignotus Peverell's tombstone. This aids in their 'master of death' research and the defeat of the Dark Lord.

Much as Arthur Holmwood is watched and almost lured into the lethal arms of Undead Lucy, Harry and Hermione are similarly eyed by the zombie-cloaked woman who turns out to be the possessed Bathilda Bagshot — the femme fatale who once accosted the pair and enticed them into her home.

The moving, raw emotion that Arthur displays at the grave of his beloved fiancé is replicated by Harry at his parents' grave. Numerous fans of the novels and films have commented that the passage was one of the most touching scenes of the series, causing many to have shed a tear with Harry. The comparison is unremittingly apparent: as Arthur is consoled by Van Helsing, Harry is comforted by Hermione.

If the authors' association with cemeteries isn't convincing enough, one can also look at the settings of each adjoining locale. For example, Lucy's grave is near St. John's church, whereas Harry's parents' grave is located next to St. Jerome's church. This detail is significant because the members' singing adds a layer of hope yet sullen ambiance to the chapter. Indeed, like Stoker's description of Lucy Westenra's tomb, no doubt the clever, vivid telling of the brooding scene augments the emotion of the events themselves:

"Behind the church, row upon row of snowy tombstones protruded from a blanket of pale blue that was flecked with dazzling red, gold, and green wherever the reflections from the stained glass hit the snow."

— Godric's Hollow

Chapter Ten

The Asylum and Azkaban

In Bram Stoker's novel *Dracula*, Dr. John Seward operates a lunatic asylum where the character Renfield is a patient. Similar to Alcatraz Island in San Francisco Bay, Azkaban is referred to in the Harry Potter series as a fortress on an island in the middle of the North Sea, which serves the magical community of Great Britain as a prison for convicted criminals. There are many striking and interesting similarities between Bram Stoker's asylum and J.K. Rowling's prison that simply cannot be ignored by literary aficionados.

Back in the Victorian age, psychological disorders were handled very differently than they are today. During this era — one often linked with graceful elegance, prim and proper conduct, and well-cultured eloquence — mentally ill people, in sharp contrast, were institutionalized, where they were experimented upon in the name of science until their ultimate demise. The Victorian classification of insanity consisted of numerous disorders, ailments, and behavior types that today are treated with commonly used medicine: learning disabilities, post-natal depression, PTSD, epilepsy, or dementia, just to name a few. Even alcoholism, antisocial or homosexual behaviors were sometimes classified as mental illness and usually resulted in radical treatment at the hands of an asylum administrator. In sum, many innocent people were falsely admitted.

"[…] he has an immense lunatic asylum all under his own care"

— Lucy Westenra to Mina Murray

Likewise, in the wizarding world of Harry Potter, the Ministry of Magic makes its fair share of blunders over the years. The most recognized error is the framing of Sirius Black. Indeed, Harry's godfather is falsely incarcerated with a life sentence for murdering the betrayer/Death Eater, Peter Pettigrew and a dozen bystanders when Pettigrew himself is the guilty one. Similarly, Care of Magical Creatures and Groundskeeper, Rubeus Hagrid is imprisoned at Azkaban for reopening the Chamber of Secrets when Ginny Weasley is the rightful culprit while under the influence of Tom Riddle. Stan Shunpike is sent to Azkaban (without sufficient evidence) for being a Death Eater. Morfin Gaunt is framed by Lord Voldemort and sent to Azkaban for life for killing the Riddle family. And finally, Sturgis Podmore is imprisoned in Azkaban for breaking into the Department of Mysteries while under Lucius Malfoy's *Imperius* curse.

However, the two reformatories share more than a propensity to punish the innocent. In fact, the censure of such blameless individuals will eventually lead to enigmatic escapes. Case in point: in *Dracula*, patient Renfield bolts numerous times from Dr. John Seward's lunatic asylum. In the Victorian age, it was so commonplace to have breakouts in state-sponsored institutions that attendants were fined for every patient that escaped on their watch. Many mental hospitals did not have the funds for qualified personnel and proper building maintenance, and patients often lived in unsafe, unsanitary conditions. Likewise, it was not unusual for smaller institutions to confine patients in cages with minimal nutrition and supervision. Therefore, any opportunity where security was lax was an invitation for the incarcerated to free themselves from what could be called a human zoo, often absconding in the uniform of an overpowered attendant.

Should we then be surprised when we see a malnourished Sirius Black escape Azkaban in 1993 after seeing Scabbers (Peter Pettigrew) in a *Daily Prophet* article? Black takes advantage of his severe weight loss to slide through his cell door in his Animagus dog form while the Dementors are bringing in his food. Then, he quickly swims across the North Sea to hunt down Pettigrew to clear his name. Consequently, in January 1996, a massive escape from Azkaban sets ten long-imprisoned Death Eaters loose when the as yet uncaptured Pettigrew aids in the Dark Lord's resurrection to humanoid form. Lord Voldemort has little difficulty arranging the mass breakout because many of the Dementors are happy to serve his sinister philosophies. Cornelius Fudge, the Minister of Magic at the time who refuses to believe that Voldemort returned and led the campaign to discredit Albus Dumbledore, expresses to the *Daily Prophet* that Sirius Black is likely responsible for the incident:

> "We have confirmed that ten high-security prisoners, in the early hours of yesterday evening, did escape. And of course, the Muggle Prime Minister has been alerted to the danger. We strongly suspect that the breakout was engineered by a man with personal experience in escaping from Azkaban; notorious mass murderer Sirius Black, cousin of the escapee Bellatrix Lestrange."
>
> — Cornelius Fudge interview to the Daily Prophet
> about the Azkaban mass breakout

One could argue the reclassification of 'prison' when closely examining the practices of a Victorian-run mental hospital. Countless documented accounts from the nineteenth century proved that persons left at lunatic asylums were treated more like forgotten inmates than cared-for patients. From being made to wear straight waistcoats for unreasonable hours to being placed into solitary confinement forever and a day, one could argue that life as a convicted felon could be more glamorous than a decorated war veteran being institutionalized for shell shock. Though Bram Stoker does not go into copious detail to describe any amenities in Dr. Seward's mental hospital, his crazed figure Renfield is confined to a room with a bed and barred window — quite often found being manhandled and forced into a straitjacket. Ironically, Renfield stands for every mental patient of this time, for being admitted to such a health care facility in the 1800s normally meant a life sentence.

"Forgive me, Doctor; I forgot myself. You do not need any help. I am so worried in my mind that I am apt to be irritable. If you only knew the problem I have to face and that I am working out, you would pity, and tolerate, and pardon me. Pray do not put me in a straight waistcoat. I want to think and I cannot think freely when my body is confined. I am sure you will understand!"

— Renfield to Dr. Seward

Though Azkaban is technically a prison and not a lunatic asylum, the similarities between the two are uncanny. According to Pottermore, only approved Ministry of Magic individuals are allowed to visit prisoners; and the few that were granted permission decline to discuss the terrors they witnessed while on the island. As a result, Azkaban earns the reputation of being a horrific place. The number of deaths that occur there far outweighs the number of prisoners that are released; therefore, a graveyard is established outside the fortress walls to bury the poor souls that perish. The conditions declined so badly that there was an uproar from the wizarding community to shut down the prison, which in turn caused the Ministry to make major reforms in 1998.

"Those who entered to investigate refused afterwards to talk of what they had found inside, but the least frightening part of it was that the place was infested with dementors."

— J.K. Rowling regarding the location of Azkaban island

Attendants that doubled as guards at early lunatic asylums were hired on more so for their brawn as opposed to their professional skills or bedside manner. Indeed, very few had nursing experience and received training in the field after being hired for such a position. Their primary focus centered around the containment and restraint of the patients instead of comfort and reform, and the majority of the attendants were burly males that could easily manhandle even the most resilient of individuals. Patients' rights as human beings were stripped as they essentially became caged captives. It was not unusual for asylum employees to be terminated after accidents, suicides, or escapes occurred while on duty — events that further publicized the horrors prisoned within. A prime example of this is in Chapter 20 of *Dracula* when the Count attacks Renfield while a guard stands watch:

> "This morning the man on duty reported to me that a little after midnight he was restless and kept saying his prayers somewhat loudly. I asked him if that was all. He replied that it was all he heard. There was something about his manner, so suspicious that I asked him point blank if he had been asleep. He denied sleep but admitted to having "dozed" for a while. It is too bad that men cannot be trusted unless they are watched. [...] The attendant came bursting into my room and told me that Renfield had somehow met with some accident. He had heard him yell; and when he went to him found him lying on his face on the floor, all covered with blood."

> — Dr. Seward's Diary

The guards at Azkaban prison do not fare any better than the accused; they are Dementors, a floating, specter-like shadowy being — deemed by Pottermore as "one of the foulest to inhabit the world" and retained by the British Ministry of Magic as the security of Azkaban Prison. Dementors held no true loyalty to anyone except whoever could offer them the greatest number of victims. The History of Magic text claims that in 1718, when Damocles Rowle was newly elected as Minister of Magic, he persisted in exploiting Azkaban's dismal pedigree, viewing the Dementors as a promising asset; for having them stand as guards would save payroll costs of hiring wizarding patrols. Despite protests, this act was set into motion, and going forward, the Dementors served the Ministry of Magic as guards of Azkaban. Under the agreement, they are allowed to feed on the emotions of the prisoners within the fortress. Fearing the retaliation of these sinister entities upon eviction, the Ministry resolves to allow the considerable colony to remain "unmolested and unchecked."

Victorian era patients in lunatic asylums were not only treated like inmates, but they also endured brutal treatment that drove many of them to insanity or death. In addition to the ever-developing depression that resulted from solitary confinement, starvation, and beatings, patients were exposed to rotation therapy, venesection, boarding, ice baths, electroshock treatments, lobotomies, and dissection. Experts that have written about such sordid practices — most of which have since been declared unlaw-

fully inhumane — and have agreed that any healthy, common, and perfectly sane individual subjected to such cruel punishment would be driven to depression and imminent insanity if continued long term. Because many were abandoned by their families
in an age that shared the belief that any misunderstood condition or behavior was a
sin against God, the majority of patients were left solely under the trusted care of the
institution.

The sentencing of a witch or wizard to Azkaban was thought of as a grim, merciless
verdict that resulted in a slow death due to the miserable influence of the Dementor
guards. Over time prisoners were driven to insanity as all happiness was sucked out of
them, and they were left with only their worst memories being replayed repeatedly in
their minds. In the wizarding world, these Dementors are known to devour human
gladness, causing depression and despair to anyone near them. But worst of all, they
long to annihilate a person's soul. Referred to as "soul-sucking," this punishment leaves
victims in an empty shell and everlasting vegetative state.

"Dementors are among the foulest creatures that walk this earth. They infest
the darkest, filthiest places, they glory in decay and despair, they grow like fun-
gus where it is decay, they drain peace, hope, and happiness out of the air
around them... Get too near a Dementor and every good feeling, every happy
memory will be sucked out of you. If it can, the Dementor will feed on you
long enough to reduce you to something like itself... soulless and evil. You will
be left with nothing but the worst experiences of your life."

— Description of Dementors

Whether one is falsely committed to the fearful reality of a lunatic asylum in the
nineteenth century or similarly sentenced to Azkaban Island in the fantastical world
of an accused witch or wizard, the end result will be the same: impending doom and
despair. Being committed to Dr. John Seward's oppressive lunatic asylum in Bram
Stoker's *Dracula* would not have been a lesser evil than receiving a life sentence to
Azkaban prison in J.K. Rowling's Harry Potter series. In either case, Dr. Seward answered the call best in his diary dated 30 September, —

"Stop; that way madness lies!"

Part Three

Themes

Chapter Eleven

Good vs. Evil

The war between good and evil has been raging since the time of Eden. Turn on the 6 o'clock news to confirm this statement. The battlefield of such adversarial forces can take on the professional form of a boardroom and the recreational rectangle of a basketball court. From the time when film and television began to entertain audiences, movies and shows which engage in the good against evil battle have proved popular. From characters, such as James Bond to DC or Marvel superheroes, to Buffy the Vampire Slayer or Supernatural, the exhausting list is hard to ignore. Literature is no different. Even though Stoker's 'good conquers evil' masterpiece was written exactly a century before the Harry Potter saga, J.K. Rowling proved that this classic formula was far from being outdated and can still be highly successful. The threads both authors spin into their respective webs are closely connected to the hero's journey, the monomythic cycle that forms the basis of *Star Wars* and *Lord of the Rings*: a dark menace presents itself, an allegiance is formed against evil; trials, setbacks, and losses occur; good prevails, and the promise of a new day arrives.

Bram Stoker's *Dracula* begins with a threat: Count Dracula is a monster, and lawyer Jonathan Harker is hired to help him relocate and spread his evil vampiric disease across London. By the end of Chapter 4, the true import of this realization begins to overwhelm the young solicitor as he gathers the wit and strength to kill his client and escape from his castle.

"Jonathan Harker's Journal — continued.

30 June, morning. [—] Then I stopped and looked at the Count. There was a mocking smile on the bloated face which seemed to drive me mad. This was the being I was helping to transfer to London, where, perhaps, for centuries to come he might, amongst its teeming millions, satiate his lust for blood, and create a new and ever-widening circle of semi-demons to batten on the helpless. The very thought drove me mad. A terrible desire came upon me to rid the world of such a monster."

Some Potter fans might suggest that Harry's threat also begins from the outset when Lord Voldemort kills his parents. Although there are mentions of He-Who-Must-Not-Be-Named scattered throughout Book One, one can argue that it is not until Chapter 15: *The Forbidden Forest* that the risk is certain. Then, like Jonathan Harker, Harry gets a glimpse of a dark blood-sucking monster feeding off the blood of unicorns.

> "Harry had taken one step toward it when a slithering sound made him freeze where he stood. A bush on the edge of the clearing quivered…Then, out of the shadows, a hooded figure came crawling across the ground like some stalking beast. Harry, Malfoy, and Fang stood transfixed. The cloaked figure reached the unicorn, lowered its head over the wound in the animal's side, and began to drink its blood."

> — describing the stumbled-upon scene in *The Forbidden Forest*

Indeed, early in both stories, an ominous intention is introduced, which becomes the building block of an ever-growing conflict that carries the novels through to Dracula and Voldemort's last stands.

Nevertheless, evil cannot be conquered alone; it sometimes takes a village or army to vanquish it. However, in these texts, it takes a small yet determined group bent on stamping out the power source. Led by a wise father-like figure who offers wisdom, reason, and protection along the way, each intrepid group is a force to be reckoned with.

Bram Stoker puts together an eclectic group from all walks of life to face Dracula: a determined attorney, a loyal schoolteacher, a leading physiatrist, a wealthy aristocrat, and a gun-slinging Texan. To ultimately lead the band to a victorious win is the Dutch professor, doctor, attorney, and vampire slayer: Abraham Van Helsing. Each person has a unique talent or gift that collectively provides the brawn, brains, funds, medicines, weapons, and leadership skills for the final conflict. Though the small clique begins to form and gel by Harker's escape from Dracula's castle, it is not until midpoint through the novel that Van Helsing comes clean on the exact cause of their sorrows. In Chapter 18, everyone joins hands and pledges their duty:

"Mina Harker's Journal.

30 September. [—] So as we all took hands our solemn compact was made. I felt my heart icy cold, but it did not even occur to me to draw back. We resumed our places, and Dr. Van Helsing went on with a sort of cheerfulness

which showed that the serious work had begun. It was to be taken as gravely, and in as businesslike a way, as any other transaction of life: —"

Exactly a century later, a gang of three eleven-year-olds begins a seven-year battle to rid the world of the most nefarious dark wizard ever to live. Just as the characters in Bram Stoker's classic prove the adage that 'two heads are better than one,' Harry Potter, Ronald Weasley, and Hermione Granger become friends very quickly, and by the end of Book One, they each lend their own distinctive flair to gain access to the sorcerer's stone. Indeed, Hermione's textbook knowledge helps recombobulate the team after helping them overcome the 'Devil's Snare' protection; Harry's flying ability progresses the team through the 'Winged Key Defense', and Ron's wizarding chess skills permit the trio to pass the strategy shield. In Chapter 20, Through the Trapdoor, Harry realizes his two compatriots are committed to his cause of ensuring Voldemort does not get the Stone:

"Seeing the open door somehow seemed to impress upon all three of them what was facing them. Underneath the Cloak, Harry turned to the other two.

"If you want to go back, I won't blame you," he said. "You can take the Cloak. I won't need it now."

"Don't be stupid," said Ron.

"We're coming," said Hermione."

And so it begins. With an extensive foundation of knowledge, skills, and abilities, coupled with the instrumental mentoring and sound leadership and guidance of the great Albus Dumbledore, the comrades in arms turn into the brave trinity that saves the wizarding world.

Despite having an assemblage prepared to overcome a malevolent menace, as with most occasions in life, the unexpected has its challenging way of stepping in often and imposing melodramatic teachable moments that show no one can be fully prepared for the future. Indeed, danger of just about any kind in life is usually dealt out in a way to prove we are ill-equipped in some fashion in one or more areas. These are referred to as trials and setbacks, and each clandestine team in both *Dracula* and the Harry Potter series has its fair share of obstacles to overcome.

The first major setback in *Dracula* is Lucy Westenra's volatile condition, death, and destruction. Over ten laborious days and nights of endless watches, blood transfusions, and decking with garlic, Lucy's on-and-off illness is causing the men much anxiety. In Chapter 12, Quincey P. Morris makes an inquiry to Dr. Seward about the situation:

"Dr. Seward's Diary.

18 September. [—]

"And how long has this been going on?"

"About ten days."

"Ten days! Then I guess, Jack Seward, that that poor pretty creature that we all love has had put into her veins within that time the blood of four strong men. Man alive, her whole body wouldn't hold it." Then, coming close to me, he spoke in a fierce half whisper: "What took it out?"

I shook my head. "That," I said "is the crux. Van Helsing is simply frantic about it, and I am at my wits' end. I can't even hazard a guess. There has been a series of little circumstances which have thrown out all our calculations as to Lucy being properly watched. But these shall not occur again. Here we stay until all be well — or ill."

The other significant setback involves chasing down Dracula when he is fleeing back to Transylvania. It appears that the Count is always one step ahead of them, using his connection with Mina's mind to navigate around the others and leading the group on a game of cat and mouse that continues until the close of the novel as they race against the sunset. In Chapter 25, the team plans proactively to arrive in Varna early to head off the vampire, only to learn that the Czarina Catherine changes its route and arrives in Galatz instead.

Dr. Seward's Diary.

"28 October. — When the telegram came announcing the arrival in Galatz I do not think it was such a shock to any of us as might have been expected. True, we did not know whence, or how, or when, the bolt would come; but I think we all expected that something strange would happen. The delay or arrival at Varna made us individually satisfied that things would not be just as we had expected; we only waited to learn where the change would occur. None the less, however, was it a surprise. I suppose that nature works on such a hopeful basis that we believe against ourselves that things will be as they ought to be, not as we should know that they will be. During both tests, however, the protagonists do not shrink back or falter; they carry on in their resolve with renewed strength and redouble their efforts until Count Dracula is destroyed."

Dumbledore's Army also experiences analogous impediments throughout the Harry Potter saga. Like the fearless five in Stoker's novel, J.K. Rowling weaves adventures in all seven books that come with their own set of trials and surprises. Perhaps Books Four and Six are the most significant in the context of this discussion.

In *The Goblet of Fire*, Voldemort finally achieves the resurrection he has been deviously yearning and manipulating others for in the previous three novels. Considered the darkest of the books thus far, the Dark Lord's quest to regain power comes with significant consequences and setbacks for the wizarding world. In fact, the impediments are so great that the Ministry of Magic refuses to believe they are due to the fear, outbreak, scandal, and finger-pointing the news creates. For not only does He-Who-Must-Not-Be-Named rise again, but his pack of Death Eaters is called back into service as well. At the end of the school term that year, Dumbledore shows great wisdom by standing up in front of Hogwarts and speaking the truth, thus going against the Ministry's wishes. Regardless of the temporary defeat, his words speak of hope and unity during the trials and fight ahead of them:

"[...] in the light of Voldemort's return, we are only as strong as we are united, as weak as we are divided. Lord Voldemort's gift for spreading discord and enmity is very great. We can fight it only by showing an equally strong bond of friendship and trust. Differences of habit and language are nothing at all if our aims are identical and our hearts are open."

— Albus Dumbledore, after Voldemort's return

As if the Dark Lord's return is not bad enough, Book Six brings about its own series of setbacks in its efforts to defeat evil. The headmaster educates Harry on the use of Horcruxes, and Dumbledore and Potter go on a dangerous adventure — one that proves brutal and fruitless in the end. Though Harry and the headmaster successfully escape with their lives and Horcrux in hand, at the end of the novel, Harry finds a mysterious note inside that proves it is a fake. To say he is devastated is an understatement.

"Harry neither knew nor cared what the message meant. Only one thing mattered: This was not a Horcrux. Dumbledore had weakened himself by drinking that terrible potion for nothing. Harry crumbled the parchment in his hand, and his eyes burned with tears as behind him Fang began to howl."

Though the sadness is bitterly real, so is the rising threat. Voldemort winning one small battle makes Harry, Ron, and Hermione's eagerness even stronger in their fight to win the war. Indeed, Book Seven finds them also fighting for Dumbledore's memory and the honor of Hogwarts.

In literature, losses often accompany significant tribulations. Thus, in *Dracula* and the Harry Potter saga, deaths at the hands of evil increase exponentially. Even though Stoker and J.K. Rowling incorporate many deaths throughout their respective stories, each tale consists of three momentous demises that are turning points as the plot thickens.

The mortal death of Lucy Westenra is the first noteworthy loss in *Dracula*. In Chapter 12, after a long, tiring vigil, Lucy's fight ends shortly after the death of her mother. The tragic death of such a sweet, innocent girl is a wake-up call for all five men and Mina: it causes them to intensify their efforts to set Miss Lucy free, form an official pact to fight Dracula, and put together an action plan. Indeed, the aforementioned matters take place in the next four chapters of the text, whereas it took twelve for their brave friend to die. Lord Godalming, who is to wed Lucy Westenra, quickly agrees to join in the vampire hunt to fight for his fiancé's honor:

"Mina Harker's Journal.

30 September. [—] "I am with you," said Lord Godalming, "for Lucy's sake, if for no other reason."

A similar jolt occurs in *The Goblet of Fire*. When Voldemort orders Cedric Diggory's death, not only does it underscore the level of the Dark Lord's selfish, evil motives, but it sets the stage for the conflicts to come and the urgent tone of the series going forward. The novels get longer, more intense, and darker — preparing readers for additional losses. What He-Who-Must-Not-Be-Named is not counting on is the fact that Cedric is the first apparition to appear following the duel between Harry and Voldemort. Cedric's echo reappears during *Priori Incantatem,* followed by Bertha Jorkins, Frank Bryce, and Harry's parents to hold off Voldemort long enough for Harry to escape. Cedric's only request is for Harry to take his body back to his parents, which Harry dutifully honors.

Thankfully, Cedric's death is not in vain: it is an inspiration to others, it is the catalyst in forming the D.A. (Dumbledore's Army), and it forces the truth to finally be spoken and faced head-on: Voldemort has returned. It is time to choose a side.

"Remember, if the time should come, when you have to make a choice between what is right and what is easy, remember what happened to a boy who was good, and kind, and brave, because he strayed across the path of Lord Voldemort. Remember Cedric Diggory."

— Albus Dumbledore's eulogy to Cedric

The second important death in Bram Stoker's most famous work is Dr. Seward's pet patient, Renfield. In Chapter 21, the lunatic bravely resists Dracula, resulting in the former being thrown and beaten severely. Clueless to what is taking place in Harker's room above, it is through the crucial final dialogue of Renfield that Seward, Van Helsing, Morris, and Holmwood are brought up to speed on the Count's sinister activities:

"Dr. Seward's Diary.

3 October. [...] Van Helsing stood up instinctively. "We know the worst now," he said. "He is here, and we know his purpose. It may not be too late. Let us be armed — the same as we were the other night but lose no time; there is not an instant to spare."

Losing Renfield, a character who is a valuable source of information, is a theme that is explored in Harry Potter as well. Just as Renfield knows of the coming and goings of the Count, Sirius Black, Harry's godfather, is an important individual to which the fearless threesome frequently turns for guidance. At the end of *The Order of the Phoenix*, Sirius is struck with a spell while fighting his reviled cousin Bellatrix — an act which causes him to fall through the Veil in the Death Chamber. The death of Sirius Black will hit Harry hard, and it will be several years before he can fully come to terms with the loss of his godfather. Dumbledore refers to Sirius as the "closest thing to a parent" Harry has ever known. Harry blames himself for Sirius's death and harbors anger and vengeance toward Bellatrix Lestrange. Oddly, these emotions strengthen his cause to fight to the end.

"Like the fact that the person Sirius cared most about in the world was you. Like the fact that you were coming to regard Sirius as a mixture of father and brother. Voldemort knew already, of course, that Sirius was in the Order, that you knew where he was, but Kreacher's information made him realize that the one person whom you would go to any lengths to rescue, was Sirius Black."

— Albus Dumbledore regarding Sirius and Harry's relationship

The third notable death in *Dracula* is Quincey P. Morris. His character dies at the end of the novel from the wound of a knife wielded by a Szgany gypsy. As Morris assists in overtaking the cart that carries the vampire's last wooden box, he also attacks one end of the chest, ultimately prizing off one end of the lid, which exposes the Count's body to the sinking sun. The Texan plunges his Bowie knife into Dracula's heart as Harker shears through the vampire's throat with his Kukri. Morris' last words are addressed to Mina Harker in Chapter 27:

"Mina Harker's Journal.

6 November. [...] "I am only too happy to have been of any service! Oh, God!" he cried suddenly, struggling up to a sitting posture and pointing to me, "It was worth for this to die! Look! Look!"

The sun was now right down upon the mountain top, and the red gleams fell upon my face, so that it was bathed in rosy light. With on impulse the men sank on their knees and a deep and earnest "Amen" broke from all as their eyes followed the pointing of his finger as the dying man spoke: —

"Now God be thanked that all has not been in vain! See! The snow is not more stainless than her forehead! The curse has passed away!"

And, to our bitter grief, with a smile and in silence, he died, a gallant gentle-man."

The end of *The Half-Blood Prince* hits everyone hard, for it verifies the death of headmaster Albus Dumbledore. Though devastating, the passing teaches a profound lesson. Dumbledore chooses to die for the greater good. Indeed, Harry has to make this choice as well in *The Deathly Hallows*. Dumbledore's death is also instructive. Selflessly, he leads by example.

Why did the headmaster have to die? Like the cherished Lucy Westenra perishes in *Dracula*, illness and death only fortify the foundation of the heroes' noble cause, feed further clues to the protagonists, and develop the thickening plot.

As Lucy lay on her bed wasting away, Dumbledore was fading as well. When he destroyed the Horcrux that was Marvolo Gaunt's ring, he placed it on his ring finger and activated a deadly curse that began to wither away at his aged body, the decay starting in his hand. The wizard wants a quick and dignified death, which he explains to Severus Snape. Professor Snape needs to be the one to kill Dumbledore because Snape must earn the trust of Voldemort and the Death Eaters. Snape's soul will not be torn apart by the act since Dumbledore is requesting death as a genuine favor. In this process, Dumbledore also prevents Draco Malfoy from becoming a murderer.

Furthermore, the death of Dumbledore strengthens Harry's character. With his mentor out of the picture, Harry has to finish the fight on his own, providing an emotional twist and a cover-up for Snape's true alliance. If the headmaster had lived, it would have made the rest of the protagonist's journey rather short and somewhat simple. Dumbledore's passing brings a strategic twist to the plot — for by remaining alive, the powerful wizard would have surpassed Harry's significance. In its place, the gifts and clues Dumbledore leaves behind keep his memory bright and reinforce the trio's central cause.

> "He did not feel the way he had so often felt before, excited, curious, burning to get to the bottom of a mystery; he simply knew that the task of discovering the truth about the real Horcrux had to be completed before he could move a little farther along the dark and winding path stretching ahead of him, the path that he and Dumbledore had set out upon together, and which he now knew he would have to journey alone." *The Half-Blood Prince* (Chapter 30)

Through all the hardships, obstacles, and costs that take place in Stoker's and J.K. Rowling's timeless masterpieces, there is a beam of brightness at the end. As with every classic epic story, one's destiny or fate is linked to one's cause. In other words, karma can be a bitch. Count Dracula and Lord Voldemort are both defeated in the end as the final showdown between good and evil plays out in front of probably the two most recognized fictional castles in the world: Castle Dracula and Hogwarts's Castle. In both battles, however, good ultimately conquers evil.

In the end, the main characters in both tales move on with their lives, work, marriages, and children. Jonathan Harker's note at the very end of *Dracula* reflects the sentiment of satisfaction:

> "In the summer of this year we made a journey to Transylvania, and went over the old ground which was, and is, to us so full of vivid and terrible memories. It was almost impossible to believe that the things which we had seen with our own eyes and heard with our own ears were living truths." Or as Harry Potter eloquently puts it, "I've had enough trouble for a lifetime."

In the final pages of *The Deathly Hallows*, Harry, Ron, and Hermione watch their own kids board the Hogwarts Express nineteen years later. As they observe their children's nervous excitement and listen to them worry about what the sorting hat will say to each, they fondly continue to practice the one weakness Dumbledore stresses the Dark Lord could not master: Love. Indeed, these precious moments and hopes for promising futures had to have brought flashbacks of their own boarding at Platform 9 ¾ in 1997. And with these three simple words, the seven-book saga comes to a close: "All was well."

Chapter Twelve

Love, Sacrifice, and Friendship

There have been countless songs written about love and friendship. Indeed, the phrase "the power of love" is significant enough to account for titles from artists like Air Supply, Huey Lewis & the News, and Celine Dion, just to name a few. Elton John sang about "Sacrifice," and James Taylor told us, "You Got a Friend." Whether it be for a shared goal, a specific season, or an entire lifetime, friends help us manage challenges, inspire our greatest efforts, and commemorate life. Taking many shapes while crossing age groups and self-imposed margins, unlikely confidants can sometimes turn out to be a godsend. So it only makes sense that this theme shows up in the most beloved of literary classics. The Holy Bible, for instance, explains in John 15:23 that Jesus addresses his disciples at the Last Supper by saying, "No one has greater love than this, to lay down one's life for one's friends...I do not call you servants any longer...but I have called you friends." Regardless of whether you prefer the term buddy, chum, amigo, dude, or BFF, the underlying meaning is the same: true friendship cannot be absent of love and sacrifice.

There are at least fourteen references to these concepts in the novel *Dracula* which attest to and eloquently illustrate their power to bind this remarkable story together.

From the despair of Castle Dracula, it is quite unlikely that the ancient Romanian vampire and Jonathan Harker have much in common — let alone friendship. Especially considering the former is holding the latter captive. Given the antagonistic relationship between these two characters, it is quite surprising and rather ironic to find them having a brief discussion about friendship. Indeed, as a justification to destroy Harker's letter in shorthand to his fiancé Mina, the Count refers to it as an "outrage upon friendship" — one which is the greatest insult he can muster. Notwithstanding their dissimilar history, both agree upon the sanctity of friendship.

Friends John Seward, Arthur Holmwood, and Quincey Morris all fall in love with the same attractive woman, Miss Lucy Westenra. However, Lucy chooses Arthur as her fiancé while sweetly letting John and Quincey down easily. The amazing route

Lucy decides to take in doing so charmingly demonstrates the supremacy of camara-
derie. Indeed, Quincey describes her as a friend, which is "rarer than a lover, it's more
unselfish anyway." Even though John and Quincey have been rejected, they both sacrifice their pride and remain loyally devoted to her. For Quincey, this powerful bond
is what initially ties him to Van Helsing and the others when it comes time to fight
the forthcoming evil of Count Dracula.

The three suitors quickly put aside their competition for Lucy for the sake of their
amity. John and Quincey genuinely congratulate Arthur. Their kinship predates Lucy,
and it only strengthens after her death — and stronger still by their subsequent killing
of the monster Dracula makes of her.

Moreover, even at the pinnacle of his despair over Lucy, when Dr. John Seward
pens an early entry in his private diary, complaining, "...nor can I be angry with my
friend whose happiness is [Lucy's]..." This devotion to his friend Arthur reflects the
moral standard that is a strong characteristic in each of the main characters.

Soon afterward, Arthur has to sacrifice his idea of decency and ask his friend John
to examine his fiancée. Dr. Seward immediately puts aside his feelings of love and
medically evaluates Lucy for the sake of his friend. In fact, Seward takes it to an even
more respectful level when he admits he can do no more and recommends Professor
Abraham Van Helsing, an expert in obscure diseases.

Van Helsing, who affectionally refers to Seward as "friend John," tells his pet pupil
that he will go to London for the sake of their friendship, even if it means breaking
promises and ignoring his duties. In Chapter 10, Van Helsing informs his old student,
"Remember, my friend, that knowledge is stronger than memory, and we should not
trust the weaker."

In the name of kinship, the doctors inadvertently cause harm to Lucy by not telling
her mother about the seriousness of Lucy's condition and the garlic cure. Van Helsing
then gives his own blood to his new friend — an act that is not only pseudo-sexual
but one that ties Van Helsing to Lucy the way Morris' devotion does earlier.

Soon afterward, Quincey arrives at Lucy's sickbed and is taken into immediate
confidence by his friend Dr. Seward. He does not hesitate in rendering his services in
any way possible — in this case, in the form of his blood — in yet another immediate
transfusion.

When Holmwood's father passes away, Arthur immediately takes on his father's
position. The newly titled Lord Godalming admits he is aware of his friend Morris'
love for his fiancée but thanks him all the more for his help. Then Lord Godalming
and Van Helsing secure their friendship after Arthur declines to use his title in the

group's presence. Close, endearing personal relationships begin to form between every main character. Van Helsing, Seward, and Morris all agree never to tell Arthur that they gave blood to Lucy — an act to save him pain, protect his pride, and simply respect someone who has just lost a loved one.

Van Helsing next meets Mina Harker and is very impressed with her — so much so that he immediately adopts her into his expanding circle of close friends. Readers who are already accustomed to the redeeming qualities of both characters see very little interaction between these two at this juncture. Indeed, it must be taken on faith that they quickly expose their noble virtues to each other.

Soon after meeting Mina Harker, Van Helsing is introduced to her husband, Jonathan. Even though the Professor has seen less of Jonathan than Mina, he befriends him by association. Van Helsing knows he needs nothing less than a completely committed group to carry out his imminent mission.

When Dr. Seward meets Mina, they swiftly begin to talk about Lucy, and soon thereafter, he freely agrees to allow her to listen to and write out all his personal phonograph entries.

"Mina Harker's Journal.

29 September. […] "It was late when I got through, but Dr. Seward went about his work of going his round of the patients; when he had finished, he came back and sat near me, reading, so that I did not feel too lonely whilst I worked. How good and thoughtful he is; the world seems full of good men—even if there are monsters in it."

Upon meeting Mina, both Quincey and Arthur feel so comfortable around her that they confide in her about their love for Miss Lucy. Arthur even ventures so far as to break down crying in her presence, and she comforts him as a mother to her child. The three bond quickly, and now virtually everyone in the group has met and formed a strong connection. Finally, in Chapter 17, Arthur asks to be a brother to Mina in a most touching dialogue of platonic kinship:

"Mina Harker's Journal.

30 September. […] "You will let me be like a brother, will you not, for all our lives — for dear Lucy's sake?"
For dear Lucy's sake," I said as we clasped hands. "Ay, and for your own sake,"
he added, "for if a man's esteem and gratitude are ever worth the winning, you

have won mine today. If ever the future should bring to you a time when you need a man's help, believe me, you will not call in vain. God grant that no such time may ever come to you to break the sunshine of your life; but if it should ever come, promise me that you will let me know." He was so earnest, and his sorrow was so fresh, that I felt it would comfort him, so I said:

"I promise."

After risking their lives for each other and destroying Dracula, an evil that cannot love, the Harkers name their first child after the members of their close-knit team of friends. The child is primarily called Quincey, who sacrifices his life for the group and whose last thought is for Mina. Seven years later, the rest remain close friends.

The same motifs are alive and well at Hogwarts, for one would be hard-pressed to have a literary conversation about the Harry Potter series without bringing up the terms 'love,' 'sacrifice,' and 'friendship.' Indeed, J.K. Rowling opens her seventh and final novel of the series with a related quote from William Penn:

"Death is but crossing the world, as friends do the seas; they live in one another still. For they must needs be present, that love and live in that which is omnipresent. In this divine glass, they see face to face; and their converse is free, as well as pure. This is the comfort of friends, that though they may be said to die, yet their friendship and society are, in the best sense, ever present, because immortal."

In Year One at the wizarding school, Harry falls in with a circle of especially close friends: Hermione Granger, Ron Weasley, and Neville Longbottom. As in *Dracula*, in due time, this coterie expands to include others such as Ginny Weasley and Luna Lovegood (the name reinforces the theme). Like Quincey P. Morris, Harry has to sacrifice his life. He needs to walk into Voldemort's presence and not only lay down his life for his friends but all the students at Hogwarts, their families, and all the wizards and Muggles in the world.

Readers see early in the Harry Potter saga that Harry is quick to make friends. Like Lucy Westenra, he is admired by many. However, the young wizard soon begins to experience the pain of loss also. Even though he is falling in love with Ginny, he begins to distance himself out of fear of endangering her. The irony in this logic is that he finally realizes an almost Biblical truth: He must die in order that others may live.

Harry's consistent goodness toward others — even in situations where others are not so deserving of kindness — only drives home a statement that headmaster Albus Dumbledore often utters: "He loved." What his good friend Hermione refers to as a "saving people thing" underscores how this immense power of love, sacrifice, and friendship will play out. It was the very reason he defeated He-Who-Must-Not-Be-

Named. Like Dracula, the Dark Lord lacks the ability to comprehend love and mocks Harry because he knows the young wizard's affection for his friends motivates him to action. Ultimately, this very reason permits Harry to walk calmly and deliberately into the Forbidden Forest and forfeit his life.

Other literary coincidences prove J.K. Rowling's preoccupation with the strong connection between love, sacrifice, and friendship. Not only are many of the lyrics of the Sorting Hat or Celestina Warbeck related to the topic, but Rowling finds other ways to reiterate these sentiments eloquently. For example, when Harry, Ron, and Hermione are on the run and decide to pay Xenophilus Lovegood a visit, they enter Luna's bedroom to find that she has painted her ceiling with five faces: Harry, Ron, Hermione, Ginny, and Neville.

> "What appeared to be fine golden chains wove around the pictures, linking them together, after examining them for a minute or so, Harry realized that the chains were actually one word, repeated a thousand times in golden ink: friends... friends... friends..." (p. 417)

Rowling leaves audiences with no doubt about her philosophical intent at the end of *The Deathly Hallows.* Indeed, there are so many allusions to love, sacrifice, and friendship from Year One that listing them all would be an impressive piece of literary commentary. The outcome becomes '*The Lifely Hallows*,' for life is born from Harry's offering of himself: the life of personal sacrifice, the life that is the master of death, the life of everlasting friendship. J.K. Rowling explains it best in her postscript appropriately titled "*Nineteen Years Later.*" Like the ending of *Dracula*, the reader is brought up to speed on events that occur outside the confines of the text. Harry and his friend Ginny are wed, and like the Harkers, they name their three children after those they lost: James, Albus Severus, and Lily. Ron and Hermione marry too and have two children, Rose and Hugo. The couples bump into each other at the famous platform 9¾, where Rose, James, and Albus are about to board the train to Hogwarts. Draco Malfoy, the notorious Slytherin of their class who is outright mean and cowardly in the novels but not completely evil, has since also married. He, his wife, and their son Scorpius are also waiting on the platform. Sadly, Draco feels awkward around his old acquaintances. He nods and quickly looks away.

> "Don't forget to give Neville our love!" Ginny told James as she hugged him goodbye.
>
> "Mum! I can't give a professor love!"
>
> "But you know Neville—"
>
> James rolled his eyes.

"Outside, yeah, but at school he's Professor Longbottom, isn't he? I can't walk into Herbology and give him love…" (p. 757).

Truly the enigma to a prosperous life can be found in one small but powerful four-letter word. Love is the foundation of friendship, and sacrifice is the framework. Jesus said, "No one has greater love than this… to lay down one's life for one's friends… I have called you friends." This truth gleams like a treasured jewel at the focus of humanity's extended conflict for purpose and reason. To be honest, compassionate, and involved in the lives of others is the answer to our very existence. And the friends in both Stoker's and Rowling's novels knew this. Without love, sacrifice, and friendship, they could not have joined forces to defeat evil.

Chapter Thirteen

Coffins and Horcruxes

Throughout history, humanity has discovered that ferocious beasts and dark beings often carry a secret weakness or soft spot that can end their sordid streaks of violence. Whether it be a small, vulnerable spot in the left breast of a mighty dragon or the sight of one's son being 'dark side electrocuted' by a hooded Empire Emperor, mass media has exposed an array of physical, psychological, and metaphysical ways to put down a demented danger. However, in *Dracula* and the Harry Potter saga, flaws arrive in the form of fifty earth boxes and seven Horcruxes. Each represents a different means to an end for the respective evil the protagonists face, yet the way they are constructed, concealed, and crushed closely parallels one another.

On the 28th of May, Johnathan Harker notices a band of Szgany gypsies encamped in the courtyard of Castle Dracula. By the 17th of June, the solicitor realizes the Slovaks are transporting great, square boxes in leiter-wagons to the awaiting Szgany. On the 24th of June, the "far-away, muffled sound as of mattock and spade" is recorded in his diary. And a day later, the hero locates the Count's secret: "There, in one of the great boxes, of which there were fifty in all, on a pile of newly dug earth, lay the Count!" Indeed, these coffins (at times in the novel referred to as earth boxes) are smuggled out of the castle and onboard the Russian schooner that runs ashore at Whitby. Readers can surmise from the many legal inquiries that Dracula asks his guest — such as can one man have multiple solicitors handling different affairs — that the vampire pre-arranges for all fifty boxes to be removed. In Chapter 18, Professor Abraham Van Helsing gives a speech that sheds some light on the mystery of the earth boxes:

"Mina Harker's Journal.

30 September. [...] "There have been from the loins of this very one great men and good women, and their graves make sacred the earth where alone this foulness can dwell. For it is not the least of its terrors that this evil thing is rooted deep in all good; in soil barren of holy memories it cannot rest."

Readers glean from this interesting lesson that the great boxes are actually coffins filled with consecrated dirt that regenerates Count Dracula's powers. One could imply from Van Helsing's idiom that the dirt obtained from the vampire's tomb in the Transylvanian castle is sacred due to its connection to his native homeland and the innocent lives he has taken over centuries. In other words, Dracula cannot sleep in 'normal dirt' because there will be no ancestral correlation between 'rudimentary dirt' and the heritage of Transylvanian soil.

After the Count cleverly constructs and transports his fifty boxes of dirt to England's shore, he hires different people to discretely scatter small groups of them around London. The vampire's identity, whereabouts, and agenda are complete mysteries until each person shares their personal information collectively, and Mina Harker then sequentially types it up in chronological order. From there, the friends begin to analyze it all and follow up on clues left by Dracula. In Chapter 18, Van Helsing continues...

"Mina Harker's Journal.

30 September. [...] "And now we must settle what we do. We have here much data, and we must proceed to lay out our campaign. We know from the inquiry of Jonathan that from the castle to Whitby came fifty boxes of earth, all of which were delivered at Carfax; we also know that at least some of these boxes have been removed. It seems to me, that our first step should be to ascertain whether all the rest remain in the house beyond that wall where we look today; or whether any more have been removed. If the latter, we must trace..."

The group splits up to track down and interview the various men the Count employs to sanitize all fifty coffins. In a matter of days, they are able to locate and place the holy Eucharist or "Host" — a consecrated unleavened bread or wafer meant to represent the body of Jesus Christ — in each box of earth, which contaminates them, making them unfit for the vampire's use.

Upon realizing the group of men are on to him, Dracula attempts to hide his fear from his pursuers as he grabs many gold coins in his Piccadilly house, crashes through a window, and hurriedly arranges to be transported back to Transylvania in his remaining coffin.

Seeing that the Count is afraid and fleeing for his life, Professor Van Helsing rallies the group as they make plans to follow in hot pursuit and head him off before he reaches Castle Dracula, ultimately crushing his evil scheme and blotting out his existence from the face of the earth.

"Dr. Seward's Diary.

3 October. [...] "We have learnt something — much! Notwithstanding his brave words, he fears us; he fears time, he fears want! For if not, why he hurries so? His very tone betrays him, or my ears deceive. Why take that money? You follow quick. You are hunters of wild beast and understand it so. [...] There is but one more earth-box, and we must try to find it; when that is done all may yet be well."

Indeed, their campaign back to Transylvania pays off: Dracula is destroyed, Mina comes back to life, and all is well in the end.

J.K. Rowling follows a very similar theme of constructing, concealing, and crushing seven Horcruxes which represent seven coffin-like objects that house a fragment of Voldemort's broken soul. While still a student at Hogwarts, Tom Riddle's agenda is suspect in the uncomfortable conversation with Professor Slughorn, who becomes ashamed by the answer he provides young Voldemort and tampers with the memory to relieve his guilt. In Book 6: *The Half-Blood Prince*, Harry is able to convince Slughorn to divulge the full, true memory with the aid of the Professor's own liquid luck potion, Felix Felicis. Finally, in Chapter 23, Professor Slughorn decides to come clean:

"Well," said Slughorn, not looking at Riddle, but fiddling with the ribbon on top of his box of crystalized pineapple," well, it can't hurt to give you an overview, of course. Just so that you understand the term. A Horcrux is the word used for an object in which a person has concealed part of their soul. [...] Well, you split your soul, you see," said Slughorn. "and hide part of it in an object outside the body. Then even if one's body is attacked or destroyed, one cannot die, for part of the soul remains earthbound and undamaged. But of course, existence in such a form..." [...] "...few would want it, Tom, very few. Death would be preferable."

"[...] How do you split your soul?"

"Well," said Slughorn uncomfortably, "you must understand that the soul is supposed to remain intact and whole. Splitting it is an act of violation, it is against nature."

"But how do you do it?"

"By an act of evil — the supreme act of evil. By committing murder. Killing rips the soul apart. The wizard intent upon creating a Horcrux would use the damage to his advantage: He would encase the torn portion —"

"[...] Wouldn't it be better, make you stronger, to have you soul in more pieces, I mean, for instance, isn't seven the most powerfully magical number, wouldn't seven —?"

"Merlin's beard, Tom!" yelped Slughorn. "Seven! Isn't it bad enough to think of killing one person? And in any case...bad enough to divide the soul...but to rip it into seven pieces..."

Readers learn from Dumbledore's magical and sleuth-like digging that the Dark Lord succeeds in killing at least seven people to create his seven Horcruxes. They likewise learn that many of the Horcruxes are placed in priceless historical artifacts and cleverly concealed. Just like Count Dracula scatters his earth boxes around, He-Who-Must-Not-Be-Named is bent on a wide-area dispersion tactic. Indeed, the well-hidden objects are placed in varied and extremely protected locations with little to no Death Eater assistance. And absolutely no one is aware that the heavily guarded objects are Horcruxes but Voldemort himself.

After Slughorn divulges the true memory of his conversation with young Voldemort, Dumbledore trusts Harry with the information that he knows. Tom Riddle's diary was one of the Horcruxes destroyed by Harry during his sophomore year at Hogwarts. The second object was Marvolo Gaunt's cursed ring that Dumbledore found and destroyed. But sadly, Salazar Slytherin's locket, the third Horcrux Harry and the headmaster risked their lives to retrieve from the dangerous cave, turns out to be a planted fake. Upon Dumbledore's death, Harry and his friends are left with little information to assist them in hunting down and destroying the remaining Horcruxes.

Rowling's final novel, similar to Van Helsing's campaign in *Dracula*, opens with several hundred pages of Harry, Ron, and Hermione carrying on Dumbledore's crusade with their own detective skills — discerning clues from memories, books, letters, and interviews that lead to the discovery of the real Horcrux locket. But without Dumbledore around to provide wisdom on methods of destruction, one in the party begins to fall prey to the evil they are fighting tirelessly to destroy. Indeed, just like Mina falls ill by the bite of Dracula, the fragment of Voldemort's soul inside Salazar Slytherin's pendant begins to make Ron unclean.

"We thought you knew what you were doing!" shouted Ron, [...] We thought Dumbledore had told you what to do, we thought you had a real plan! "

"[...] Well, sorry to let you down," said Harry, his voice quite calm even though he felt hollow, inadequate. "I've been straight with you from the start, I told you everything Dumbledore told me. And in case you haven't noticed, we've found one Horcrux —"

"Yeah, and we're about as near getting rid of it as we are to finding the rest of them — nowhere effing near, in other words!"

"Take off the locket, Ron," Hermione said, her voice unusually high. "Please take it off. You wouldn't be talking like this if you hadn't been wearing it all day." (p. 307)

However, Professor Snape's Patronus Charm — a white doe, the same as Lily Potter's — soon leaves the Sword of Godric Gryffindor in a frozen pond. Ron uses this famed weapon to destroy the locket, releasing its spell and altering Ron's erratic behavior. Over the course of several more chapters in Book 7, the concealments of the remaining Horcruxes are identified: Helga Hufflepuff's Cup (found in Bellatrix Lestrange's vault at Gringotts Wizarding Bank), Rowena Ravenclaw's lost Diadem (found in the Room of Requirement revealed as the Room of Hidden Objects), Voldemort's pet snake Nagini (which never left the Dark Lord's side once he realized the other Horcruxes were being destroyed), and Harry Potter himself.

Much like securing Dracula's earth boxes, finding the Horcruxes is only fifty percent of the work; they need to be crushed first to make Voldemort vulnerable and susceptible to being trapped in a corner. Since He-Who-Must-Not Be-Named considers himself to be the seventh Horcrux, he is unaware that the rebounded spell used on Harry as an infant makes Harry the final Horcrux. As the race against time to save the school unfolds at the end of the novel, Ron and Hermione destroy the cup in the Chamber of Secrets with the Basilisk fang, and Crabbe unknowingly obliterates the Lost Diadem of Ravenclaw with his Fiendfyre spell, which got out of control.

In the final chapters of *The Deathly Hallows*, Harry bravely allows himself to be killed at the hands of He-Who-Must-Not-Be-Named. As Quincey P. Morris dies a hero, so does Harry, understanding that in order to defeat Voldemort, he — the Horcrux the Dark Lord never intended to make — has to be destroyed first. Yet Harry is in possession of *The Deathly Hallows* and has the power to overcome death.

Once Harry is resurrected and Neville Longbottom kills Nagini with the sword of Gryffindor, Harry reveals to the Dark Lord that he is the rightful owner of the Elder Wand. However, when the wand refuses to kill its rightful owner, the elder wand flies to Harry (who casts a disarming spell) with Voldemort's killing curse rebounding on him, as a mortal, as no Horcruxes are left.

Parallel to the last stand at the end of Bram Stoker's novel, The Dark Lord disintegrates at the famous castle while the sun transitions in the sky and all the main characters watch in exhausted relief.

"We did it! We bashed them, wee Potter's the one! And Voldy's gone mouldy, so now let's have fun!"

—Peeves the Poltergeist sings a victory song

In summary, two famous villains decide to scatter their means of protecting their immortality across fifty coffins of moldy earth and ripped pieces of soul in seven coffin-like objects. But in their respective demises, both monsters face their vulnerable, weakened states for a moment, exposing their soft spots to others. Indeed, no matter how eternal one thinks one may be, even the bloodthirstiest of vampires and the darkest of powerful wizards can reach their setting sun. And at final dissolution, may they be granted a look of peace — such as one never could have imagined — resting on their vanishing visage.

Chapter Fourteen

Death

Ask any living soul about their greatest fear, and next to public speaking, death ranks at the top of the list. Experts have named this condition Thanatophobia, as the sometimes obsessional thoughts surrounding the condition affect millions of people worldwide. Over decades, studies of the commonplace phobia have sought to root out the reason for such dread. A large number of subjects are afraid of dying due to an underlying belief that the process of death will be physically painful, while others are distressed at the thought of leaving the material objects or people they are attached to in human life. Therefore, it is not surprising that the theme of death has shown up repeatedly in works dating back to the earliest examples of written form.

Indeed, death in classic literature is time and again utilized to levy structure on the physical and spiritual worlds. Fatality can be exploited in symbolic or non-representative fashions, but regardless of the method, the greatest impact is on readers' emotions. For example, how many adults — let alone children — shed a tear after reading Shel Silverstein's *The Giving Tree*? Yours truly certainly did. And forty years later, the scene repeated itself as the credits rolled for *The Half-Blood Prince*. Regardless of the intensity of the emotional impact, however, there can be no doubt that the theme of death runs rampant throughout *Dracula* and the Harry Potter series.

Life. Death. Undead. Those three words and the relationship between them are perhaps the prevalent themes in Bram Stoker's work. That is to say, the association between life, death, and the state in between ("undeadness") is a frequent topic explored by all the central characters. In Chapter 15, the misunderstanding between this trio of terms leads to an emotionally charged conversation between Professor Abraham Van Helsing and the honorable Arthur Holmwood several days after Lucy is lain to rest:

"Dr. Seward's Diary.

29 September. [...] Arthur jumped to his feet, "Good God!" he cried. "What do you mean? Has there been any mistake, has she been buried alive?" He groaned in anguish that not even hope could soften.

"I did not say she was alive, my child. I did not think it. I go no further than to say that she might be UnDead."

"UnDead! Not alive! What do you mean? Is this all a nightmare, or what is it?"

"There are mysteries which men can only guess at, which age by age they may solve only in part. Believe me, we are now on the verge of one. But I have not done. May I cut off the head of dead Miss Lucy?"

"Heavens and earth, no!" cried Arthur in a storm of passion. "Not for the wide world will I consent to any mutilation of her dead body. Dr. Van Helsing, you try me too far. What have I done to you that you should torture me so? What did that poor, sweet girl do that you should want to cast such dishonour on her grave? Are you mad, that you speak of such things, or am I mad to listen to them? Don't dare think more of such a desecration. I shall not give my consent to anything you do. I have a duty to do in protecting her grave from outrage, and by God, I shall do it!"

While the great mysteries of life and death can provoke fear in many, in the case of Arthur Holmwood, the notion that an 'Undead' world exists brings consternation to the heart. In fact, the belief is so fantastical that it isn't until the mid-point of the text that all leading characters are on board to even open their minds to the possibility of such a metaphysical concept.

Van Helsing explains that Dracula is a creature of the undead, and the touchstone of his undeadness is his inability to die. In other words, his mid-world immortal reality traps him in a dark prison for eternity. To release the Count out of this supernatural realm equates with death by an unthinkable supernatural means, a job that Van Helsing himself calls "butcher work."

Other characters in the novel hover between the categories of living and dying while suffering from mental illness. For example, upon leaving Dracula's castle, Jonathan Harker spends several months recovering from brain fever. During this time, he agonizes horribly, often raving about blood, death, and other nightmarish images. Likewise, Lucy's sleepwalking is an 'in-between' state — that is, not waking and not sleeping — which helps the Count to find, bite, and eventually turn her into a vampire. Continuing with this theme, Mina becomes hypnotized on numerous occasions by Professor Van Helsing in order to extract information concerning Dracula's location. This hypnotic state is another kind of 'in-between' undeadness. Jonathan Harker and Abraham Van Helsing turn gray and aged as the book progresses—alive in spirit but near death physically, as they deliberately place their lives in danger. Once Dracula becomes 'true dead,' they regain their total health. And then there is Renfield, Dr. Seward's pet patient, who is mentally in-between worlds and quite fanatically preoccupied with the life-giving blood of the animals he eats. Regardless of whether he is ingesting flies, spiders, birds, or cats, his obsessive belief is that they all must die to give him life. The 'zoophagous maniac' also trusts the Count will provide him with the supernatural knowledge of undeadness.

"Dr. Seward's Diary.

3 October. [...] "Then he began to whisper 'Rats, rats, rats! Hundreds, thousands, millions of them, and everyone a life, and dogs to eat them, and cats too. All lives! All red blood, with years of life in it; and not merely buzzing flies!

Remarkably, undeadness appears to diametrically contradict the traditional Christian views of the afterlife. In the latter, the soul is granted immortal life in heaven, in proximity to God, once it has been freed from the earthly body as it transitions from life to death. However, in the case of undeadness, the living body is shifted to a state of "almost dead" — thus, maintaining a sort of purgatorial existence in which it feasts on the blood of the living. The soul, ensnared inside, cannot abide with God in heaven; the vessel becomes a parasite, eking out a presence pilfered from the vital energy of others. Seemingly, Bram Stoker argues that in order to maintain the conventional biotic processes of living and dying, and the customary, moral, "Christian" processes of death and resurrection, undeadness has to be eliminated: souls must be allowed to rise to heaven. This concept is recognized at the end of the novel by Mina's gladness when Dracula is destroyed. As the undead soul is released from his body, a sudden expression of peace flashes across his face, and she feels a sense of empathy. In this vantage point, even the evil one is saved as he becomes "true dead."

In her own fictional offerings, J.K. Rowling advances the notion of death. Pottermore claims she once stated, "My books are largely about death. They open with the death of Harry's parents. There is Voldemort's obsession with conquering death and his quest for immortality at any price, the goal of anyone with magic. I so understand why Voldemort wants to conquer death. We're all frightened of it."

When the last page is turned in the Harry Potter series, audiences feel burdened with a sense of loss — not only in a physical sense but from psychological and spiritual perspectives as well. Main and supporting characters perish throughout the saga, but there are also wizards, such as Neville Longbottom's parents, who are admitted into St. Mungo's mental ward due to unforgivable curses, rebounding memory charms, and extreme torment. Indeed, Frank and Alice Longbottom are tortured to insanity by Bellatrix Lestrange. Though they do not die from the agony the ruthless Death Eater imposes upon them, Neville's parents are not really living either. Like Jonathan Harker, when he suffers from brain fever, they hover between life and death, unable to even recognize their son.

Neville's mother had come edging down the ward in her nightdress. She no longer had the plump, happy-looking face Harry had seen in Moody's old photograph of the original Order of the Phoenix. Her face was thin and worn now, her eyes seemed overlarge, and her hair, which had turned white, was wispy and dead looking. She did not seem to want to speak, or perhaps she was not able to, but she made timid motions toward Neville, holding something in her outstretched hand.

"Again?" said Mrs. Longbottom, sounding slightly weary. "Very well, Alice dear, very well—Neville, take it, whatever it is…"

But Neville had already stretched out his hand, into which his mother dropped an empty Drooble's Blowing Gum wrapper.

"Very nice, dear," said Neville's grandmother in a falsely cheery voice, patting his mother on the shoulder. But Neville said quietly, "Thanks Mum."

His mother tottered away, back up the ward, humming to herself. Neville looked around at the others, his expression defiant, as though daring them to laugh, but Harry did not think he'd ever found anything less funny in his life.

— *Harry Potter and the Order of the Phoenix* (p. 514-515)

Though Barty Crouch Senior does not make it to St. Mungo's like Frank and Alice Longbottom, he very well could have, providing he had lived long enough. Indeed, in *The Goblet of Fire*, Crouch is placed under the Imperius curse by He-Who-Must-Not-Be-Named. When he manages to break free due to Wormtail's neglect, he escapes and flees to Hogwarts to warn the headmaster of Voldemort's plans. Fatigued and marginally mad from the effects of Voldemort's mind-bending spell, he teeters through the Forbidden Forest and onto the Hogwarts grounds, where he stumbles upon Harry and Viktor Krum. Resisting Voldemort's spells, Harry and Viktor witness Crouch having a continuous conversation with a tree, believing it to be his assistant "Weatherby" (Percy Wesley).

"Thank you, Weatherby, and when you have done that, I would like a cup of tea. My wife and son will be arriving shortly, we are attending a concert tonight with Mr. and Mrs. Fudge."

Crouch was now talking fluently to a tree again, and seemed completely unaware that Harry was there, which surprised Harry so much he didn't notice that Crouch had released him.

"[…] He is mad," said Krum doubtfully, staring down at Crouch, who was still gabbling to the tree, apparently convinced it was Percy.

— *Harry Potter and the Goblet of Fire* (p. 555-556)

While Harry goes to get Dumbledore, Barty Jr arrives (as Alastor Moody) and stuns Krum. Barty Jr then murders his father and transfigures the corpse into a bone, burying it in Rubeus Hagrid's garden. Indeed, in a very short time, the troubled Barty Crouch Sr. fluctuates from being alive to a period of 'undeadness' to being killed true dead. The rhetorical question is, 'Was the murder one of sympathy or not?'

Another key concept explored in the saga is the acceptance of death. In *The Deathly Hallows*, the Peverell brothers struggle to conquer death and magical items, which, when reunited, make one a Master of Death. Their adventures are less about attaining immortality but more about accepting death. A wise man once said, 'The only true way someone can defeat death is when they no longer fear it.' Just like the vampire hunters in Dracula strived to help Mina and Lucy cheat death using various superstitious magical means (i.e., garlic, wild rose, crucifixes, etc.), the two elder brothers are not as clever as their younger sibling. Much like Renfield, the youngest brother decides to conceal himself from the world with the cloak of invisibility until he is a ripe old age. He then passes his secret on to his son and bravely greets Death as 'an old friend.' Indeed, throughout the series, Rowling reinforces the notion that death is a natural process that should not be feared; rather, it should be regarded as "life's next big adventure."

The Harry Potter books teach that a loved one's passing can be beheld as a magnificent process and more profound in other spheres than it appears on earth. Thus, the series symbolizes loss and grief. For example, Dumbledore comforts Harry when he realizes his father does not come back to life to help him, and in doing so, he instructs him on the merit of acceptance, "You think the dead we loved ever truly leave us? You think we don't recall them more clearly than ever in times of great trouble?" Just as the spirit of Quincey P. Morris lives on in the Harker's son, Dumbledore's spirit lives on in Harry's and Ginny's youngest son Albus.

Finally, there is a close connection between Dracula's 'undead' status and the 'ripped times seven' state of Voldemort. Indeed, when the rebounded curse strikes the Dark Lord the first time when he tries to kill Harry as an infant, He-Who-Must-Not-Be-Named is no longer alive in a physical sense. However, he is not 'true dead' either. His soul is torn into seven objects, yet he is too weak to find a means to resurrect himself until *The Goblet of Fire*. As Dracula needs followers and victims to stay alive, Voldemort hovers in limbo for fourteen years without a physical body — caught somewhere between life and death: undead, awaiting the blood of Harry to bring him back to life.

"I was ripped from my body, less than spirit, less than the meanest ghost, but still, I was alive."

— Lord Voldemort regarding his fall from power

So, death in literature is a diverse concept, just as it is in culture. While it is an inevitable fate for all human beings, it is not experienced and wrestled with in the same fashion. Even as it continuously pervades our beliefs at all levels, from the instant feeling of devastation that personal bereavement provides to the ways in which we process the concept of death by pushing it onto the surface, it remains an enigma. If the *Dracula* and Harry Potter franchises give us any boon, it is this: As remarkably reassuring and horrifyingly entertaining the downfall of a monster might be, don't get so occupied with the fear of dying that you forget to live. If that sounded a lot like a Van Helsing or Dumbledore, it was meant to be!

Chapter Fifteen

Magic & Mesmerism

An innate border separates the realm of the real and the world of fantasy. As a reader, our physical bodies are positioned in the globe we know, but our metaphysical forms can occupy a space that is unreal. The bookworm's hesitation between the two spheres helps define the space between them while providing a path from one to the other — that is to say, their uncertainty assists in crossing each universe. Without the reader's cooperation, without their twinkling of indecision and eagerness for adventure, the magic of the fantastical narrative is absent. For most children, the grand quest for an imaginative escape can drive them excitably to the library; but sadly, as one ages, the decreasing lack thereof can cause many enchanted great books to begin collecting dust.

What is magic, anyway? Quite simply, it can be defined as the power of influencing the course of events by using mysterious or supernatural forces. Whether one chooses to use such synonyms as sorcery, witchcraft, or voodoo, the translation and end results are the same: a supernatural power-altering reality. Most comic books, cartoons, and children's literature can be placed in this category. From a superhero with amazing powers to a sleeping princess cursed by a queen, these stories bring — and continue to bring — joy to thousands, with particular favorites often passed down from generation to generation.

It is a given that children are the targeted audience for Harry Potter books, but the stigma that adults cannot appreciate them is an injustice to anyone over age eighteen. The reverse is true for *Dracula*. Indeed, both are magical — regardless of the age of the reader. Unfortunately, the labels 'Gothic Horror" or "Young Adult Fantasy" can sometimes segregate a reading audience.

On the surface, one might not recognize the "Gothic Horror" masterpiece as fantasy. Indeed, there are no magic wands, Hogwarts, or broomsticks in the novel. But if one were to look closer, there are several connections that prove otherwise.

To begin with, vampirism has been documented in folklore as being a form of sorcery — a curse performed on a human considered evil or one desperate to give up his soul for an unattainable price on earth. Early legends reflected the premise that the curse was passed down from a powerful witch or the devil himself. As mentioned in an earlier chapter of this book, the conversation Abraham Van Helsing has in *Dracula* with the other protagonists mentions Mount Hermannstadt, which, according to lore, carries rooted knowledge of alchemy and magic. Though Stoker leaves many details of his vampire villain's early life obscure, it was said "he was in life a most wonderful man. Soldier, statesman, and alchemist. He had a mighty brain, a learning beyond compare, and a heart that knew no fear and no remorse... there was no branch of knowledge of his time that he did not essay." He studies the black arts at the academy of Scholomance in the Carpathian Mountains, overlooking the town of Sibiu (also known as Hermannstadt), and has a deep knowledge of alchemy and magic.

Though Bram Stoker takes this reference from Emily Gerard's 1885 article on 'Transylvanian Superstitions,' there has been much speculation about the origin and meaning of the Scholomance. Since the publication of *Dracula*, a folklorist by the name of R.C. Maclagan was able to produce a report which included a more accurate version of the story Gerard referred to during the then-circulated Hermannstadt region of Transylvania:

> "Here we find that the *drac* is the devil in person, who instructs certain persons to be magicians and medicine men in a college under the earth. Of these, one in eight receives instruction for fourteen years, and on his return to earth he has the following power. By means of certain magical formulae he compels a dragon to ascend from the depths of a *loch*. He then throws a golden bridle with which he has been provided over his head, and rides aloft among the clouds, which he causes to freeze and thereby produces hail."

Since the Scholomance was referenced as being 'under the earth,' it makes perfect sense that the mountains of Hermannstadt are the ideal location for the school. To better understand the remaining passage, one should first consider that before Transylvania was a Christian region, it was part of the pre-Christian Roman province of Dacia — one that, prior to the Roman conquest, was traditionally joined with Thrace. Priests of the pagan gods in both of these territories were known to retreat into the woods to undisclosed locations to learn the secrets of the gods. The Transylvanian scholars of the Scholomance studied to control the weather and ride dragons. What might seem to be a bizarre lesson for the devil to teach becomes clearer upon realizing that the country had an indigenous legend of wandering wizards that performed those same two miracles.

Henceforth referred to as the Solomanari, after a connection between Solomon and alchemy, the Zgriminties or Hultan were shaman-priests who seized power over storms and could summon a balaur (dragon) to ride. According to author Jason Colavito, "Before Christianity, they were seen as benevolent forces able to implore the gods to deliver much-needed rain to fertilize the crops. Christians defamed the Solomonari as devil-worshippers, but in reality, they originated as pre-Christian pagan priests." Greek reports suggest these priests worshipped Zalmoxis (or Salmoxis), whose power they were able to wield. The ancients declared this god taught astrology and the doctrine of immortality. It was asserted that those who were scholars of this god did so in secluded, subversive chapels.

Not only did the text of *Dracula* shed light on a connection between the origin of vampirism and sorcery, but it also provided a list of supernatural powers to accompany the curse. Indeed, from shapeshifting to appearing out of the mist, the Count is given enough magical skills to become his own supervillain Marvel comic book in the 1970s, often fighting werewolves, Doctor Strange, Frankenstein's Monster, Blade or Van Helsing himself. In Chapter 18, the lengthy famous speech of Professor Van Helsing records numerous superstitions found in folklore, including a history of what could arguably be based on the historical Vlad Dracula III, commonly known as Vlad Țepeș or Vlad the Impaler.

"Mina Harker's Journal.

30 September. [...] "Now let us see how far the general powers arrayed against us are restrict, and how the individual cannot. In fine, let us consider the limitations of the vampire in general, and of this one in particular.

"All we have to go upon are traditions and superstitions. These do not at the first appear much, when the matter is one of life and death, nay of more than either life or death. Yet must we be satisfied, in the first place because we have to be, no other means is at our control, and secondly, because, after all these things, tradition and superstition, are everything. Does not the belief in vampires rest for others, though not, alas! for us, on them? A year ago which of us would have received such a possibility, in the midst of our scientific, sceptical, matter of fact nineteenth century? We even scouted a belief that we saw justified under our very eyes. Take it, then, that the vampire, and the belief in his limitations and his cure, rest for the moment on the same base. For, let me tell you, he is known everywhere that men have been. In old Greece, in old Rome, he flourishes in Germany all over, in France, in India, even in the Chermosese, and in China, so far from us in all ways, there even is he, and the peoples for him at this day. He has followed the wake of the berserker Icelander, the devil-begotten Hun, the Slav, the Saxon, the Magyar.

"So far, then, we have all we may act upon, and let me tell you that very much of the beliefs are justified by what we have seen in our own so unhappy experience. The vampire lives on, and cannot die by mere passing of the time, he can flourish when that he can fatten on the blood of the living. Even more, we have seen amongst us that he can even grow younger, that his vital faculties grow strenuous, and seem as though they refresh themselves when his special pabulum is plenty.

"But he cannot flourish without this diet, he eats not as others. Even friend Jonathan, who lived with him for weeks, did never see him eat, never! He throws no shadow, he makes in the mirror no reflect, as again Jonathan observed. He has the strength of many of his hand, witness again Jonathan when he shut the door against the wolves, and when he helps him from the diligence too. He can transform himself to wolf, as we gather from the ship arrival in Whitby, when he tear open the dog, he can be as bat, as Madam Mina saw him on the window at Whitby, and as friend John saw him fly from this so near house, and as my friend Quincey saw him at the window of Miss Lucy.

"He can come in mist which he creates, that noble ship's captain proved him of this, but from what we know, the distance he can make this mist is limited, and it can only be round himself. "He come on moonlight rays as elemental dust, as again Jonathan saw those sisters in the castle of Dracula. He became so small, we ourselves saw Miss Lucy, ere she was at peace, slip through a hair-breadth space at the tomb door. He can, when once he finds his way, come out from anything or into anything, no matter how close it be bound or even fused up with fire, solder you call it. He can see in the dark, no small power this, in a world which is one half shut from the light. Ah, but hear me through.

"He can do all these things, yet he is not free. Nay, he is even more prisoner than the slave of the galley, than the madman in his cell. He cannot go where he lists, he who is not of nature has yet to obey some of nature's laws, why we know not. He may not enter anywhere at the first, unless there be some one of the households who bid him to come, though afterwards he can come as he please. His power ceases, as does that of all evil things, at the coming of the day.

"Only at certain times can he have limited freedom. If he be not at the place whither, he is bound, he can only change himself at noon or at exact sunrise or sunset. These things we are told, and in this record of ours we have proof by inference. Thus, whereas he can do as he will within his limit, when he have his earth-home, his coffin-home, his hell-home, the place unhallowed, as we saw when he went to the grave of the suicide at Whitby, still at other time he can only change when the time come. It is said, too, that he can only pass running water at the slack or the flood of the tide. Then there are things which so afflict him that he has no power, as the garlic that we know of, and as for things sacred, as this symbol, my crucifix, that was amongst us even now when we resolve, to them he is nothing, but in their presence he take his place far off and silent with respect. There are others, too, which I shall tell you of, lest in our seeking we may need them.

"The branch of wild rose on his coffin keep him that he move not from it, a sacred bullet fired into the coffin kill him so that he be true dead, and as for the stake through him, we know already of its peace, or the cut off head that giveth rest. We have seen it with our eyes.

"Thus when we find the habitation of this man-that-was, we can confine him to his coffin and destroy him, if we obey what we know. But he is clever. I have asked my friend Arminius, of Buda-Pesth University, to make his record, and from all the means that are, he tells me of what he has been. He must, indeed, have been that Voivode Dracula who won his name against the Turk, over the great river on the very frontier of Turkeyland. If it be so, then was he no common man, for in that time, and for centuries after, he was spoken of as the cleverest and the most cunning, as well as the bravest of the sons of the 'land beyond the forest.' That mighty brain and that iron resolution went with him to his grave and are even now arrayed against us."

Thus, it is clear that certain elements of magic from Hermannstadt, such as controlling the weather, transfer into Van Helsing's presentation. While most of the supernatural powers, vampiric traits, and methods of destruction can be traced back to early lore, Stoker invokes literary license by expounding upon a few to develop his plot. A perfect example of this is Dracula filling coffins with his native soil. Though the vampire legend across numerous countries shares in the supernatural, life-sustaining power of resting in the ground of indigenous dirt, transporting coffins around like luggage is a new twist to an old myth. Though Van Helsing's explanation of how the vampire curse is spread by being a victim of one stands prevalent today, the magic of the Scholomance still carries a thread of reference in modern vampire stories when explaining the origin of the first vampires. Indeed, the long-running series *The Vam-*

pire Diaries, including its spin-off *The Originals*, purports that the first family of vampires sprouted fangs after being cursed by their witch mother after she performed a magical blood ritual.

Another form of magic that is an important theme in *Dracula* is the use of hypnotism. Often referred to as mesmerism or mind control, during Stoker's day, the concept of influencing one's mind and manipulating a response was widely considered an occult practice. Many referred to those who claimed to practice hypnosis or mesmerism during that time as imposters, fakes, or quacks, and even the most learned and scientific of men had closed minds when it came to embracing the subject.

"Dr. Seward's Diary.

26 September. [...] "I suppose now you do not believe in corporeal transference. No? Nor in materialization. No? Nor in astral bodies. No? Nor in the reading of thought. No? Nor in hypnotism —" [Van Helsing speaking]."

Indeed, mind control is the only eccentricity or 'possible possibility' that Van Helsing dishes out that Seward can support based on Jean-Martin Charcot's international reputation and case studies in the field. However, the other men in the group resolve their doubts once Van Helsing himself begins placing Mina under hypnosis to help pinpoint the vampire's whereabouts.

However, Van Helsing is not the only person in Stoker's novel with the skill of mesmerism. Dracula has the supernatural power to control the actions of even the most resistant victims. From Lucy's entranced sleepwalking adventures to Jonathan's compelled trance while Mina is magnetically drinking from his breast, the spell-binding Count uses his hypnotic abilities for personal gain:

"Dr. Seward's Diary.

3 October. [...] "Jonathan is in a stupor such as we know the Vampire can produce [Van Helsing speaking]."

[...] "I felt my strength fading away, and I was in a half swoon. How long this horrible thing lasted I know not; but it seemed that a long time must have passed before he took his foul, awful, sneering mouth away." [Mina Harker speaking].

The appearances of alchemy, vampires, shapeshifting, mesmerism, blood rituals, curses, magic, and witches are not isolated to the novel *Dracula*. Indeed, they all appear in the Harry Potter series as well. Depicted as supernatural energy that can be used to overrule the laws of nature, J.K. Rowling's wizarding world looks at magic as an extremely rare gift inherited by a dominant resilient gene, with less common exceptions, such as 'Mudbloods' and 'squibs.' There are several branches or categories of magic that Rowling thought through carefully, specifying their laws, limits, and history. For the purposes of this chapter, three of these will be broken down which share a connection with Stoker's *Dracula*: alchemy, shapeshifting, and mesmerism.

According to Merriam-Webster's definition of alchemy, the word represents "a medieval chemical science and speculative philosophy aiming to achieve the transmutation of the base metals into gold, the discovery of a universal cure for disease, and the discovery of a means of indefinitely prolonging life."

Just as the doctors in *Dracula* practice alchemy professionally in an attempt to 'prolong life' as good Samaritans, the Count studies it as a man in the Scholomance from a black arts perspective. The same scenario unfolds in Rowling's tale a century later. At Hogwarts, the subject of alchemy was an optional sixth- and seventh-year class, especially for those interested in the field of advanced potion-making.

"The best known goals of the alchemists were the transmutation of common metals into Gold or Silver (less well known is plant alchemy, or "Spagyric"), and the creation of a "panacea", a remedy that supposedly would cure all diseases and prolong life indefinitely, and the discovery of a universal solvent. Although these were not the only uses for the science, they were the ones most documented and well known. Starting with the Middle Ages, European alchemists invested much effort on the search for the philosopher's stone, a legendary substance that was believed to be an essential ingredient for either or both of those goals."

— Libatius Borage, *Advanced Potion-Making*

In the magical world of Harry Potter, great wizards Nicolas Flamel and Albus Dumbledore are mentioned as being alchemists. Similar to Seward and Van Helsing, their study and practice of the subject matter is altruistic. Nicolas Flamel is the only known maker of the Philosopher's Stone, a legendary substance with incredible powers. He owes his considerable age to the Elixir of Life. He and his wife Perenelle create this Elixir utilizing the Stone. As of 1992, he is six hundred and ninety years old.

"Nicolas Flamel is an historical character. Flamel lived in France in the fourteenth century and is supposed to have discovered how to make a philosopher's stone. There are mentions of sightings of him through the centuries because he was supposed to have gained immortality. There are still streets named after Flamel and his wife Perenelle in Paris."

— J.K. Rowling on Nicolas Flamel

Like Dracula uses the study of alchemy for the dark arts, Lord Voldemort intends to steal the Philosopher's Stone to resurrect himself and spread evil across the land. The Dark Lord fails, for, at Dumbledore's appeal, the stone is abolished. Nicolas Flamel reserves enough Elixir of Life to set his affairs in order, and then he passes away. Harry, Ron, Hermione, and Neville are awarded 170 points overall for Gryffindor — a grand total responsible for them winning the House Cup in 1997 — and Lord Voldemort's return is further delayed three years.

The magical skill of shapeshifting into a different animal form in the Harry Potter saga is referred to as Animagi. According to Pottermore, an Animagus is a "witch or wizard who could morph him or herself into an animal at will. It was a learned, rather than hereditary skill, unlike those of a Metamorphmagus." To clarify, the latter is a hereditary magical skill that allows a witch or wizard to alter their physical appearance without the aid of Polyjuice potion, such as the witch character Nymphadora Tonks, who is habitually changing the color of her hair throughout the series. As Dracula learns this skill from the Scholomance, the Animagi process is taught to Hogwarts students during their third year Transfiguration class.

"The process is extremely difficult and can result in disaster (such as permanent half-human, half-animal mutations) if done incorrectly. A witch or wizard must keep a single mandrake leaf in their mouth for an entire month (from full moon to full moon). If the leaf is removed or swallowed, the witch or wizard will have to start over again. At the next visible full moon (if the night happens to be cloudy one will have to start over), the wizard must spit the leaf in a phial within range of the moon's pure rays. To the moon-struck phial, the wizard or witch must add one of their own hairs, a silver teaspoon of dew that has not seen sunlight or been touched by human feet for seven days, and the chrysalis of a Death's-head Hawk Moth. The mixture must be put in a quiet, dark place and be in any way disturbed. The next thing that must happen is for the wizard to wait for an electrical storm, whenever that might be. During this waiting period the wizard must, at sunrise and sundown without fail, chant the incantation Amato Animo Animato Animagus with the tip of their wand placed over the heart. When, at last, there is a lightning storm, the wizard ought to move immediately to a large and secure place, recite the incantation one final time, and then drink the potion."

— Pottermore, on Acquiring the Amimagus Skill

An Animagus registration exists to keep track of those that have learned this challenging ability, though some wizards, such as Peter Pettigrew, fail to register in order to fake their deaths and remain hidden.

Unlike the Count, who practices this learned skill as a vampire and often shapeshifts into wolves and bats, an Animagus can only take on the form of one specific animal. This animal shape is not chosen by the wizard; however, it is determined by their personality and inner traits. It can also be that the full-bodied Patronus charm reveals what form a witch or wizard might shift into if they are an Animagus. Case in point, Minerva McGonagall, a known cat Animagus, also has the Patronus of a cat. This proves the theory that the form a Patronus takes is determined by the same inner traits as the Animagus.

Just like Dracula, who is not confined by the lifespan limit of the creature he chooses to manifest, the same logic applies in the wizarding world. For example, in the instance of Animagus Peter Pettigrew, who takes the form of a rat, he remains in Animagi shape for at least a dozen years, remaining alive notwithstanding the fact that rodents have a brief lifespan.

Just as with alchemy and shapeshifting, mesmerism (or mind control) is another form of magical ability that can be used for the power of good or evil. In Bram Stoker's novel, Van Helsing uses the skill to help locate and ultimately destroy Dracula, while the vampire uses it to trap and feed on the helpless. Likewise, in the Harry Potter books, Legilimency, Occlumency, and the Imperius Curse are used numerous times, and dependent upon the witch or wizard casting the spell, the intent can benefit or harm the recipient of the charm.

Legilimency is known in Rowling's series as the magical skill of circumnavigating through the stratosphere of a person's mind and properly interpreting one's discoveries. Though Dumbledore, who is known as a master 'Legilimens,' readers can be confident that the power is wielded for such responsible purposes, as in reading Harry Potter's thoughts to ensure his personal safety:

> "Professor Dumbledore was now looking down at Harry, who looked right back at him, trying to discern the expression of the eyes behind the half-moon spectacles…. [Harry] really couldn't think of anything to say. The inside of his head seemed to be in complete disarray, as though his brain had been ransacked." — *The Goblet of Fire*

The reverse form of Legilimency is Occlumency — a magical counter skill to safeguard one's mind from the intrusion and influence of Legilimens. At the request of the headmaster, Professor Snape is asked to teach Occlumency to Harry out of fear that He-Who-Must-Not-Be-Named will invade Potter's mind in order to lure him out of Dumbledore's protection. As played out sometimes ruthlessly in *The Order of the Phoenix*, the professor used Legilimency on Harry so that Snape could instruct him, with mixed results, at best.

"The mind is not a book, to be opened at will and examined at leisure. Thoughts are not etched on the inside of skulls, to be perused by any invader. The mind is a complex and many-layered thing, Potter. Or at least most minds are... It is true, however, that those who have mastered Legilimency are able, under certain conditions, to delve into the minds of their victims and to interpret their findings correctly."

— Severus Snape regarding the art of Legilimency

Because Harry fails to master Occlumency, two-thirds into Book 5, Voldemort is able to invade Potter's mind, read his thoughts, and conclude that the love of Sirius Black will bring Harry to the Department of Mysteries if he believes his godfather is in danger.

The Imperius curse, the other form of mesmerism linked to mind control, is one of the three Unforgiveable Curses outlawed in 1717. Pottermore states that the curse was invented during the Middle Ages by dark witches or wizards as a means of coercion and brainwashing victims into slavery. As explored in the previous chapter, Barty Crouch Sr. is a misfortunate recipient of this spell, along with Alastor Moody, Katie Bell, Lavender Brown, and many, many others, as Lord Voldemort begins his campaign to full power.

As Dracula gives Lucy orders to rise from bed, open a window or door, and walk outside up to the Whitby churchyard, the Dark Lord blames his victims for heinous crimes such as slaughter, political exploitation, and theft. Death Eater Barty Crouch, Jr., disguises himself as Alastor Moody while teaching the unforgivable curses to a group of fourth-year students that include Harry Potter. Crouch (disguised as Moody) sinisterly explains as he holds a cursed spider dangling by his wand: "I could make her jump out a window, drown herself, or even launch herself down one of your throats."

Indeed, Harry Potter is placed under the Imperius curse briefly by Barty Crouch Jr. and even by Lord Voldemort himself for an extremely brief time, resisting both attempts. Though the feeling can be freeing, the lasting effect and implications are rather severe and awful.

"It was the most wonderful feeling. Harry felt a floating sensation as every thought and worry in his head was wiped gently away, leaving nothing but a vague, untraceable happiness. He stood there feeling immensely relaxed, only dimly aware of everyone watching him."

        — Harry Potter while under the Imperius Curse
        by Barty Crouch Jr. (disguised as Professor Moody)

In sum, regardless of whether the use of magic in *Dracula* or the Harry Potter saga is for good or evil, book sales over the years can attest that readers continue to locate that inherent border separating the realm of the real and fantasy world to cross over. Bookworms could probably attest that escaping into these novels could very well carry a feeling similar to the Imperius curse — that is, wonderful.... worry-free.... happiness — under the control of the late, great Bram Stoker or the talented storyteller J.K. Rowling. Though neither writer claimed to be a practitioner of mesmerism by profession, many fans would probably argue the case in theory: indeed, children and adults continue to be mesmerized by the imaginative escape each tale excites, and there is no enchanted sign suggesting either will be collecting dust soon.

Part Four

Symbolisms

Chapter Sixteen

Stakes & Wands

The use of symbolism in literature was a nineteenth-century French movement that spilled over into the art world. Still widely used today, symbolism is a creative, useful way for the author to communicate an important, deeper idea through vivid images that are more profound than literal word choice. For example, a writer who is attempting to convey the subject of peace might use a dove in the text to underscore the message of calm, or, as in *Dracula*, the use of the crucifix to ward off evil is a representational image of the pureness of Christ.

In the case of Bram Stoker and J.K. Rowling, both utilize symbolism throughout their respective works as a means to drive home the numerous themes. This chapter is devoted to two long, wooden instruments of power: stakes and wands.

In the most simplistic terms, the wooden stake carries the potential to destroy a vampire. Author and vampire guru J. Gordon Melton, Ph.D., had the following to say in *The Completely Revamped Vampire Book: The Encyclopedia of the Undead* © 1999 Visible Ink Press:

> "The most well-known way to kill a vampire was by staking it in the heart. This method was prescribed by Sheridan Le Fanu in his novella, *Carmilla*, (1872) and was a remedy later lauded by Bram Stoker for his novel, *Dracula*, and repeated in numerous vampire movies."

The ancient superstition of corpse staking of a rogue vampire was a practice found across Europe before the conception of coffins was popularized. By keeping a corpse attached to the ground below its body, a wooden stake would usually be driven through the stomach for easier penetration. Lore in some areas recommended turning the suspect corpse face down while the wooden stake was driven through the back. Regardless of the country, however, it is interesting to note that the heart was often avoided, for it was difficult to penetrate the rib cage. Vampire myths in some locations actually prescribed the type of wood the stake needed to be carved from to avoid these mistakes: ash, aspen, juniper, or hawthorn. Some legends went as far as recommending that a stake be driven into the ground over the grave as a way to block the suspected vampire from rising.

However, once coffins became widespread, the purpose of staking changed some-what. J. Gordon Melton went on to say,

"Where previously the object of the staking was to fix the body to the ground, the purpose of the staking became a frontal assault upon the corpse itself. By attacking the heart, the organ that pumped the blood, the bloodsucking vam-pire could be killed. Staking the heart was somewhat analogous to the practice of driving nails into a vampire's head."

The power of the stake led to much conjecture in numerous novels and movies concerning the rationale for wooden stakes. Some believed the power of the stake was in the 'end result' — that is to say, the brute physical damage to the heart — while others felt the vampire was directly affected by wood. There seemed to be a strong argument for the latter, as much modern lore adopted the belief that wooden bullets could strike down a vampire. For some, the stake being driven into the vampire was a measure of finality, while other believers viewed the act as a temporary, blood-sucking hiatus. Indeed, the removal of the stake became a popular means to revive fan-favorite vampires for literary and film sequels.

In Bram Stoker's *Dracula*, Arthur Holmwood (a.k.a. Lord Godalming) drives the wooden stake into Lucy Westenra's heart, finally giving her peace.

"Dr. Seward's Diary — continued.

[29 September.] "Take this stake in your left hand, ready to place the point over the heart, and the hammer in your right. Then when we begin our prayer for the dead—I shall read him, I have here the book, and the others shall follow — strike in God's name, that so all may be well with the dead that we love, and that the Un-Dead pass away." [Van Helsing speaking]."

When Holmwood buries the wooden stake deep into Lucy's heart, it is with the power to execute the demon she has become and return her to the state of purity and innocence he so values. Indeed, the language with which Stoker describes this violent act is unmistakably erotic — "The body shook and quivered and twisted in wild con-tortions" — and the wooden stake is a covert phallic symbol. In this context, it is fitting that the blow came from Lucy's fiancé, Arthur Holmwood:

"Dr. Seward's Diary —continued.

[29 September.] "So that, my friend, it will be a blessed hand for her that shall strike the blow that sets her free. To this I am willing; but is there none amongst us who has a better right? Will it be no joy to think of hereafter in the silence of the night when sleep is not: 'It was my hand that sent her to the stars; it was the hand of him that loved her best; the hand that of all she would herself have chosen, had it been to her to choose? Tell me if there be such a one amongst us?"

We all looked at Arthur. He saw, too, what we all did, the infinite kindness which suggested that his should be the hand which would restore Lucy to us as a holy, and not an unholy, memory; he stepped forward and said bravely, though his hand trembled, and his face was as pale as snow: —" My true friend, from the bottom of my broken heart I thank you. Tell me what I am to do, and I shall not falter.!"

One could argue that Lucy is being punished not only for being a vampire but also for being open to the vampire's seduction. However, when Holmwood eradicates the demonic Lucy, he returns her to the role of an authentic, monogamous lover, reinvesting his fiancée with her initial Victorian virtue.

Indeed, a similar process is used for the three weird sisters who reside in Castle Dracula; however, this time, it is Van Helsing himself who frees them of the vampire curse:

"Dr. Van Helsing's Memorandum.

5 November, afternoon. — "Oh, my friend John, but it was butcher work; had I not been nerved by thoughts of other dead, and of the living over whom hung such a pall of fear, I could not have gone on. I tremble and tremble even yet, though till all was over, God be thanked, my nerve did stand. Had I not seen the repose in the first face, and the gladness that stole over it just ere the final dissolution came, as realization that the soul had been won, I could not have endured the horrid screeching as the stake drove home; the plunging of writhing form, and lips of bloody foam. I should have fled in terror and left my work undone. But it is over! And the poor souls, I can pity them now and weep, as I think of them placid each in her full sleep of death, for a short moment ere fading."

Again, one could argue the presence of sexually charged tones in this entire passage, including a previous line where Van Helsing states, "She was so fair to look on, so radiantly beautiful, so exquisitely voluptuous that the very instinct of man in me, which calls some of my sex to love and to protect one of hers, made my head whirl with new emotion." Henceforth, these are the same three creatures that begin seducing

Jonathan at the beginning of the novel; and now Professor Van Helsing has the power of his 'wood' as he 'plunge[s]' it into all three women and returns them into the Victorian ladies they were before being poisoned by Dracula's tainted blood.

Similarly, as reflected in the Harry Potter series, the wand is a long wooden object that contains magical properties granted to a witch or wizard. According to Pottermore:

> "A wand is the object through which a witch or wizard channels his or her magic. It is made from wood and has a magical substance at its core. Wands made by Ollivander have cores of phoenix feather, unicorn hair or dragon heartstring, and are of varying woods, lengths, and flexibilities."

> — Description of a wand

As with 'stakelore,' 'wandlore' is the study of the history and the magical properties of wands. All of Rowling's novels make it clear that a wand chooses its owner and works best in his or her possession. Pottermore further reasons a wand to be a quasi-sentient, magical tool through which a witch or wizard channels his or her magical powers to centralize the effects for more complex results. Most spells are performed with the aid of a wand, although certain incantations can be cast without one. Performing magic without using a wand is extremely difficult and requires much concentration and incredible skill. Advanced wizards and some enchanted creatures, such as house-elves, are said to perform wandless magic.

In J.K. Rowling's wizarding world, wands are manufactured and sold by wandmakers; the most renowned of these is Garrick Ollivander in Great Britain, and Mykew Gregorovich in Eastern Europe. Like wooden stakes that must be fashioned from specific trees, each wand consists of a particular type of wood that surrounds a core of magical substance. Although the wand cores may come from the same magical creature or the wood from the same tree, no two existing wands are exactly alike.

Wandlore noted that wands were developed in Europe at an unknown point, though it is recognized that it was in the B.C. era. Indeed, the Ollivander family started manufacturing wands in 382 B.C.; and over time, their business earned a worldwide following. In the 13th century, the notorious Elder Wand, which would become known as the most powerful wand in existence, was created.

Like so much in the Harry Potter saga, symbolic meaning can be found in the most minute details. By looking at folklore, the properties of British trees, and Garrick Ollivander's personal notes, a clear picture can be painted regarding how a wand reflects its owner's personality, power (good or bad), and fate.

On the surface, some have thought it strange that Harry Potter and He-Who-Must-Not-Be-Named share twin wand cores — phoenix feathers, both taken from Dumbledore's pet bird Fawkes. However, if one looks deeper, it quickly becomes apparent that these characters have a lot in common. Apart from Lord Voldemort's relation to Harry as a Horcrux — one that also gives them involuntary similarities such as the power of Parseltongue — their backgrounds are complimentary. They are orphans raised by Muggles and totally unaware they are wizards until Dumbledore invites them to Hogwarts. Because they each own Peverell family heirlooms, they are probably blood-related as well. Although to understand the key differences between Harry and Voldemort, one would need to look no further than the supernatural power of the different wood of their wands.

Bram Stoker referenced the symbolic, venomous yew tree countless times in *Dracula*, such as in Chapter 15 when Dr. Seward writes:

"I took up my place behind a yew-tree, and I saw his dark figure move until the intervening headstones and trees hid it from sight."

Lord Voldemort's wand is made from the poisonous yew tree. Indeed, except for the flesh of the berry (the seeds are toxic), the alkaloids contained in the tree are lethal to humans. Like the yew, He-Who-Must-Not-Be-Named is deadly and claims the lives of many. His belief system, such as pure-blood supremacy, is equally as contaminated. It is also important to note that the power of the yew tree poison remains active after the tree has died. This truth is remarkably akin to the Dark Lord's Horcruxes and Death Eater followers, which loiter on after his downfall at Godric's Hollow, polluting minds and devastating lives.

In contrast, Harry's wand cannot have been any more different. Indeed, holly is a traditional symbol of luck, prosperity, and protection from evil. Holly has been hung on doors to ward off vampires, and it has been used in celebration rituals throughout history — including the Roman festival of Saturnalia, the pagan Winter Solstice, and, of course, Christmas. Like holly, Harry repelled evil in the form of Lord Voldemort and his cohorts and unified the wizarding world in commemoration as they proudly toast 'The Boy Who Lived.'

And then there is Dumbledore's powerful Elder Wand. Elder trees have played a peculiar role in Druidic mythology. These revered plants are alleged to possess medicinal powers and an association with the supernatural world. Indeed, chopping an elder tree or burning the wood is understood to enrage the Mother Goddess and incite her to pursue vengeance. For example, the following line from the Wiccan Rede suggests that the Elder Wand is hexed from the instant the wood is cut: "Elder is the Lady's Tree, burn it not or cursed ye be!"

Undeniably, illustrations of blessings and misfortunes rung true with Albus Dumbledore, who held the Elder Wand since defeating Gellert Grindelwald in 1945. Dumbledore is gifted with immeasurable talent; however, the powerful wizard is equally cursed by a heartrending family past. Once he fully comprehends the many perils of abusive power, the Elder Wand proceeds into his possession. That powerful instrument which, when ill-used, hastily turns its proprietor into a target. Dumbledore's unique destiny is to utilize his exceptional wisdom to shield others from corruption. Indeed, it is interesting to point out that this all-powerful and mighty wand — the one that Voldemort used to destroy Harry's Horcrux — will be the very tool that will kill the Dark Lord himself. The Elder Wand recognizes that Harry is its proper master and will only wield to him. And it is not mere fortune that certain wands are paired with certain wizards to underwrite such power.

Thus, in both texts, the stake and the wand are lengthy, wooden, symbolic, supernatural instruments used to channel power. In both stories, whether or not this authority will be used for good or evil is up to the holder. Indeed, Stoker and Rowling successfully communicate in their brilliant pages that the ideal of love carries the power to build up while the dogma of hate carries the power to tear down.

Chapter Seventeen

Diaries, Letters & Newspapers

Throughout the ages, diaries (or journals) have been used as a written form of expression, normally documenting real-life events. Perhaps one of the most famous diaries belonged to Anne Frank, the German-born diarist and one of the most discussed Jewish victims of the Holocaust. Her diary was a symbol of comfort and independence when the world around her was full of unrest and oppression. Letters can be viewed as a selected few pages of a diary addressed to a loved one as a tool to express personalized messages or 'epistles' (as they were commonly referred to in Biblical times). The Apostle Paul's epistles to the Romans and Corinthians were almost compositions in prose or poetry written in the form of formal letters as symbols of hope, peace, and love. In contrast, newspapers can be symbolic of pessimism, conflict, and hate that is often expressed on the daily front page of almost every publication.

The entire novel *Dracula* is written in the form of diary and journal entries, letters, telegrams, memorandums, and newspaper clippings. Since its publication in 1897, scholars have debated about the reason Bram Stoker chose to compose such an odd collection of correspondence, but in truth, one needs not look any further than the novel itself for answers.

Stoker's dedication to his dear friend 'Hommy-Beg' (or "little Tommy"), a Manx name of endearment for Hall Cain, the English novelist) reads as follows:

"How these papers have been placed in sequence will be made manifest in the reading of them. All needless matters have been eliminated, so that a history almost at variance with the possibilities of later-day belief may stand forth as simple fact. There is throughout no statement of past things wherein memory may err, for all the records chosen are exactly contemporary, given from the standpoints and within the range of knowledge of those who made them."

Even though many of the events in the novel are hard to conceive, the author refers to them "as simple fact." Indeed, the plethora of documents is symbolic of the central character's hope and sanity being presented in court as a stack of evidence. However, the reader serves as both judge and jury. The myriad diaries, journals, letters, telegrams, and memorandums that Jonathan and Mina Murray Harker, Lucy Westenra, Dr. John (Jack) Seward, and Professor Abraham Van Helsing carefully write are in a style that is straightforward, immediate, and presented in chronological order. Because the characters compose in their journals practically as events are happening, the evidence is presented fresh and firsthand, so the readers experience the proceedings almost as the protagonists do. Though Stoker was a man of faith, he was also a man of science. Though he never practiced law, he took and passed the bar exam; and, therefore, used his knowledge of legal matters in his writing. Having Jonathan write in shorthand, Dr. Seward enter his diary via phonograph, and Mina transfer all accounts into a typed document are symbolic ways to show the importance and advantageous ways modernity could play in the legal system.

Details. Dates. Times. Logistics. From what might be the dull or boring account of a man looking through an atlas to something more thrilling as the seduction by the weird sisters, readers consistently receive a full, immediate description — a 'script,' which Jonathan Harker describes in Chapter 25 "[that] may be evidence to come between some of us and a rope." Even though the Count's body immediately crumbles to dust — thus protecting the group from being suspected of murder — their sanity is constantly being tested. Even the lunatic asylum owner and physiatrist, Dr. Seward himself, writes on October 2nd, "I sometimes think we must be all mad and that we shall wake to sanity in strait-waistcoats." Nevertheless, despite how bizarre their individual accounts could get, even the early and alarming entry by Harker proves to be a key that opens the doorway to reason — that is, once shared and validated by Van Helsing:

"Jonathan Harker's Journal — continued.

12 May, Later. — "What I saw was the Count's head coming out from the window. I did not see the face, but I know the man by the neck and the movement of his back and arms. In any case I could not mistake the hands which I had had so many opportunities of studying. I was at first interested and somewhat amused, for it is wonderful how small a matter will interest and amuse a man when he is a prisoner. But my very feeling changed to repulsion and terror when I saw the whole man slowly emerge from the window and begin to crawl down the castle wall over that dreadful abyss, face down, with his cloak spreading out around him like great wings. At

first, I could not believe my eyes. I thought it was some trick of the moonlight, some weird effect of shadow; but I kept looking, and it could be no delusion. I saw the fingers and toes grasp the corners of the stones, worn clear of the mortar by the stress of years, and by thus using every projection and inequality move downwards with considerable speed, just as a lizard moves along a wall."

"Letter (By Hand), Van Helsing To Mrs. Harker.

"25 September, 6 o'clock.

"Dear Madam Mina, —

"I have read your husband's so wonderful diary. You may sleep without doubt. Strange and terrible as it is, it is true! I will pledge my life on it. It may be worse for others; but for him and you there is no dread. He is a noble fellow; and let me tell you from experience of men, that one who would do as he did in going down that wall and to that room — ay, and going a second time — is not one to be injured in permanence by a shock. His brain and his heart are all right; this I swear before I have even seen him; so be at rest. I shall have much to ask him of other things. I am blessed that today I come to see you, for I have learn all at once so much that again I am dazzle — dazzle more than ever, and I must think.

"Yours the most faithful,

"Abraham Van Helsing."

Aside from Van Helsing writing letters symbolic of hope and sanity, Mina Murray Harker, Lucy Westenra, and Dr. John Seward join in, spreading the prudent message of maintaining an optimistic outlook and sound reason during such a horrible ordeal in the form of a telegram or memorandum.

The text of *Dracula* is was made up of several newspaper clippings: the *Pall Mall Gazette* (concerning the escaped wolf Bersicker from the London Zoo), the *Dailygraph* (covering the Demeter, the Russian schooner that runs aground), and the *Westminster Gazette* (covering the Undead Lucy as the 'Bloofer Lady'). Though all of these reports unleash further turmoil on the intrepid group, they are necessary for connecting the dots in the incredible mystery that pulls their band together. When Mina merges these crucial pieces of news into a typewritten, chronological heap of proof, even the Count recognizes the danger of leaving their documented detective work preserved. As a result, the vampire burns the papers after his nighttime snack with Madame Mina, unaware of the 'manifold' copy placed in Harker's safe. Arthur Holmwood provides an account of the event in Chapter 21:

"Dr. Seward's Diary.

3 October. — "He had been there, and though it could only have been for a few seconds, he made rare hay of the place. All the manuscript had been burned, and the blue flames were flickering amongst the white ashes; the cylinders of your phonograph too were thrown on the fire, and the wax had helped the flames." Here I interrupted. "Thank God there is the other copy in the safe!" His face lit for a moment but fell again as he went on: "I ran downstairs then but could see no sign of him. I looked into Renfield's room; but there was no trace there except —!" Again he paused. "Go on," said Harker hoarsely; so he bowed his head and moistening his lips with his tongue, added: "except that the poor fellow is dead."

When the boon of sleep becomes a 'presage of horror,' while one's long, shadowy days are laden with sordid events so terrifying they only bridge a thread to the same wicked nightmare, where can one find refuge and catharsis? Writing. Indeed, the answer to this question is each leading character's consistent daily input, fully documenting the evidence uncovered during their grueling, gruesome, six-month-long adventure. Similar to Anne Frank's famous diary, the symbolic inference of comfort and independence shine through their individual and collaborative efforts during a period when Dracula strives to wreak pain and control over their lives. Seven years after the Count's death, Jonathan writes a postscript to the narrative where he shares the sentiment that it no longer matters if anyone believes; as long as Quincey Harker grows up knowing how brave and loved his mother was, the terrible trial was worth it....

Note:

"It was almost impossible to believe that the things which we had seen with our own eyes and heard with our own ears were living truths [...] I took the papers from the safe where they had been ever since our return so long ago. We were struck with the fact, that in all the mass of material of which the record is composed, there is hardly one authentic document; nothing but a mass of typewriting, except the later notebooks of Mina and Seward and myself, and Van Helsing's memorandum. We could hardly ask anyone, even did we wish to, to accept these as proofs of so wild a story. Van Helsing summed it all up as he said, with our boy on his knee: —

"We want no proofs; we ask none to believe us! This boy will someday know what a brave and gallant woman his mother is. Already he knows her sweetness and loving care; later on he will understand how some men so loved her, that they did dare much for her sake."

— Jonathan Harker.

Like Bram Stoker's most famous work, the Harry Potter series devotes the entire second book to the infamous diary of Tom Riddle. Though it is hinted that other Hogwarts students keep journals, it is Voldemort's first Horcrux that stands out as also a tool to reopen the Chamber of Secrets in year two. J.K. Rowling once commented in an interview, "My sister used to commit her innermost thoughts to her diary. Her great fear was that someone would read it. So that's how the idea came to me of a diary that is itself against you. You would be confiding everything to pages that aren't inanimate."

Symbolically speaking, the diary turns out to be a useful piece of evidence to prove that Voldemort is lingering around Hogwarts — actively scheming to be reborn — and has the means to charm, influence, and even possess others. Though it would take several more years before the wizarding world at large would believe that He-Who-Must-Not-Be-Named was back, Harry, Ginny, Ron, Hermione, and Professor Dumbledore know better.

The diary is not only a symbolic piece of evidence that foreshadows events to come, but it invokes a remarkable plot twist that brings young Harry face-to-face with young Voldemort. Via this magical tool, readers realize there are many distinguishing yet similar factors between the two characters while affirming Harry's desire to take a different path.

The leading characters in *Dracula* record most events and dialogue exchanged during the day to look back on for clues to identify and destroy the evil that begins to ruin their lives. In the same sense, Riddle describes his ghostly presence as "a memory [...] Preserved in a diary for fifty years." Yet the Dark Lord begins to possess Ginny through the diary as an exchange of souls. In Chapter 17 of *The Chamber of Secrets*, the sixteen-year-old Riddle speaks of Ginny Weasley's abashed connection with the book by cunningly relating to Harry:

"The diary. My diary. Little Ginny's been writing in it for months and months, telling me all her pitiful worries and woes... So Ginny poured out her soul to me, and her soul happened to be exactly what I wanted... I grew stronger and stronger on a diet of her deepest fears, her darkest secrets. I grew powerful, far more powerful than little Miss Wesley. Powerful enough to start feeding Miss Weasley a few of my secrets, to start pouring a little of my soul back into her..."

— Ginny Weasley's emotional dependency on the diary

In *Dracula*, the vampire himself destroys the original diary manuscript, which can be used as evidence to prove his existence. Oddly enough, the reverse concept takes place in Book Two when Harry destroys the Horcrux diary with a Basilisk fang, banishing the sixteen-year-old Riddle from Hogwarts.

As with the many letters, telegrams, and memorandums that contribute to the manuscript *Dracula*, it would be fascinating to know the collective number of letters delivered by the Owl Postal Service to the Hogwarts students and their families over the seven-year span of the Harry Potter series. The significant count would be staggering and probably second to the sizable number of Educational Decrees set forth by the vicious Professor Umbridge during her reign of terror in Year Five. Regardless if it is a 'Howler' by Molly Weasley, warning her son Ron to "NOT PUT ANOTHER TOE OUT OF LINE!" or from Sirius Black, Potter's godfather, writing Harry to "hereby give him permission to visit Hogsmeade on weekends," the underlying sentiment is one of love and safety. While the many letters written in *Dracula* are symbolic of the necessity for hope and sanity to be reinforced during dark trials, the same message holds true in the Harry Potter saga. A seamless example of this happens in *The Prisoner of Azkaban* when Harry receives a letter from his best mate Ron:

Dear Harry,

Happy birthday!

Look, I'm really sorry about that telephone call. I hope the Muggles didn't give you a hard time. I asked Dad, and he reckons I shouldn't have shouted.

It's amazing here in Egypt. Bill's taken us around all the tombs and you wouldn't believe the curses those old Egyptian wizards put on them. Mum wouldn't let Ginny come in the last one. There were all these mutant skeletons in there, of Muggles who'd broken in and grown extra heads and stuff.

I couldn't believe it when Dad won the Daily Prophet Draw. Seven hundred galleons! Most of it's gone on this trip, but they're going to buy me a new wand for next year.

We'll be back about a week before term starts and we'll be going up to London to get my wand and our new books. Any chance of meeting you there?

Don't let the Muggles get you down!

Try and come to London,

Ron

P.S. Percy's Head Boy. He got the letter last week.

Page two

Harry — this is a Pocket Sneakoscope. If there's someone untrustworthy around, it's supposed to light up and spin. Bill says it's rubbish sold for wizard tourists and isn't reliable, because it kept lighting up at dinner last night. But he didn't realize Fred and George had put beetles in his soup.

Bye — Ron

As Van Helsing often finds himself in the position of sound mind and reason — though fantastically 'unsound' the circumstances are– Hermione Granger similarly assumes the role as the educated, thoughtful, rule-abiding go-to-person who ensures her clan is safe and 'in bounds.' Hermione's desire to keep Ron and Harry within the good graces of the legal system is communicated clearly in her letter addressed to both her friends in Book 2:

Dear Ron, and Harry if you're there,

I hope everything went all right and that Harry is okay and that you didn't do anything illegal to get him out, Ron, because that would get Harry into trouble, too. I've been really worried and if Harry is all right, will you please let me know at once, but perhaps it would be better if you used a different owl because I think another delivery might finish your one off.

I'm very busy with schoolwork, of course and we're going to London next Wednesday to buy my new books. Why don't we meet in Diagon Alley? Let me know what's happening as soon as you can.

Love from Hermione

Newspapers and periodicals referred to in the Harry Potter saga — such as *The Daily Prophet, The Quibbler,* and *Witch Weekly* — are symbolic of the negativity, fighting, vanity, and discrimination taking place in the wizarding world. Often sensationalized by acid-penned 'quick quotes quill' writers like Rita Skeeter, most subscribers are left feeling more discouraged and afraid than before reading, when in fact, the magical community desperately needs the direct opposite. On the other hand, numerous articles shared throughout the seven books provide insight into what is going on outside of Hogwarts and, at times, supply clues to Harry, Ron, and Hermione as they engage in their ongoing, extra-curricular detective work about the castle. Indeed, just like the Bloofer Lady article in the *Westminster Gazette* alerts Van Helsing's reaction to Lucy's un-deadness, "Mein Gott… so soon!" in the *Philosopher's Stone*, Chapter Eight, helps Harry glean a clue from *The Daily Prophet*:

"Gringotts Break-In Latest

Investigations continue into the break-in at Gringotts on 31 July, widely believed to be the work of Dark wizards or witches unknown. Gringotts goblins
today insisted that nothing had been taken. The vault that was searched had in
fact been emptied the same day. "But we're not telling you what was in there,
so keep your noses out if you know what's good for you," said a Gringotts spoke
goblin this afternoon."

Harry recalls Ron telling him on the train that someone tried to rob Gringotts, but
Ron fails to tell him the date. When Harry immediately reminds Hagrid that they
were at the bank the same day — his eleventh birthday, in fact — removing a small
package which Hagrid refers to as "Hogwart's business." Hagrid does not meet Harry's
eyes; instead, he grunts and offers him another piece of rock cake. Rowling concludes
the chapter as Harry contemplates several enlightening thoughts:

"As Harry and Ron walked back to the castle for dinner, their pockets weighed
down with rock cakes they'd been too polite to refuse, Harry thought that none
of the lessons he'd had so far had given him as much to think about as tea with
Hagrid. Had Hagrid collected that package just in time? Where was it now?
And did Hagrid know something about Snape that he didn't want to tell
Harry?"

Though editorial bias in mass media can cause the truth of events, topics, and
stories to be overhyped, misrepresented, and manipulated, the readers of Stoker and
Rowling can find comfort in the fact that such clippings are reacted upon by both
bands of heroes in a way to ultimately promote hope, harmony, and assurance when,
symbolically speaking, most media can be looked upon as a cancer that multiplies despair, discord, and fear.

In conclusion, written expression — whether in diary form, letters, or editorials —
is unique. Unlike spoken words that are fleeting, the formal genres of memoirs, epistles, or journalistic prose carry on indefinitely. Were he alive today, Bram Stoker would
likely be surprised that over a hundred years later, Jonathan Harker's early memorandum, "Must get recipe for Mina," has an exorbitant number of readers on the internet
searching on how to prepare Paprika Hendl, Impletata, and Robber Steak. Likewise,
what will J.K. Rowling think when she is eighty and realizes that Harry Potter's acceptance letter to Hogwarts continues to be circulated and replicated as readers peruse
school supply stores for dragonhide protective gloves, a live snowy owl, and a copy of
One Thousand Magical Herbs and Fungi by Phyllida Spore? Keep the faith,
folks…search on….and by all means, journal about it.

Chapter Eighteen

Blood

Since recorded time, blood has symbolically been used to represent life. In the Old Testament, this life source is used in sacrifices to preserve life, but prophets warned against eating it because the life of all flesh is in its blood, representing the divine function taking place inside the body. In the New Testament, blood and wine became interchangeable symbols when Jesus and his disciples participated in the last supper, where the fruit of the vine represented the blood of Christ.

Since *Dracula* was published in 1897, literary scholars have written countless reviews and articles about the significance of the references to the vital fluid in the text. Because Dracula participates in the unholy consumption of human plasma to remain alive, thus defiling the sacred Biblical text of not eating blood, he is looked upon as an evil monster. However, Renfield's character proves that a human suffering from mental illness can be profoundly influenced by the Un-dead without being turned into a vampire. Indeed, Chapter 11 shows that the 'life eating lunatic' graduates from the lifeblood of smaller beings, such as flies and birds, thus testing his gory preoccupation with a human:

"Dr. Seward's Diary.

17 September. "[...] Suddenly, the door was burst open, and in rushed my patient, with his face distorted with passion. I was thunderstruck, for such a thing as a patient getting of his own accord into the Superintendent's study is almost unknown. Without an instant's pause he made straight at me. He had a dinner knife in his hand, and, as I saw he was dangerous, I tried to keep the table between us. He was too quick and too strong for me, however; for before I could get my balance, he had struck at me and cut my left wrist rather severely. Before he could strike again, however, I got in my right, and he was sprawling on his back on the floor. My wrist bled freely, and quite a little pool trickled on to the carpet. I saw that my friend was not intent on further effort, and occupied myself binding up my wrist, keeping a wary eye on the prostrate figure

all the time. When the attendants rushed in, and we turned out attention to him, his employment positively sickened me. He was lying on his belly on the floor, licking up, like a dog, the blood which had fallen from my wounded wrist. He was easily secured, and, to my surprise, went with the attendants quite placidly, simply repeating over and over again: "The blood is the life! the blood is the life!"

Nevertheless, Renfield is not the only human who is poisoned by the Count's influence into believing the blood of man is essential to healthy living. Indeed, Dracula's numerous attacks on Lucy place her into an anemic-like stupor, pallid and clinging to life; but in a few days, she has the blood of several strong men pulsing through her veins, a condition which prolongs her life until the vampire successfully transitions her into his own. In Chapter 13, Dr. Seward becomes annoyed with Van Helsing when he laughs and cries at the irony of their band of men giving their blood to save Lucy, only to have her die and come back as a vampire. However, since Seward still was unaware of Lucy's 'un-deadness,' he rebukes the professor's words and laughter, feeling he is insensitive and possibly coming unhinged:

"Dr. Seward's Diary.

22 September. "[...] Well, for the life of me, Professor," I said, "I can't see anything to laugh at in all that. Why, your explanation makes it a harder puzzle than before. But even if the burial service was comic, what about poor Art and his trouble? Why, his heart was simply breaking."

"Just so. Said he not that the transfusion of his blood to her veins had made her truly his bride?"

"Yes, and it was a sweet and comforting idea for him."

"Quite so. But there was a difficulty, friend John. If so that, then what about the others? Ho, ho! Then this so sweet maid is a polyandrist, and me, with my poor wife dead to me, but alive by Church's law, though no wits, all gone — even I, who am faithful husband to this now-no-wife, am bigamist."

"I don't see where the joke comes in there either!" I said; and I did not feel particularly pleased with him for saying such things."

If blood is considered symbolic of healthy living for Dracula, Renfield, and Lucy, it is regarded as the complete opposite for Wilhelmina Murray Harker. Indeed, when the Count forces Mina to feed on his own blood in Chapter 21, her reaction afterwards — including the retelling of the sordid event — is communicated with an angst of repulsion, self-loathing, and horror. As the blood from her mouth and wound from her neck stain her husband's white robe, she immediately recoils from him and exclaims amidst choking sobs:

"Unclean, unclean! I must touch him or kiss him no more. Oh, that it should be that it is I who am now his worst enemy, and whom he may have most cause to fear."

Though Jonathan claims her reaction is nonsensical and the other men do not discriminate against her plight, Mina still cannot hide her shame any more than her husband can conceal his hair, which turns white overnight.

"Dr. Seward's Diary.

3 October. "[…] Oh my God! My God! What have I done? What have I done to deserve such a fate, I who have tried to walk in meekness and righteousness all my days. God pity me! Look down on a poor soul in worse than mortal peril; and in mercy pity those to whom she is dear!"

Then she began to rub her lips as though to cleanse them from pollution."

This reaction is very reminiscent of Lady Macbeth, who washes her hands repeatedly after the killing of King Duncan. Shakespeare uses the cleansing of the blood as a metaphor for guilt. Though Mina is the victim, the Victorian woman often blamed herself after attacks, very much so as many victims of rape or abuse do so today. Though Mina did nothing to cause the assault, the blood no doubt reminds her of when the vampire preyed on her friend Lucy and the terrible ordeal and demise which followed. Indeed, in Mina's mind, blood is not life: it is contamination. She prefers to die by her own hand rather than follow Lucy's path.

The adage "Blood is thicker than water" is symbolically linked to Bram Stoker's narrative. The quote itself comes from the Bible. Proverbs 27:10 reads: "The blood of the covenant is thicker than the water of the womb." In context, this verse implies that bloodshed in battle bonds soldiers more strongly than simple genetics. Even though society today commonly uses this scripture to speak to the bond of family ties, it doesn't refer to lineage at all.

In *Dracula*, the band of protagonists is not blood-related. Indeed, the seven main characters are not even formally introduced to each other until Lucy's illness and subsequent death. However, the love they all share for Lucy causes a swift friendship to form between them that is just as deep — if not deeper, even — than that of an ancestral nature. In Chapter 24, Van Helsing records a message on Dr. Seward's phonograph for Jonathan Harker, which illustrates beautifully the fact that the blood of united friends, in combat for a good cause, can be tighter than one of a familial nature:

"Dr. Seward's Phonograph Diary Spoken by Van Helsing

This to Jonathan Harker.

We go off now to find what ship, and whither bound. When we have discovered that, we come back and tell you all. Then we will comfort you and poor Madam Mina with new hope. For it will be hope when you think it over, that all is not lost. This very creature that we pursue, he takes hundreds of years to get so far as London. And yet in one day, when we know of the disposal of him, we drive him out. He is finite, though he is powerful to do much harm and suffers not as we do. But we are strong, each in our purpose, and we are all stronger together. Take heart afresh, dear husband of Madam Mina. This battle is but begun and in the end we shall win. So sure as that God sits on high to watch over His children. Therefore be of much comfort till we return."

Indeed, to some characters in the novel, blood is symbolic of life, while to others, it is representative of contamination. However, to the collective group, blood stands for the strength of an indestructible tie. The heroes pray together, plan together and travel together. They protect the group, fight for the group, and put their lives at risk for the group. They cry as one, laugh as one, and gain victory as one. Even though Lucy and Quincy die in the fight, their bond does not, and their fallen friends' memories live on in the next generation.

History has proven to society that no war can be fought without bloodshed. In the case of Stoker's masterpiece, while blood is symbolic of life for the vampire, it is symbolic of death for its victims and those that war against him. Indeed, from the bagged baby that the Count delivers to the weird sisters to the infant's mother that pleads for her child in the castle courtyard, Dracula snuffs out the life of many. However, most bloodshed occurs 'off camera' (using the Texan phrase of Quincey P. Morris) and is presented in a PG13, gore-less manner.

As the vampire grows stronger while feeding on the women of his enemies, the women lose all of their life liquid. Dr. Seward compares Lucy's anemic likeness to "a corpse after a prolonged illness." Remarkably, the author applies Enfield's "the blood is the life!" theology by minimizing its very presence in the novel. If, indeed, "the blood is the life!" then Dracula is but a pale and waning magnum opus — or "bloodless" to use the word Dr. Seward selects in diagnosing Lucy's condition — that is, great quantities of vital fluid vanish from Lucy's veins without a trace. However, preceding the mortal wound Quincey Morris suffers at the very end of *Dracula's* three hundred plus pages, it is astonishing to state very little blood is lost — save for a shaving cut, a shallow wound from a dinner knife, minimal droplets of coagulated blood observed at the corners of uncleaned mouths, and a valuable few "gouts of fresh blood" leaking over to punctuate the manuscript in certain scenes. As opposed to indulging the audience in a series of bloodlust, the proper Victorian approach is taken: the entire novel meditates upon the idea that where there is no blood, death follows. Indeed, its mysterious absence, coupled with the ill-phased inquiry: "And how the blood lost or waste?" — meaning, "Where did the blood go?" — underscores its importance and absence when vampires are present.

Hitherto Quincey's self-sacrificing end, death only touches the reader through Lucy's extended, desperate scuffle. Indeed, with the exception of Lucy's mother, all other deaths occur outside of the plot. Previous to the Count's arrival in London, Mrs. Westenra has "got her death warrant" — her doctor having already "told her that within a few months, at most, she must die, for her heart [was] weakening." Arthur Holmwood is already preparing for the end of August, still weeks before her ultimate demise, by warning Dr. Seward and Van Helsing, "Her doom is spoken — disease of the heart," with the agreement that "any shock could prove fatal." Indeed, Mrs. Westenra's expiration is a bloodless and mercifully quick conclusion: she dies "as if struck by lightning."

One could view *Dracula* as an anemic vessel, for the few vampiric attacks that the novel depicts are due in part to a surrender of will as confused victims yield themselves to the shrewd and deductive demands of Morpheus. Perhaps it is the concepts of the crimes committed in *Dracula* that still shake generations of readers today rather than their portrayal.

Renfield's motto, "The Blood is the Life!" is, in fact, a truth-seeker's curvaceous phrase, articulated to form an identity between 'blood' and 'life.' The uniquely applied definite article adjective 'The' effusively reassures universality. The question of "Where did the blood go?" thus becomes identical to the question of "Where did the life go?" Most importantly, the question, "Where did the Life go?" is, in the reasoning of Dracula, merely another way of asking, "From where did the Life come?" for it has been determined that it comes from and goes to the equal unbegotten pre-mythic state. The vehicle Stoker employs to position and personify this transformational question is, indeed, Lucy Westenra. Symbolically, Bram Stoker constructs his most celebrated classic with this clever thought in mind (both literally and figuratively speaking): the presence of blood equates to life; the absence of blood equates to death.

The use of blood in the Harry Potter series holds many symbolic similarities one century later. Just as Count Dracula needs blood to remain alive, Lord Voldemort believes in "The Blood is the Life" mantra as well. Indeed, in Book One, He-Who-Must-Not-Be-Named uses unicorn blood to sustain his life until he can steal the Philosopher's Stone and regain his true body. As the Dark Lord possesses the back of Quirinus Quirrell's head, the stuttering professor drinks the blood on Voldemort's behalf because Quirrell's body is dying from sharing it with Voldemort's fragmented soul.

Professor Firenze, the friendly centaur that lives in the Forbidden Forest, explains to Harry in *The Philosopher's Stone* the forbidden and plagued act of feeding on a beloved unicorn:

> "That is because it is a monstrous thing, to slay a unicorn," said Firenze. "Only one who has nothing to lose, and everything to gain, would commit such a crime. The blood of a unicorn will keep you alive, even if you are an inch from death, but at a terrible price. You have slain something pure and defenseless to save yourself, and you will have but a half-life, a cursed life, from the moment the blood touches your lips." — Chapter 15, page 155.

In 1994, Peter Pettigrew utilizes a mixture of unicorn blood and Nagini's venom to form a potion that creates a temporary body for He-Who-Must-Not-Be-Named, until he can regain his true body. It is unknown if creating such a potion and proceeding to consume it fashions a similar hex upon the user's life. In the Dark Lord's instance, his re-usage of unicorn blood (having indirectly consumed some two years prior) could have produced a cumulative effect on the curse's potency. However, Voldemort's questionable degree of humanity may have diluted, or even canceled entirely, the effectiveness of the spell. Regardless, a sign above the Hog's Head tavern forbids the trade of unicorn's blood and warns patrons not to ask about it.

The Dark Lord's blood consumption continues into the saga and expands into human usage. The Goblet of Fire sees Wormtail forcibly taking the blood of Harry Potter to aid in the spell to resurrect He-Who-Must-Not-Be-Named back to his original form. As discussed earlier in this book, the use of Harry's blood in the rebirth potion will turn out to be a mistake for it thwarts Voldemort from murdering Harry as the blood passes Lily Potter's protection to the Dark Lord and cements Harry to the living world through him, ensuring He-Who-Must-Not-Be-Named's downfall three years later.

"— it is an old piece of dark magic, the potion that revived me tonight…"
—Lord Voldemort's description of the Regeneration Potion

As Mina Harker is sobbing over her unclean blood status upon exchanging vital fluids with Count Dracula, wars are being fought over blood status in the wizarding world. Indeed, blood status, or purity of blood, is a concept in the Harry Potter novels that distinguishes between family trees that have alternate levels of magically-endowed members. It often results in prejudice toward those who have a great number of Muggles in their families. As Sirius Black informs Harry Potter, almost all wizards of their time have Muggles in their family trees, though some claim otherwise. Indeed, this concept plays an important role in both the First and Second Wizarding Wars. Families that claim to be pure, to whatever extent they ever really are, dwindle in number. Salizar Slytherin does not trust students born of Muggle parents — or 'Mudbloods' if using the derogatory reference — which creates friction and ultimately segregation and parting of the Hogwarts founders. This belief system rooted in equality spreads so much hate that it overtly manifests itself to Harry, Ron, and Hermione in *The Chamber of Secrets*. For example, Draco Malfoy calls Hermione a "filthy little Mudblood" when she interjects her opinion, inciting Ron's anger in Chapter 7:

"It's about the most insulting thing he could think of," gasped Ron, coming back up. "Mudblood's a really foul name for someone who is Muggle-born — you know, non-magic parents. There are some wizards — like Malfoy's family — who think they're better than everyone else because they're what people call pure-blood… I mean, the rest of us know it doesn't make any difference at all."
— Chapter 7, pages 115-116

In time, Salazar Slytherin leaves Hogwarts permanently, vowing never to return, after creating the Chamber of Secrets to purge the school of all Mudblood pupils. However, regardless if one is considered a Mudblood, half-blood, pureblood, or Muggle-born, it is ultimately the choices and actions of the individual that determines greatness. Perhaps Albus Dumbledore sums it up best:

"You place too much importance, and you always have done, on the so-called purity of blood! You fail to recognize that it matters not what someone is born, but what they grow to be!"
— Albus Dumbledore's stance on blood status

Even though Mina Harker considers her blood to be unclean, those that love her best disagree and treat her no differently. The same holds true for Hermione Granger. And as tainted as their blood may seem, both heroines go on to pursue greatness that many 'untainted blood' individuals could not have expected combined.

The "Blood is Thicker than Water" adage also carries on in the Harry Potter books. Like the band of heroes that fights the vampire Dracula as a 'battle blood family,' J.K. Rowling's seven-book tale proves that the strong bond between Harry, Ron, and Hermione in Book One becomes contagious. Indeed, as five strong men give their blood for a good cause in Stoker's novel, no less than thirty individuals decide to join the trio in their fight against the Dark Arts when they all sign on as D.A. (or Dumbledore's Army) members and converge at the Hogs Head in *The Order of the Phoenix*. Aside from the Weasleys, Patils, and Creeveys, the group is not blood-related; yet they become bonded in battle as they pour their hearts and souls into the fight to help destroy Voldemort's reign.

> "Every great wizard in history has started out as nothing more than what we are now: students. If they can do it, why not us?"
>
> — Harry Potter

With battle comes bloodshed, and J.K. Rowling's tour de force proves that though blood is symbolic of regenerating Voldemort's life, it is also symbolic of death for many victims who stand in his way — the most significant, perhaps, being Harry's parents.

As with the deaths in *Dracula*, many occur 'off-camera' in the wizarding world, and the ones written inside the plot are usually described in a 'bloodless' fashion. For example, the death of Harry's parents, whom the Dark Lord murders with the killing curse, occurs before the series begins and is only reenacted through Harry's dreams and visions. The effect of the Avada Kedavra curse is an instantaneous 'bloodless' death for both of them. Or as Rowling describes James' death, [James falls] like a marionette whose strings [are] cut."

In fact, with a few exceptions — such as the Sectrumsempra, which Harry uses to unknowingly slash Draco Malfoy — most spells used or described in the Harry Potter saga are blood-free.

Another significant death, and one which Harry witnesses in person, is that of his godfather, Sirius Black. This takes place at the height of the Battle of the Department of Mysteries at the conclusion of *The Order of the Phoenix*. Most of the fighting is set in the Death Chamber, and Death Eater Bellatrix Lestrange hits her cousin Sirius Black squarely on the chest with a curse, throwing him off balance and sending him through the Veil to his death. Indeed, this exit happens so peacefully (especially coming from loud and evil incarnate Lestrange) that Harry refuses at first to believe that Sirius has died. Sadly, he keeps repeating to Ron and Hermione that he will come out of the archway from the other side of the curtains, much like how — when he was a baby — he believed his parents would get up after being hit with the Killing Curse. When Harry questions his godfather's spirit through the Resurrection Stone at the end of *The Deathly Hallows*, an ethereally reassuring response is provided, which gives Harry the courage to allow Voldemort to use the killing curse on him:

Harry Potter: "Does it hurt?"

Sirius: "Dying? Not at all. Quicker and easier than falling asleep."

— Sirius' spirit speaks to Harry through the Resurrection Stone

With the exception of the few wounded during the Battle of Hogwarts, the blood spilled in the entire series is minimal, especially considering the 4,224 pages in length. When Rowling stated in a 2006 interview, "My books are largely about death," it begs to question, how can there be so much death with so little blood? Symbolically, Rowling's magical masterpiece had the same clever idea in mind that Stoker shared a hundred years before: the presence of blood equates to life; the absence of blood equates to death. The psychological impact of death is sometimes far scarier than the bloody, disgusting, gore-filled portrayals that sadly make up many manuscripts today. Indeed, the answer to the question "Where did the blood go?" can be more frightening if left to the imagination.

Chapter Nineteen

Sexuality

Sex. There. The taboo term has been uttered. As the Hip Hop group, Salt-N-Pepa sang in the 90s, "Let's talk about it." In the midst of a serious analysis of character actions, themes, and settings, it is natural to wonder why this chapter is necessary, but a hundred years since its publication, one is never hard-pressed to find opinions, articles, dissertations, or even entire books analyzing the sexuality within the pages of *Dracula*. This is amazing — especially considering Bram Stoker wrote his most famous work in the Victorian age when the word was undoubtedly prohibited. Indeed, it would have been deemed ungentlemanly for a well-educated and proper Irish nobleman, much like himself, to market such a scandalous tale. Though the subject was less inviolable when J.K. Rowling wrote the Harry Potter series a century later, a similar sentiment rings true: it would be shocking for a well-educated and proper British lady to explore an adult topic in a scholastic book series. Yet the subject of sex in the seven-book saga has been brought up often, even though sex education was not on any student's syllabus at Hogwarts. Perhaps that is the common link worth exploring: how can there be so much hype about a topic both authors avoid like the Forbidden Forest?

If one were to time travel back to the age of the 'new woman,' it would be apparent that British women were urged to remain virgins until marriage and show no outward sexual behavior. Of all the characters in *Dracula*, there are only two married leading men: the young Jonathan Harker (who marries Wilhelmina Murray about a third of the way through the novel) and the elderly Professor Abraham Van Helsing (who has been married for years). Readers must surmise that Jonathan and Mina cannot consummate their wedding vows until the very end of the novel. Indeed, with Jonathan suffering from 'brain fever,' Lucy passing away, and Mina being turned into the Undead, the mood is most likely ill-fitting. Van Helsing refers to his relationship situation as complicated: "and me, with my poor wife dead to me, but alive by Church's law, though no wits, all gone...." From the busy professor's teaching commitments and countless days traveling abroad to assist others, it is obvious he uses his profession to fill his loneliness.

If the married men and women are sexually oppressed, one could make a good argument that the single folk are equally as restrained. Certainly, one would not need to look any further than Lucy Westenra's opening letter to Mina: "Why can't they let a girl marry three men, or as many as want her, and save all this trouble? But this is heresy, and I must not say it."

Indeed, just as the Victorian women were often looked at as being promiscuous for acting out on such sexual frustrations, men during this era were held and graded by high gentlemanly standards, thus repressing their sexual desires until marriage. As a result, Bram Stoker's unmarried men look elsewhere for happiness: Dr. Seward seeks comfort in his lunatics and morphine; Arthur Holmwood uses his money and power for consolation; and Quincy P. Morris holds his horses, firearms, and strong drink in proximity.

When the king vampire orders them to leave Jonathan Harker be, the weird sisters even remind Count Dracula that he is sexually repressed:

"Jonathan Harker's Journal.

15 May. "[…] "You yourself never loved; you never love!" On this the other women joined, and such a mirthless, hard, soulless laughter ran through the room that it almost made me faint to hear; it seemed like the pleasure of fiends. Then the Count turned, after looking at my face attentively, and said in a soft whisper:

"Yes, I too can love; you yourselves can tell it from the past."

And past knowledge of sexual relations is about all the acknowledgment that readers can glean from the Harry Potter books because children do not receive a welcoming letter to Hogwarts until they are at least eleven years of age. Understandably, parents do not expect their kids to be exposed to *Fifty Shades of Gray* material at Hogwarts; but on the other hand, in a coming-of-age series, puberty cannot be ignored, and Harry, Ron, and Hermione somehow learn outside of the plot that baby wizards are not delivered by Owl Post.

Of all the students at Hogwarts, Harry himself receives the most coverage in the arena of carnal exasperation. His adolescence crush on Cho Chang is described in a gentlemanly, almost Victorian manner as readers learn she makes his stomach 'feel funny,' and when she kisses him, it is 'very wet.' However, it is Ginny Weasley who ultimately forces Harry's transition from boy to man.

"Harry, you've got a maggot in your hair," said Ginny cheerfully, leaning across the table to pick it out; Harry felt goosebumps erupt up his neck that had nothing to do with the maggot."

— Harry Potter and the Half-Blood Prince,
Chapter 16: A Very Frosty Christmas

Of all of the parents of the magical children fully characterized in the series, it is, no doubt, Arthur and Molly Weasley's 'caldron that is full of hot, burning love,' resulting in a houseful of seven children. However, it appears this steamy pot has run cold at the point where the series picks up. Indeed, with Arthur Weasley working overtime at the Ministry of Magic and Molly Weasley preoccupied over which of her children would be in 'mortal peril' next, the couple falls in line with the other sexually repressed characters of the saga. Molly Weasley's oppression is reflected colorfully when her significant crush on Gilderoy Lockhart is brought to light in Year Two. As she picks up a copy of his guide to household pests, her cheeks turn pink, and she confesses to Ron, Harry, George, and Fred:

"Oh, he is marvelous," she said. "He knows his household pests, all right, it's a wonderful book." If sexual frustration is not obvious enough in this moment, it is reinforced a few pages later as she takes the children to purchase their schoolbooks.

"Harry, Ron and Hermione squeezed inside. A long queue wound right to the back of the shop, where Gilderoy Lockhart was signing his books. They each grabbed a copy of Break with a Banshee and sneaked up the line to where the rest of the Weasleys were standing with Mr. and Mrs. Granger.

'Oh, there you are, good,' said Mrs. Weasley. She sounded breathless and kept patting her hair. 'We'll be able to see him in a minute ...'

— Harry Potter and the Chamber of Secrets, page 59

Shifting focus from parents to instructors, this author would be remiss not to point out that not a single teacher or administrator at Hogwarts claims a spouse or child. Indeed, except for Severus Snape, who sometimes resides at the House at Spinner's End when school is not in session, readers are led to believe that all other castle employees live on campus year-round. Indeed, only Hagrid and Lupin act out their carnal repression. In *The Goblet of Fire*, Hagrid desperately tries to romance French mistress Madame Maxime on the dark school grounds, failing miserably.

"'Ow dare you! I 'ave nevair been more insulted in my life! 'Alf-giant? Moi? I 'ave — I 'ave big bones!"

— Madame Maxime's words leave Hagrid heartbroken

Of all the Hogwarts employees, ex-instructor and werewolf-wizard Remus Lupin, though temperamental and short-lived, makes it to the farthest base in the love department. Nymphadora Tonks fancies Lupin and nags after him until he agrees to marry her. However, after Lupin finds out Tonks is pregnant, he suffers considerable mental distress, tearing out a tuft of his hair in anxiety over the likelihood that his child will be a werewolf. Harry becomes so hurt that his ex-teacher, mentor, and friend would even consider leaving his wife alone while pregnant, and eventually denounces him after doing so, calling him a coward for his unkind words:

"Don't you understand what I've done to my wife and my unborn child? I should never have married her; I've made her an outcast! And the child — the child...my kind don't usually breed! It will be like me; I am convinced of it! How can I forgive myself when I knowingly risked passing on my own condition to an innocent child?! And if, by some miracle, it is not like me, then it will be better off, a hundred times so, without a father of whom it should always be ashamed!"

— Remus' view of his marriage to Tonks and her pregnancy

In time, Lupin comes to his senses and returns to Tonks and their son Edward but tragically dies in the Battle of Hogwarts, fighting the dark wizard Dolohov. Sadly, Tonks, too, is killed by her aunt, Bellatrix Lestrange, in their third and final duel.

As portrayed in both tales, when a supernatural twist plays into sexual relationships, the additional wrench creates newfangled challenges that usually work against both parties: they become difficult, dangerous, and downright life-threatening. Like the Harkers in *Dracula*, Harry, Ron, and Hermione all wait until the very end to pursue love and start families. This ideology should bring readers to a subsequent question worth further exploration: if opposite-sex relationships cannot be pursued while the main characters are under evil threats, where do they go for comfort? The answer is same-sex relationships.

For over a hundred years, much has been said about implied homosexuality within the context of Bram Stoker's famous text. If one were to look at each main character, there are, undeniably, same-sex pairings that cannot be ignored: Jonathan Harker has Peter Hawkins; Count Dracula has R. M. Renfield; Wilhelmina Murray has Lucy Westenra; Dr. John (Jack) Seward has Professor Abraham Van Helsing; Arthur Holmwood (Lord Godalming) has Quincey P. Morris; and the Weird Sisters — well, they have each other. Regardless if same-sex bonding occurs over late-night dinners, summer sleepovers, or rambunctious campfires, no reader can argue their existence. However, because there is no explicit sexual behavior described in the plot — straight, gay, or otherwise — fifty different readers could perceive these relationships in fifty different ways. A good example of this is Dracula's harsh words to the Weird Sisters upon finding them hovering over Jonathan Harker's swooned body:

"Jonathan Harker's Journal.

15 May. — "How dare you touch him, any of you? How dare you cast eyes on him when I had forbidden it? Back, I tell you all! This man belongs to me! Beware how you meddle with him, or you'll have to deal with me."

The five words "This man belongs to me!" have been looked at by many fans, readers, and scholars alike as a direct reference to classify the infamous vampire's sexual identity as homosexual. On the other hand, the dispute that the Count is simply using the solicitor strictly for selfish business purposes is equally convincing. In fact, continuing the text and taking it into consideration with the previous sentence only assists in supporting this notion as he further explains to the gruesome threesome:

"Well, now I promise you that when I am done with him you shall kiss him at your will. Now go! go! I must awaken him, for there is work to be done."

Since so much surrounding the hidden meanings, subliminal connotations, and inner workings of the famous novel may never be fully known — that is without additional *Dracula* notes, diaries, and interviews of Bram Stoker appearing in attics, barns, and archives in years to come — we can only speculate based on the facts we know.

It is a known fact that Bram Stoker established a pattern throughout all his works in describing his male characters comprehensively while leaving the features of his female characters generally up to the reader's imagination. A good example of this was Professor Abraham Van Helsing's description written from Mina Harker's point of view:

"Mina Harker's Journal.

25 September. — "I rose and bowed, and he came towards me; a man of medium weight, strongly built, with his shoulders set back over a broad, deep chest and a neck well balanced on the trunk as the head is on the neck. The pose of the head strikes one at once as indicative of thought and power; the head is noble, well-sized, broad, and large behind the ears. The face, clean-shaven, shows a hard, square chin, a large, resolute, mobile mouth, a good-sized nose,

rather straight, but with quick, sensitive nostrils, that seem to broaden as the big, bushy brows come down and the mouth tightens. The forehead is broad and fine, rising at first almost straight and then sloping back above two bumps or ridges wide apart; such a forehead that the reddish hair cannot possibly tumble over it, but falls naturally back and to the sides. Big, dark blue eyes are set widely apart, and are quick and tender or stern with the man's moods."

In stark contrast, the only physiognomy provided for Lucy Westenra is Arthur Holmwood's much shorter and rather monstrous description of where he finds his former fiancé's features evil and revolting:

"Never did I see such baffled malice on a face; and never, I trust, shall such ever be seen again by mortal eyes. The beautiful color became livid, the eyes seemed to throw out sparks of hellfire, the brows were wrinkled as though the folds of the flesh were the coils of Medusa's snakes, and the lovely, blood-stained mouth grew to an open square, as in the passion masks of the Greeks and Japanese. If ever a face meant death — if looks could kill — we saw it at that moment."

— Chapter 16

Did Stoker just feel more comfortable describing his own sex, or did he find the male physique more attractive than the opposite sex? To help answer this question, one would need to look outside of the man's works and into what is known about the personal life of Bram Stoker. Though the author married the beautiful Florence Balcombe, and they had one son together, Irving Noel Thornley Stoker, it has been stated that their marriage was more platonic than sexual. In addition, the author's closest friends were writers who were rumored to be homosexual: Walt Whitman, Hall Caine, and Oscar Wilde. But perhaps the most convincing evidence to suggest that Bram Stoker was attracted to men was a letter he wrote Walt Whitman, made available in its entirety for the first time in *Something in the Blood: The Untold Story of Bram Stoker, the Man Who Wrote 'Dracula'* by David J. Skal.

"DUBLIN, IRELAND, FEB. 18, 1872

If you are the man I take you to be you will like to get this letter. If you are not I don't care whether you like it or not and only ask that you put it into the fire without reading any farther. But I believe you will like it. I don't think there is a man living, even you who are above the prejudices of the class of small-minded men, who wouldn't like to get a letter from a younger man, a stranger, across the world—a man living in an atmosphere prejudiced to the truths you sing and your manner of singing them. The idea that arises in my mind is whether there is a man living who would have the pluck to burn a letter in

which he felt the smallest atom of interest without reading it. I believe you
would and that you believe you would yourself. You can burn this now and test
yourself, and all I will ask for my trouble of writing this letter, which for all I
can tell you may light your pipe with or apply to some more ignoble purpose—
is that you will in some manner let me know that my words have tested your
impatience. Put it in the fire if you like—but if you do you will miss the pleasure of the next sentence which ought to be that you have conquered an unwor-
thy impulse. A man who is certain of his own strength might try to encourage
himself a piece of bravo, but a man who can write, as you have written, the
most candid words that ever fell from the lips of a mortal man—a man to whose
candor Rousseau's Confessions is reticence—can have no fear for his own
strength. If you have gone this far you may read the letter and I feel in writing
now that I am talking to you. If I were before your face I would like to shake
hands with you, for I feel that I would like you. I would like to call YOU Com-
rade and to talk to you as men who are not poets do not often talk. I think that
at first a man would be ashamed, for a man cannot in a moment break the habit
of comparative reticence that has become second nature to him; but I know I
would not long be ashamed to be natural before you. You are a true man, and
I would like to be one myself, and so I would be towards you as a brother and
as a pupil to his master. In this age no man becomes worthy of the name without an effort. You have shaken off the shackles and your wings are free. I have
the shackles on my shoulders still—but I have no wings. If you are going to
read this letter any further, I should tell you that I am not prepared to "give up
all else" so far as words go. The only thing I am prepared to give up is prejudice,
and before I knew you, I had begun to throw overboard my cargo, but it is not
all gone yet. I do not know how you will take this letter. I have not addressed
you in any form as I hear that you dislike to a certain degree the conventional
forms in letters. I am writing to you because you are different from other men.
If you were the same as the mass, I would not write at all. As it is I must either
call you Walt Whitman or not call you at all—and I have chosen the latter
course. I do not know whether it is unusual for you to get letters from utter
strangers who have not even the claim of literary brotherhood to write you. If
it is, you must be frightfully tormented with letters and I am sorry to have
written this. I have, however, the claim of liking you—for your words are your
own soul and even if you do not read my letter it is no less a pleasure to me to
write it. Shelley wrote to William Godwin and they became friends. I am not
Shelley and you are not Godwin and so I will only hope that sometime I may

meet you face to face and perhaps shake hands with you. If I ever do it will be one of the greatest pleasures of my life … The way I came to you was this. A notice of your poems appeared some two years ago or more in Temple Bar magazine. I glanced at it and took its dictum as final and laughed at you among friends. I say it to my own shame but not to regret for it has taught me a lesson to last my life out—without ever having seen your poems. More than a year after I heard two men in College talking of you. One of them had your book (Rossetti's edition) and was reading aloud some passages at which both laughed. They chose only those passages which are most foreign to British ears and made fun of them. Something struck me that I had judged you hastily. I took home the volume and read far into the night. Since then I have to thank you for many happy hours, for I have read your poems with my door locked late at night and I have read them on the seashore where I could look all round me and see no more sign of human life than the ships out at sea: and here I often found myself waking up from a reverie with the book open before me. I love all poetry, and high generous thoughts make the tears rush to my eyes, but sometimes a word or a phrase of yours takes me away from the world around me and places me in an ideal land surrounded by realities more than any poem I ever read. Last year I was sitting on the beach on a summer's day reading your preface to the Leaves of Grass as printed in Rossetti's edition … One thought struck me and I pondered over it for several hours—" the weather-beaten vessels entering new ports," you who wrote the words know them better than I do: and to you who sing of your land of progress the words have a meaning that I can only imagine. But be assured of this Walt Whitman—that a man of less than half your own age, reared a conservative in a conservative country, and who has always heard your name cried down by the great mass of people who mention it, here felt his heart leap towards you across the Atlantic and his soul swelling at the words or rather the thoughts. It is vain for me to quote an instances of what thoughts of yours I like best—for I like them all and you must feel you are reading the true words of one who feels with you. You see, I have called you by your name. I have been more candid with you—have said more about myself to you than I have said to anyone before. You will not be angry with me if you have read so far. You will not laugh at me for writing this to you. It was no small effort that I began to write, and I feel reluctant to stop, but I must not tire you anymore. If you would ever care to have more you can imagine, for you have a great heart, how much pleasure it would be to me to write more to you. How sweet a thing it is for a strong healthy man with a woman's eye and a child's wishes to feel that he can speak to a man who can be if he wishes father, and brother and wife to his soul. I don't think you will laugh, Walt Whitman, nor despise me, but at all events I thank you for all the love and sympathy you have given me in common with my kind.

— Bram Stoker"

So did Bram Stoker write *Dracula* with hidden homosexual undertones? The plausibility leans toward the 'most likely' side of the suspect spectrum.

The Harry Potter series, too, has its fair share of same-sex companionship: Harry Potter has Ronald Weasley; Hermione Granger has Ginny Weasley and Luna Lovegood; Albus Dumbledore has hosteller Grindelwald; Lord Voldemort has Peter Pettigrew; Draco Malfoy has Vincent Crabbe and Gregory Goyle, and Sirius Black has Remus Lupin. Similar to Stoker's vampire classic, although same-sex coupling occurs throughout Harry's seven years at Hogwarts Castle, nothing sexual overtly manifests within the plot. Indeed, the bonding remains strictly platonic between the pages; however, speculation that plenty transpires between the sheets outside of the plot has been a popular topic with fans for years to the extent that many have written their own R-Rated or Mature stories (see https://www.fanfiction.net/book/Harry-Potter/ for example).

Unlike Bram Stoker, who is sadly not with us to join in the discussion, J.K. Rowling frequently holds interviews, answers fan mail, and posts many enlightening facts, thoughts, and behind-the-scenes inter-workings of the characters and plot that went into the genesis of the series. At an October 2007 conference at Carnegie Hall, a question from the panel forwardly projected a hotly-debated topic regarding the beloved Hogwarts headmaster:

"Did Dumbledore, who believed in the prevailing power of love, ever fall in love himself?

J.K. Rowling's response was, "My truthful answer to you... I always thought of Dumbledore as gay. [ovation.] ... Dumbledore fell in love with Grindelwald, and that added to his horror when Grindelwald showed himself to be what he was. To an extent, do we say it excused Dumbledore a little more because falling in love can blind us to an extent? But he met someone as brilliant as he was, and rather like Bellatrix he was very drawn to this brilliant person, and horribly, terribly let down by him. Yeah, that's how I always saw Dumbledore. In fact, recently I was in a script read through for the sixth film, and they had Dumbledore saying a line to Harry early in the script saying I knew a girl once, whose hair... [laughter]. I had to write a little note in the margin and slide it along to the scriptwriter, "Dumbledore's gay!" [laughter] If I'd known it would make you so happy, I would have announced it years ago!"

The writer followed up with another statement at a Toronto authors' festival, adding, "It has certainly never been news to me that a brave and brilliant man could love other men. He is my character. He is what he is, and I have the right to say what I say about him."

In December 2014, a Twitter exchange took place between a fan and Rowling when this statement was posed: "It's safe to assume that Hogwarts had a variety of people, and I like to think it's a safe place for LGBT students." To which the writer replied: "But of course. If Harry Potter taught us anything, it is that no one should live in a closet."

Still another undertone between the binary works can be considered sexual, for the consumption, transfusion, and exchange of blood symbolizes sexual desire and intercourse. For the vampires in *Dracula*, it is also the means of reproduction, but for Lord Voldemort, it is the means of resurrection. Indeed, Stoker's novel is full of the exchange of the bodily fluid, blood. Blood, like semen, brings new life to the vampire victims. As an exasperated Dr. Seward points out in Chapter Twelve, "Once again we went through that ghastly operation."

Though Lucy has given her heart to Holmwood, suiters Seward and Morris give their blood in lieu of seed to replenish the blood that the Count takes. And Van Helsing and Arthur do the same under the Professor's belief "A brave man's blood is the best thing on this earth when a woman is in trouble." Though sperm and blood are two very distinctive and different bodily fluids, they each share the property of sexual intimacy and life-giving-bond. For example, the old-school childhood ritual of becoming blood brothers requires two friends to cut themselves and press their wounds together, exchanging blood to form an unbreakable, life-long protection pact. Potter fans see this same concept play out magically when Severus Snape and Narcissa Malfoy create an Unbreakable Vow in *The Half-Blood Prince* to protect Draco Malfoy for life.

In previous chapters, much has been discussed about blood and the unique fluid exchanges shared between lifelong friends, vetoed marriage proposals, and sworn enemies — including Wilhelmina Harker and Count Dracula and Harry Potter and Lord Voldemort. Sweat and tears are certainly other bodily liquids provided to each other and risked freely for the greater good. However, one relationship that has been slightly ignored is the peculiar love-hate association between Severus Snape and Harry Potter.

Indeed, this unusual pair proves that there is one additional biological substance frequently shared between intimate wizards: one that is silvery blue and neither gas nor liquid.

At the end of Chapter Thirty-Two in *The Deathly Hallows*, the Dark Lord orders his pet snake Nagini to kill Snape. They leave the professor to die, not realizing that Harry and Hermione are present, hiding under the Cloak of Invisibility. As Harry reveals himself and rounds on Snape, his wide black eyes find Harry and labor to speak:

"Take...it...Take...it..."

Something more than blood was leaking from Snape. Silvery blue, neither gas nor liquid, it gushed from his mouth and his ears and his eyes, and Harry knew what it was but did not know what to do—

A flask, conjured from thin air, was thrust into his shaking hands by Hermione. Harry lifted the silvery substance into it with his wand. When the flask was full to the brim, and Snape looked as though there was no blood left in him, his grip on Harry's robes slackened.

"Look...at...me..." he whispered.

The green eyes found the black, but after a second, something in the depths of the dark pair seemed to vanish, leaving them fixed, blank, and empty. The hand holding Harry thudded to the floor, and Snape moved no more. — p. 657-658

The dying memory Snape shares with the confused Harry is the secret he has been carrying for Harry's lifetime and 4,224 pages across seven novels. When Harry returns to the castle and places the vile of memory into the swirling pensive, the truth sets both characters free: Snape loved Lily Potter romantically, Snape swore his allegiance to Dumbledore, and Snape acted as a spy against He-Who-Must-Not-Be-Named. Once these critical facts are revealed, Harry finally understands that Snape's harshness toward him was a cover-up for the lingering Death Eaters and returned Dark Lord. In the end, Harry feels so much affection for Snape that he names his youngest son Albus Severus. In the Epilogue of *The Deathly Hallows*, Potter reassures Albus as he boards the Hogwarts Express that being sorted into Slytherin will not be a bad thing.

"Albus Severus," Harry said quietly, so that nobody but Ginny could hear, and she was tactful enough to pretend to be waving to Rose who was now on the train, "you were named for two headmasters of Hogwarts. One of them was a Slytherin and he was probably the bravest man I ever knew." P. 758

Without a doubt, this is a prime testament to how the sharing of bodily fluids is symbolic of intimacy and reproduction — that is, bringing two opposing characters together in the end and creating a new life to carry on the legacy of the initial pair.

The unrequited love that Severus Snape guards for Harry's mother, Lily, can be compared to Dr. John Seward's one-sided love for Lucy Westenra. Parallels can be made between the loneliness, pining, and depression both characters feel as they witness their respective women commit to another man — one they each know — and then suffer untimely deaths soon afterward. Their obsessions and loss drive both men to overwork to mask the pain. Dr. Seward turns to opiates to numb his feelings while Professor Snape's Patronus becomes a doe — as Lily's was — in loving remembrance of his undying love for her. Furthermore, both men feel considerable guilt after the women they loved pass away. When Seward realizes that the monster that is responsible for Lucy's death has lived right next door to him all along, he notes in his diary:

"Dr. Seward's Diary.

30 September. — "Strange that it never struck me that the very next house might be the Count's hiding place! Goodness knows that we had enough clues from the conduct of the patient Renfield! The bundle of letters relating to the purchase of the house were with the transcript. Oh, if we had only had them earlier, we might have saved poor Lucy! Stop! That way madness lies!"

Similarly, Snape feels so guilty that Voldemort kills Lily that he goes to Dumbledore, redeems himself, and carries out the rest of his life as a double agent for the headmaster while protecting Harry from harm.

Albus Dumbledore: "If you loved Lily Evans, if you truly loved her, then your way forward is clear. You know how and why she died. Make sure it was not in vain. Help me protect Lily's son."

Snape: "Very well. But never — never tell, Dumbledore! This must be between us! Swear it! I cannot bear... especially Potter's son..."

— Snape switches sides after Lily's murder

Finally, from obsession to seduction, possibly the most discussed sexual scene in *Dracula* is Harker's "almost being raped by the weird sisters sequence." For the Victorian age, the depiction verged on the obscene. The fact that the gender roles were reversed from the usual 'man-on-woman' violation, coupled with the fact that it was an orgy, raised many eyebrows in baffled astonishment.

Stoker scholars suggest that it may have been the author's intent that the trio are Dracula's daughters, extending the sexuality metaphor of vampirism to incest. Even though it is never stated, it might be that the term 'sister' is not meant in the literal connotation. Perhaps it is more akin to the relationship between the women and not as they are to Dracula. Such an interpretation seems more valid because the three also refer to Mina Harker as 'sister' after she is forced to drink the blood of Dracula and afflicted with signs of vampirism herself. Furthermore, Mina and Lucy also call each other 'sister' in the novel despite not having any blood relation. Nevertheless, one cannot debate the sexually-charged scene itself: there can be no doubt regarding the intent of the women and the arousal Jonathan Harker feels from the encounter. Indeed, it is so vivid and strong that even when he awakens from their spell, the prisoner recounts every detail in his own words:

"Jonathan Harker's Journal.

15 May. — "I was afraid to raise my eyelids but looked out and saw perfectly under the lashes. The girl went on her knees, and bent over me, simply gloating. There was a deliberate voluptuousness which was both thrilling and repulsive, and as she arched her neck, she actually licked her lips like an animal, till I could see in the moonlight the moisture shining on the scarlet lips and on the red tongue as it lapped the white sharp teeth. Lower and lower went her head as the lips went below the range of my mouth and chin and seemed about to fasten on my throat. Then she paused, and I could hear the churning sound of her tongue as it licked her teeth and lips, and I could feel the hot breath on my neck. Then the skin of my throat began to tingle as one's flesh does when the hand that is to tickle it approaches nearer, nearer, until I could feel the soft, shivering touch of the lips on the super-sensitive skin of my throat, and the hard dents of two sharp teeth, just touching and pausing there. I closed my eyes in a languorous ecstasy and waited, waited with beating heart."

A more family-oriented version of the 'weird sisters' scene' turns up a century later in *The Goblet of Fire*. As the scholars of Beauxbaton dance their way into the grand hall, most male students (and even some female pupils) become very light-headed as if entranced. This is because the female pupils of the French academy are full- (or part-) blooded Veela. Their beautiful appearance, seductive magic, and irresistible charm cause others to engage in strange behavior in order to get nearer to the Veela. For example, at the 1994 Quidditch World Cup, the irascible Veela are sent away because both teams begin fighting each other while Harry and Ron want to throw themselves off the Top Box in a fit of hormonal teenage gallantry. In addition, their enchanted, seductive speaking and singing voices hypnotize those who hear them, very like the Sirens of Greek mythology.

Ron Weasley (who will later become Fleur Delacour's brother-in-law) is perhaps the student most affected by the Veelas' seduction spell. Indeed, he habitually makes a fool of himself in an attempt to get Fleur to kiss him on the cheek or agree to escort him to the Yule Ball (having blurted out the question and then quickly running away). Ginny Weasley and Hermione Granger remark on this riling conduct as "pathetic."

In the woods at the Quidditch World Cup, Ron is so oversexed by the Veela that he becomes totally disorientated:

> Further still along the path, they walked into a patch of silvery light, and when they looked through the trees, they saw three tall and beautiful Veela standing in a clearing, surrounded by a gaggle of young wizards, all of whom were talking very loudly.
>
> "I pull down about a hundred sacks of Galleons a year," one of them shouted. "I'm a dragon-killer for the Committee for the Disposal of Dangerous Creatures."
>
> "No, you're not," yelled his friend, "you're a dishwasher at the Leaky Cauldron... but I'm a Vampire Hunter, I've killed about ninety so far—"
>
> A third young wizard, whose pimples were visible even by the dim silvery light of the Veela, now cut in, "I'm about to become the youngest ever Minister for Magic, I am."
>
> Harry snorted with laughter. He recognized the pimply wizard; his name was Stan Shunpike, and he was in fact a conductor on the triple-decker Knight Bus.
>
> He turned to tell Ron this, but Ron's face had gone oddly slack, and next second Ron was yelling, "Did I tell you I've invented a broomstick that'll reach Jupiter?"
>
> "Honestly!" said Hermione again, and she and Harry grabbed Ron firmly by the arms, wheeled him around and marched him away.
>
> — *Goblet of Fire*, Chapter 9, The Dark Mark.

Chapter Twenty

Immortality

The theme of death was discussed in detail in a former analysis in this book. This author stressed the pursuit of immortality in both *Dracula* and the Harry Potter series, arguing that to overcome death, antagonists and protagonists in each text are heavily motivated by the underlying fear of the unknown. Both authors ingeniously use objects and ideals in their respective works which symbolize immortality, thus driving plot twists and fueling the characters' actions.

The subject of vampirism is representative of the term 'undead.' Indeed, a vampire's victim grows a set of elongated canine teeth (or fangs) and lives on after their human heart stops beating. Neither alive nor dead, the vampire is cursed to walk the earth forever, feeding on blood with its soul trapped in purgatory — much like that of a ghost but rather in solid form.

In Chapter 16 of *Dracula*, Van Helsing gives a brief lecture on vampire lore immediately before a stake is driven into Lucy Westenra's heart:

"Dr. Seward's Diary — continued.

29 September, night. — "Before we do anything, let me tell you this; it is out of the lore and experiences of the ancients and of all those who have studied the powers of the Un-Dead. When they become such, there comes with the change the curse of immortality; they cannot die, but must go on age after age adding new victims and multiplying the evils of the world; for all that die from the preying of the Un-Dead become themselves Un-Dead and prey on their kind. And so the circle goes on ever widening, like as the ripples from a stone thrown in the water. Friend Arthur, if you had met that kiss which you know of before poor Lucy die; or again, last night when you open your arms to her, you would in time, when you had died, have become nosferatu, as they call it in Eastern Europe, and would all time make more of those Un-deads that so have fill us with horror. The career of this so unhappy dear lady is but just begun. Those children whose blood she sucks are not as yet so much the worse; but if she lives on, Un-dead, more and more they lose their blood, and by her

power over them they come to her; and so she draws their blood with that so wicked mouth. But if she dies in truth, then all cease; the tiny wounds of the throat disappear, and they go back to their plays unknowing ever of what has been."

It is cleverly curious — and perhaps amusingly ironic to a certain extent — that Bram Stoker bestows the curse of vampirism (sometimes referred to as the dark gift derived from Satan's power) against the victim's will. In other words, those who do not want it, such as Lucy Westenra, are forced to take it, while those who seek it out, like R. M. Renfield, die begging for it. Dracula makes promises to Renfield — not by words but by doing things, or as the patient tells the band of men in Chapter 21, "by making them happen." However, the Count uses Renfield only for direct access to the asylum and denies the madman's obsessive plea for immortality. The vampire leads the man on by tempting him with the lives of many animals.

Renfield recounts, "He seemed to be saying: "All these lives will I give you, ay, and many more and greater, through countless ages, if you will fall down and worship me." As soon as Renfield lets Dracula into his cell, the rats disappear. "All day I waited to hear from him, but he did not send me anything, not even a blow-fly, and when the moon got up, I was pretty angry with him," the dying patient explained to the group.

Just as the 'dark gift' is a symbol of the evil vampire's undeadness in Stoker's narrative, J.K. Rowling's wicked Lord Voldemort uses the darkest of all magic to grant him seven Horcruxes. These cursed objects are symbolic of He-Who-Must-Not-Be-Named's 'ripped soul,' allowing him to live forever at a steep price. Indeed, from a very early age, Tom Riddle breeds a disturbing, insalubrious fixation with immortality. Two critical conversations during year four and year six speak to this obsession:

"I, who have gone further than anybody along the path that leads to immortality [said Voldemort] You know my goal — to conquer death. And now, I was tested, and it appeared that one or more of my experiments had worked... for I had not been killed, though the curse should have done it"

— *Harry Potter and the Goblet of Fire*

And...

"Well, Harry,' said Dumbledore, 'I am sure you understood the significance of what we just heard. At the same age as you are now, give or take a few months, Tom Riddle was doing all he could to find out how to make himself immortal.'

— *Harry Potter and the Half-Blood Prince*

The childhood of Tom Riddle is defined by fear of death, beginning with the passing of his mother. In the pensive scene at the orphanage, Riddle reacts to Dumbledore's magical abilities news accordingly:

"My mother can't have been magic, or she wouldn't have died," said Riddle, more to himself than Dumbledore."

— *The Half-Blood Prince*, Chapter 13 — The Secret Riddle —

It could be that Voldemort's unhealthy preoccupation and quest for immortality begins with the thought of viewing his mother as being a weakling for deserting him, submitting to death and leaving him to be raised in an orphanage. This negative viewpoint is undoubtedly fueled when he learns the circumstances of her upbringing, his birth, and the fact that she is a "disgusting little Squib."

This childhood belief system is the genesis of Voldemort's birth. It sets up the idea that death is a human frailty — an Achilles' heel meant to be bested. Pursuing immortality gives him a way to prove that he is better than his mother. With no prior awareness of the magical community, Riddle straightaway assumes that wizards have the upper hand — that is to say, magical folk are superior to Muggles, and their power renders them immortal and different.

"There he showed his contempt for anything that tied him to other people, anything that made him ordinary. Even then, he wished to be different, separate, notorious."

— *The Half-Blood Prince*, Chapter 13 — The Secret Riddle

Truly, there aren't many ways to be more diverse than to embrace eternity. It is the decisive standout instance: a moment that will certainly place him apart forever — asserting his self-believed superiority over all living beings.

Fear. Power. Diversity. All these pre-adolescent ideas are symbolic of He-Who-Must-Not-Be-Named's horrid future fueled with murder, Horcrux creation, the journey toward immortality, and world domination. J.K. Rowling labels Voldemort a psychopath in many interviews. Indeed, from his early days bullying other children in the orphanage, he did not just want to be different; he wanted to be better, regardless of the extent and expense to others, at any selfish cost. Just like vampirism, the act of murdering many so one might live is an existence not worth living for.

Both authors write of other supernatural objects which also symbolize immortality. However, this second 'branch of magic' is different from vampirism or Horcruxes, both of which are considered evil bequests from the Dark One himself. The following look at other 'mysteries of life' are dissimilar in the fact that their origin, purpose, and

outcome are not as direct as 'murder;' and dependent on the heart and intent of the
bestowed 'owner' of the gift. Nevertheless, their usage can bring good into the world.

In Chapter 14 of *Dracula*, Professor Abraham Van Helsing prepares his friend,
pupil, and associate Dr. John Seward for the cold hard truth. His means of doing so is
thoughtfully and exceptionally cushioned by a plea to simply believe:

"Dr. Seward's Diary.

26 September. — "Let me tell you, my friend, that there are things done today
in electrical science which would have been deemed unholy by the very man
who discovered electricity, who would themselves not so long before been
burned as wizards. There are always mysteries in life. Why was it that Methu-
selah lived nine hundred years, and 'Old Parr' one hundred and sixty-nine, and
yet that poor Lucy, with four men's blood in her poor veins, could not live even
one day? For, had she lived one more day, we could save her. Do you know all
the mystery of life and death? Do you know the altogether of comparative anat-
omy and can say wherefore the qualities of brutes are in some men, and not in
others? Can you tell me why, when other spiders die small and soon, that one
great spider lived for centuries in the tower of the old Spanish church and grew
and grew, till, on descending, he could drink the oil of all the church lamps?
Can you tell me why in the Pampas, ay and elsewhere, there are bats that come
out at night and open the veins of cattle and horses and suck dry their veins,
how in some islands of the Western seas there are bats which hang on the trees
all day, and those who have seen describe as like giant nuts or pods, and that
when the sailors sleep on the deck, because that it is hot, flit down on them and
then, and then in the morning are found dead men, white as even Miss Lucy
was?"

"Good God, Professor!" I said, starting up. "Do you mean to tell me that Lucy
was bitten by such a bat, and that such a thing is here in London in the nineteenth century?"

He waved his hand for silence, and went on, "Can you tell me why the tortoise
lives more long than generations of men, why the elephant goes on and on till
he have seen dynasties, and why the parrot never die only of bite of cat of dog
or other complaint? Can you tell me why men believe in all ages and places that
there are men and women who cannot die? We all know, because science has
vouched for the fact, that there have been toads shut up in rocks for thousands
of years, shut in one so small hole that only hold him since the youth of the

world. Can you tell me how the Indian fakir can make himself to die and have been buried, and his grave sealed and corn sowed on it, and the corn reaped and be cut and sown and reaped and cut again, and then men come and take away the unbroken seal and that there lie the Indian fakir, not dead, but that rise up and walk amongst them as before?"

In an instrumental passage in the novel, Van Helsing builds a case that essentially science and magic are cohesive facts — that is, 'magic' in this intellect can be confirmed via meticulous means, providing the human mind is open enough to embrace the possibilities. In this context, there is no division between science and belief—each necessitates an openness of brain and heart, and both require the scientist to never spring to conclusions but to honor time's call to assemble and analyze facts. The key argument in the Professor's declaration is that we think we discern phenomena to be false, but we do not know that they are untrue; we only think they are implausible. Indeed, true faith translates that we can believe beyond our individual prejudices and be open to a universe that is more complex and extraordinary than we once thought. Only then can we view immortality in an alternate light.

In the Harry Potter series, J.K. Rowling introduces readers to two other magical possibilities symbolic of immortality: *The Philosopher's (Sorcerer's) Stone* and *The Deathly Hallows*. Created by Nicolas Flamel and Death (or the Peverell brothers), these enchanted objects are not linked to Satan, so they are free to be utilized by the holder to dispense good or evil into the world.

Rowling did not invent the Philosopher's Stone. References to the object date back to 300 AD in Ancient Greece, where it was referenced as the source of Biblical longevity. Known for being made from an alchemical ingredient proficient in altering base metals into gold or silver, the stone was likewise referred to as the elixir of life, thus valuable for rejuvenation and attaining immortality. The object remained the crucial symbol of the mystical lexicon of alchemy for many centuries, embodying perfection at its optimum, illumination, and spiritual nirvana. Exertions to unearth the Philosopher's Stone were known as the Magnum Opus (or Great Work), rendering it the highest hunted artifact of alchemy.

"The Stone was not such a wonderful thing. As much money and life as you wanted, the two things most human beings would choose above all. The trouble is, humans do have a knack of choosing precisely those things that are worst for them."

—Albus Dumbledore regarding the true nature
of the Philosopher's Stone

Nicolas Flamel was also a real person who lived in the 14th and 15th centuries and contributed financially to many churches. Being well respected for philanthropy, this evidence suggests that the renowned alchemist used the Stone for good.

"Nicolas Flamel is an historical character. Flamel lived in France in the fourteenth century and is supposed to have discovered how to make a philosopher's stone. There are mentions of sightings of him through the centuries because he was supposed to have gained immortality. There are still streets named after Flamel and his wife Perenelle in Paris."

— J.K. Rowling on Nicolas Flamel

In the Harry Potter universe, however, Voldemort, while occupying the back of Professor Quirrell's head and living off unicorn plasma, attempts to steal the Stone for egotistical, malicious reasons: to rejuvenate himself, take over the world, and start the next wizarding war, killing countless innocent people. With this misadventure, the Dark Lord decorously deduces that the headmaster will destroy the Stone to prevent it from falling into the wrong hands. Quickly, Voldemort begins scheming for another method to regenerate his body which later comes to be known as the 'Rudimentary Body Potion.'

Flash forwarding six school years, Book Seven: *The Deathly Hallows* introduces readers to another supernatural set of magical icons symbolic of immortality. *The Tales of Beedle the Bard* is an assortment of bedtime stories written for young wizards and witches. *The Tale of the Three Brothers* presents Harry Potter followers with the Deathly Hallows objects: The Elder Wand, the Resurrection Stone, and the Cloak of Invisibility. According to the fable, the trio reaches a river too deep to wade across; thus, they conjure a bridge using magic. Death then appears, commends them for their ingenuity, and offers them each a reward. This Grim Reaper conceals his true intent to trap all of them because he is cheated by their survival. The story continues as the first brother requests a weapon that will continuously win any battle, an armament laudable of one who had duped Death. Death breaks a branch from an elder tree and gifts him the Elder Wand. The second brother solicits something to bequeath power over Death, having recently lost his loved one. Death reaches into the river and hands him the Resurrection Stone. The third brother, on the other hand, is suspicious of Death's intentions and thus inquires about a recompense that will permit him to evade Death. Cornered by his words, Death turns over his personal Cloak of Invisibility. The three brothers finish their journey and travel their separate ways.

Soon, the first brother incites a duel with a wizard he abhors and leaves him for dead. Consequently, the first brother is murdered that very same night by someone who has heard his boasting about his 'unbeatable wand' and decided to steal it for himself. The second brother discovers despair when he raises his former lover from the grave with the Resurrection Stone but realizes she had been happier dead. In desperation, he takes his own life to join her. The third brother, however, conceals himself from Death for his entire life by wearing the Cloak of Invisibility. When he attains a desired old age, he decides to regift the Cloak to his son, and he and Death finally 'meet as old friends' and depart as equals.

It is important to mention that Death serves himself — neither God nor Satan. Furthermore, the magical gifts he hands out can be used for good or evil, dependent upon the heart of the owner. If joined together, however, the three mythological relics will make the wielder the exceedingly powerful 'Master of Death.'

"I was fit only to possess the meanest of them, the least extraordinary. I was fit to own the Elder Wand, and not to boast of it, and not to kill with it. I was permitted to tame and to use it, because I took it, not for gain, but to save others from it."

—Albus Dumbledore on the Deathly Hallows and the Elder Wand

Dumbledore reveals to Harry that the true Master of Death is one who accepts that death is inevitable, in much the same way Ignotus Peverell, the third brother, does. Dumbledore further admits that his obsession with finding all three legendary objects has blinded him at times and caused him to sacrifice the safety of others, clouding his decision-making. Therefore, in preparation for his own demise, he makes certain that the objects wind up in Harry's hands instead of Voldemort's — for he knows the most deserving owner will be one who does not search for or desire the objects at all.

Lord Voldermort selfishly seeks the Elder Wand, for he trusts it will allow him to defeat Harry Potter. Nevertheless, in an unexpected twist of fate Harry himself briefly becomes the Master of Death when he unites all three artifacts at the end of the series, ultimately destroying He-Who-Must-Not-Be-Named a second time.

"I'm putting the Elder Wand back where it came from. It can stay there. If I die a natural death like Ignotus, its power will be broken, won't it? The previous master will never have been defeated. That'll be the end of it."

— Harry, on his decision to give up the Elder Wand

After purposely dropping the Resurrection Stone on the floor of the Forbidden Forest, Harry chooses only to keep the Cloak of Invisibility, which will eventually pass down to James Sirius Potter, his and Ginny's eldest son, as written in the screenplay for *Harry Potter and the Cursed Child.*

The opening section of this chapter originated out of Satan's Hell and the process of exchanging one's soul for the 'dark gift/magic' of immortality through vampirism or Horcruxes. The middle dealt with the undead icons of earthly power, which could be used for a product of good or evil. Therefore, it would seem appropriate to close out this topic by discussing immortality in the context of God's heaven and the Christianity concept of being 'true dead.'

When reading Gothic fiction, one can bet that religion will play a critical role in the inclusive development of the literary genre itself. A critical analysis of the text of *Dracula* reflects copious spiritual illustrations and Christian aspects. Most notably is the crucifix, symbolizing not only the power of Christ Jesus' resurrection but also the redemption of mankind, thus allowing God's children to live on in heaven forever after death. Indeed, true death within Stoker's story is parallel to the Christian faith, and Professor Abraham Van Helsing harnesses the full force of God and His religious symbols to avail against the undead. This tactic fully plays out with Lucy Westenra after she is turned by the Count. Van Helsing uses the crucifix to keep her from attacking her fiancé Arthur; he seals up her tomb with a paste made out of the holy communion wafer. However, it is not until a wooden stake is plunged into her heart and her head is removed and stuffed with garlic that her soul is free to transition to heaven.

"Dr. Seward's Diary — continued.

29 September, night. — "But of the most blessed of all, when this now Undead be made to rest as true dead, then the soul of the poor lady whom we love shall again be free. Instead of working wickedness by night and growing more debased in the assimilating of it by day, she shall take her place with the other Angels."

Furthermore, Van Helsing's undying religious faith and belief in Christian immortality shine again in the text in his own countless praises of Mina's moral character. Indeed, he testifies repeatedly to the fact that she is the embodiment of the virtues of the Victorian era. In his own words, she is, "one of God's women, fashioned by His own hand to show us men and other women that there is a heaven where we can enter, and that its light can be here on earth. So true, so sweet, so noble."

A century later, J.K. Rowling admitted to injecting Christian beliefs into the Harry Potter series. "To me, the religious parallels have always been obvious," Rowling said in 2007. "But I never wanted to talk too openly about it because I thought it might show people who just wanted the story where we were going." Therefore, it makes logical sense that she crafted many characters and events in a Christian light. For example, readers learn that Hogwarts celebrates Christian holidays, that Albus Dumbledore owns a copy of the Holy Bible, and that Harry Potter is christened shortly after his birth. To further strengthen these claims, fans recall the heartfelt gesture of Harry gouging a small cross, the major symbol of Christianity, into the tree under which he buries Professor Moody's magical eye.

Furthermore, places of worship typically do not allow non-members of their church to be buried in their cemeteries, making it highly probable that the wizards buried in the parish church of St. Clementine graveyard in Godric's Hollow are, indeed, Christian. Notable figures buried there include Ignotus Peverell, Ariana and Kendra Dumbledore, and James and Lily Potter. If this alone did not communicate the concept of the Christian afterlife, then certainly the tombstones of Ariana and Kendra Dumbledore and Lily and James Potter solidify the belief: "For where your treasure is, there will your heart be also" and of "The last enemy that shall be destroyed is death" allude to Matthew 6:21 and 1 Corinthians 15:26 respectively. In 2007, Rowling said: "On any given moment if you asked me if I believe in life after death, I think if you polled me regularly through the week, I think I would come down on the side of yes — that I do believe in life after death."

Indeed, the essential Christian motif that runs through the series is the belief in life after death. This idea continues to build throughout the saga and matures fully in *The Deathly Hallows*. There are many references to 'moving on' at the end of life as opposed to remaining behind as a ghost. Indeed, it seems that everyone, excluding Lord Voldemort and the Hogwart's ghosts, embraces the true death. The Veil, a reference to the English phrase, 'beyond the veil,' originated from Hebrew tradition as a veil or curtain that separated the main body of the Temple from the Tabernacle. When Sirius Black accepts his fate of going beyond the veil, it can be said he is entering the holiest of places where the presence of God is manifested. Indeed, intimate fellowship with God — or communing with God at the deepest level — requires transformation.

The Deathly Hallows itself begins with two religiously themed epigraphs, one from *The Libation Bearers* by Aeschylus, which calls on the gods to "bless the children," and one from William Penn's *More Fruits of Solitude*, which speaks of death as but 'crossing the world, as friends do the seas.' Indeed, this is the only book in the series which begins with epigraphs — a curious fact, perchance, but one that Rowling means to be a guiding light.

"I really enjoyed choosing those two quotations because one is pagan, of course, and one is from a Christian tradition," Rowling said of their inclusion in 2007. "I'd known it was going to be those two passages since 'Chamber' was published. I always knew [that] if I could use them at the beginning of book seven then I'd cued up the ending perfectly. If they were relevant, then I went where I needed to go."

Though the book began with a quote on the immortal soul, and although Harry found peace with his own mortality at the end of his journey, it is the struggle itself that mirrors Rowling's own.

"The truth is that, like Graham Greene, my faith is sometimes that my faith will return. It's something I struggle with a lot," she revealed.

In the end, *The Deathly Hallows* can most simplistically and categorically be described as a resurrection story and, in many respects, parallel with the Bible's New Testament. When Harry freely allows Voldemort to kill him, he ventures to a way station that is white, peaceful, and very heavenly in appearance. There he finds an elderly man in white robes and beard, who turns out to be Professor Dumbledore. Before he is resurrected and returned to earth to conquer evil, Rowling injects a final piece of wisdom; a statement enlightened by Biblical truth:

"Do not pity the dead, Harry. Pity the living, and above all, those who live without love."

— Albus Dumbledore on death

Chapter Twenty-One

Scars

Scars are imprints of the past. They can appear on the outside or inside of the body. Because such marks are personal and unique to the owner, the stories and life lessons that typically accompany a scar are vast and varying. However, most can agree on one concept: physical scars are the supreme, prominent souvenirs of trauma to the body. Yet all scars are not negative. Though their lasting marks are continual visible reminders of experiences we have endured, physical scars can be symbolic — bearing a spiritual significance that goes beyond the traditional strength and bravery that surviving soldiers of war boast about. Scars are visible reminders of discipline, sacrifice, mercy, and healing. Simply put, they reinforce Biblical messages. Scars also point to greater problems or illnesses in society.

Authors Bram Stoker and J.K. Rowling inflict scars throughout their most famous works to symbolize the unfolding evil threats — ones that only grow as their respective plots uncoil — but also to remind readers of the importance of undying faith and hope in this world.

In Chapter 4 of *Dracula*, imprisoned hero Jonathan Harker discovers his host's daytime lair, which, correspondingly, unravels the rolling mysteries and sinister secret of the man that has been assembling in the previous three chapters:

"Jonathan Harker's Journal — continued.

30 June, morning. — The great box was in the same place, close against the wall, but the lid was laid on it, not fastened down, but with the nails ready in their places to be hammered home. I knew I must reach the body for the key, so I raised the lid, and laid it back against the wall; and then I saw something which filled my very soul with horror. There lay the Count, but looking as if his youth had been half renewed, for the white hair and moustache were changed to dark iron-grey; the cheeks were fuller, and the white skin seemed ruby-red underneath; the mouth was redder than ever, for on the lips were

gouts of fresh blood, which trickled from the corners of the mouth and ran over the chin and neck. Even the deep, burning eyes seemed set amongst swollen flesh, for the lids and pouches underneath were bloated. It seemed as if the whole awful creature were simply gorged with blood. He lay like a filthy leech, exhausted with his repletion. I shuddered as I bent over to touch him, and every sense in me revolted at the contact; but I had to search, or I was lost. The coming night might see my own body a banquet in a similar way to those horrid three. I felt all over the body, but no sign could I find of the key. Then I stopped and looked at the Count. There was a mocking smile on the bloated face which seemed to drive me mad. This was the being I was helping to transfer to London, where, perhaps, for centuries to come he might, amongst its teeming millions, satiate his lust for blood, and create a new and ever-widening circle of semi-demons to batten on the helpless. The very thought drove me mad. A terrible desire came upon me to rid the world of such a monster. There was no lethal weapon at hand, but I seized a shovel which the workmen had been using to fill the cases, and lifting it high, struck, with the edge downward, at the hateful face. But as I did so the head turned, and the eyes fell full upon me, with all their blaze of basilisk horror. The sight seemed to paralyse me, and the shovel turned in my hand and glanced from the face, merely making a deep gash above the forehead. The shovel fell from my hand across the box, and as I pulled it away the flange of the blade caught the edge of the lid which fell over again and hid the horrid thing from my sight. The last glimpse I had was of the bloated face, blood-stained and fixed with a grin of malice which would have held its own in the nethermost hell."

What might appear to be an isolated misadventure at first is, in fact, an instrumental encounter as it saves Jonathan Harker's life. Indeed, the grim answers the young solicitor receives in these two pages give him the hope, strength, and courage needed to escape the castle. Simultaneously, he leaves a physical and mental scar on the vampire, which communicates to the vampire that he is not going to go down without a fight.

Rarely in literature does the hero mark the villain prematurely in the tale. Case in point: future appearances of the Count reinforce Harker's journal to be shockingly true:

Mina Harker recounts in her diary in Chapter 21: "I knew, too, the red scar on his forehead where Jonathan had struck him." Dr. Seward similarly calls Dracula's scar to the group's attention in his diary on October 3rd: "His waxen hue became greenish-yellow by the contrast of his burning eyes, and the red scar on the forehead showed on the pallid skin like a palpitating wound."

Even though the unsightly mark is a recurring vile reminder to the intrepid vampire hunters that evil is afoot, the implied symbolism of the Count's scar calls out his weaknesses and hope for defeat. Indeed, the end of the novel carries forth their abiding faith in deliverance as Dracula's nasty scar disintegrates with the rest of him.

In contrast, another mark on the forehead was created a century later by fellow British author J.K. Rowling. This time it was the monster at the beginning of the tale, however, that left a scar on the infant hero in the form of an infamous lightning bolt. Many parallelisms can be drawn between the Harker/Dracula and the Potter/Voldemort links that go beyond the forehead.

"All anyone knows is, he turned up in the village where you were all living, on Hallowe'en ten years ago. You was just a year old. He came ter yer house an' — an' — 'You-Know-Who killed 'em. An' then — an' this is the real myst'ry of the thing — he tried to kill you, too... But he couldn't do it. Never wondered how you got that mark on yer forehead? That was no ordinary cut. That's what yeh get when a powerful, evil curse touches yeh — took care of yer mum an' dad an' yer house, even — but it didn't work on you, an' that's why yer famous, Harry."

— Rubeus Hagrid, describing the attack

Undoubtedly, the lightning bolt scar proves to be the saving factor for young Harry Potter, just as Dracula's shovel mark saves Jonathan Harker. The lasting message on the villain, Lord Voldemort, consequently, echoes loudly that 'The Boy Who Lived' is a force to be reckoned with. Though The Dark Lord frequently boasts about his plan to kill Harry, there is a vague fear in He-Who-Must-Not-Be-Named, which causes him to proceed with caution, much like Dracula when he dodges Harker's Kukri knife and crashes hurriedly through the window, fleeing the grounds after grasping a handful of money.

"The one with the power to vanquish the Dark Lord approaches... Born to those who have thrice defied him, born as the seventh month dies... And the Dark Lord will mark him as equal, but he will have power the Dark Lord knows not... And either must die at the hand of the other for neither can live while the other survives... The one with the power to vanquish the Dark Lord will be born as the seventh month dies..."

— Sybil Trelawney's first prophecy

Because Voldemort fears death and Harry is prophesized to destroy him, the Dark Lord is very cautious around his opponent, usually surrounding himself with Death Eaters for security.

Harry's scar is symbolic of He-Who-Must-Not-Be-Named's many malevolent moods. Indeed, as Dracula's red scar seems to palpitate when the group closes in on him, Potter's lightning bolt often burns and aches. In a 2007 podcast, Rowling elaborated on this phenomenon:

> "Well, of course the pain he feels [in his scar] whenever Voldemort's particularly active is this piece of soul seeking to rejoin the master soul. When his scar is hurting him so much, that's not scar tissue hurting him. That's this piece of soul really wanting to get back out the way it entered. It really wants to — it entered this boy's body through a wound, and it wants to rejoin the master. So when Voldemort's near him, when he's particularly active, this connection, it was always there. That's what I always imagined this pain was. Yes, so there you go." — J.K. Rowling — The Leaky Cauldron — Pottercast's Interview with J.K. Rowling — 12.23.2007

It is curious and slightly amusing that Harry's scar can be compared to Renfield's character in *Dracula*, for it seems so mixed up with Voldemort "in an indexy kind of way."

Harry's lightning bolt is a lifelong reminder of the Dark Lord's real existence, heinous actions, and ultimate defeat. All through the series Harry and others alike cannot ignore the imminent return of He-Who-Must-Not-Be-Named. Though some individuals here and there wish to ignore or deny the news (even Harry himself thinks he is going crazy hearing voices in his second year), the truth prevails: the scar that the monster made turns The Boy Who Lived into the unsung hero, and it is this twist of fate that ultimately defeats the monster — not once, but twice. The spiritual significance of that statement touches all life's lessons mentioned at the start of this chapter: strength, bravery, discipline, sacrifice, mercy, and healing. While Dracula's scar fades to dust at the conclusion of Stoker's novel, Harry's lightning bolt has behaved for eons:

> "The scar had not pained Harry for nineteen years. All was well."
>
> — The last two sentences of Book 7: *The Deathly Hallows*

A bite from a human — of any kind, for that matter — is usually symbolic of violence. Dream experts have believed for years that when one is bitten in a reverie, the dreamer must remain cognizant that people who conceal secrets might intend to cause harm. In a comparable fashion, buried information in one's psyche is poised to cause all sorts of problems in one's life. Therefore, dreaming of being bitten — or seeing bite marks on one's body — can symbolize secrets within the mind as well as unseen (or 'violent") things other people are keeping from the dreamer. More interestingly, though, it is said that if one were to dream of being bitten by a vampire, however, the victim should make a special note of people that may be using the dreamer for their own selfish purposes; for, unfortunately, once one realizes what is going on, it may be too late to stop the violence and simultaneously unmask these mysterious predators.

Regardless of era or region, vampire lore has remained consistent in the sense that the undead bite for blood and that these bites leave scars. Indeed, Bram Stoker freely incorporates this mythology into his novel, which begins with Lucy Westenra, continues with the 'Bloofer Lady' victims, and ultimately ends with Wilhelmina Harker.

As Professor Van Helsing does not reveal the esoteric evidence to the group until halfway through the novel, readers wince and recoil at the ignorance of the main characters as they do their best to logically explain away all behavior and symptoms. However, when science and reason cannot justify the unknown, the supernatural scars of vampirism remain. For example, when Mina rescues Lucy from her infamous sleepwalking adventure to the cemetery of St. Mary's churchyard, her reaction to the bite marks on her friend's neck is quickly explained away as Mina's own act of carelessness:

"Mina Murray's Journal.

Same day, noon. — "I was sorry to notice that my clumsiness with the safety-pin hurt her. Indeed, it might have been serious, for the skin of her throat was pierced. I must have pinched up a piece of loose skin and have transfixed it, for there are two little red points like pin-pricks, and on the band of her nightdress was a drop of blood."

Similarly, the reporter that is involved in the 'Hampstead Mystery/Horror' or 'Bloofer Lady' investigation gets creative with the interpretation of the children's bite marks on the neck:

"The Westminster Gazette," 25 September
A Hampstead Mystery

The neighborhood of Hampstead is just at present exercised with a series of events which seem to run on lines parallel to those of what was known to the writers of headlines and "The Kensington Horror," or "The Stabbing Woman," or "The Woman in Black." During the past two or three days several cases have occurred of young children straying from home or neglecting to return from their playing on the Heath. In all these cases the children were too young to give any properly intelligible account of themselves, but the consensus of their excuses is that they had been with a "bloofer lady." It has always been late in the evening when they have been missed, and on two occasions the children have not been found until early in the following morning. It is generally supposed in the neighborhood that, as the first child missed gave as his reason for being away that a "bloofer lady" had asked him to come for a walk, the others had picked up the phrase and used it as occasion served. This is the more natural as the favorite game of the little ones at present is luring each other away by wiles. A correspondent writes us that to see some of the tiny tots pretending to be the "bloofer lady" is supremely funny. Some of our caricaturists might, he says, take a lesson in the irony of grotesque by comparing the reality and the picture. It is only in accordance with general principles of human nature that the "bloofer lady" should be the popular role at these al fresco performances. Our correspondent naively says that even Ellen Terry could not be so winningly attractive as some of these grubby-faced little children pretend, and even imagine themselves, to be.

There is, however, possibly a serious side to the question, for some of the children, indeed all who have been missed at night, have been slightly torn or wounded in the throat. The wounds seem such as might be made by a rat or a small dog, and although of not much importance individually, would tend to show that whatever animal inflicts them has a system or method of its own. The police of the division have been instructed to keep a sharp lookout for straying children, especially when very young, in and around Hampstead Heath, and for any stray dog which may be about."

Vampires have a history of feeding, manipulating, and engaging in violence. In the above passage, the freshly turned vampire Lucy Westenra demonstrates all three actions to a small group of children playing on the heath in the early evenings. Circling back to the dream interpretation concept, a dreamer biting others is indicative of possible violence and manipulation taking place in waking life. Whether awake or asleep or alive or dead (or in this case, 'undead'), evil habitually inflicts violence; and violence customarily leaves mutilations — both outward and internal scarring.

Though the Harry Potter saga does not have vampires scarring the bodies of the innocent in the literal sense, there is plenty of evil afoot, manipulating and leaving its mutation on anyone who gets in its way. The Boy Who Lived is not the only one scarred by the profuse wickedness that He-Who-Must-Not-Be-Named and his followers dish out upon the wizarding world.

For example, in Chapter 34: 'The Department of Mysteries' of *The Order of the Phoenix*, Dumbledore's Army fights the Death Eaters in the Brain Room. After Ron Weasley is 'confunded,' he finds the brains amusing and summons them. When the thoughts leap upon him, they begin to wrap themselves around Ron's arms, almost asphyxiating him.

"Hey, Harry, there are brains in here, ha, ha, ha, isn't that weird, Harry?...Honest, Harry, they're are brains — look — Accio Brains!" The scene seemed momentarily frozen. Harry, Ginny, and Neville and each of the Death Eaters turned in spite of themselves to watch the top of the tank as a brain burst from the green liquid like a leaping fish...The moment they came in contact with his skin, the tentacles began wrapping themselves around Ron's arms like ropes... "Harry, it'll suffocate him!" screamed Ginny."

— Ron's attack by thought

In the aftermath of the battle, Madam Pomfrey says that it will leave a scar since nothing leaves deeper scarring than thought. It is curious of the three protagonists that 'thought' will be the scar that chooses Ron. Indeed, of the trio of friends, Ron is the least academic of them and the one more apt to spring into action without thinking through the plan and considering consequences. In this context, 'thought' symbolically scars him for life.

In *The Deathly Hallows*, Hermione Granger is the victim of scarring as she is held, interrogated, and tortured by Bellatrix Lestrange:

"You're lying, filthy Mudblood, and I know it! You have been inside my vault at Gringotts!... What else did you take? Tell me the truth or, I swear, I shall run you through with this knife! What else did you take, what else? ANSWER ME! CRUCIO! How did you get into my vault? Did that dirty little goblin in the cellar help you?"

— Overheard parts of Hermione's brutal interrogation

During the skirmish at Malfoy Manor, Hermione suffers cuts and bites from the incident, including "the thin cut Bellatrix had made, scarlet against her throat." In Hermione's case, Lestrange is about to slit her jugular amidst all kinds of discriminating slurs before Dobby's chandelier distraction saves her. Back at Shell Cottage, Hermione boldly reveals the scar claiming that she is not ashamed to be a Mudblood, thus ultimately using the mark as a symbolic reminder of her purpose in the fight.

"Why shouldn't I?' said Hermione. 'Mudblood, and proud of it! I've got no higher position under this new order than you have, Griphook! It was me they chose to torture, back at the Malfoys!"

In addition, Lord Voldemort taints all his Death Eaters by ensuring the 'dark mark' appears on their forearms. And one could not mention scars in the Harry Potter world without bringing up Dumbledore's bizarre emblem. Indeed, in *The Philosopher's Stone*, Dumbledore replies to McGonagall's question as to whether he can do something about the scar infant Harry has on his forehead:

"Even if I could, I wouldn't. Scars can come in handy. I have one myself above my left knee that is a perfect map of the London Underground." — Chapter 1, The Boy Who Lived.

How the headmaster gets this most unusual scar is never elaborated further; however, we fans can be sure it would make for a supremely interesting and enlightening tale in its own right.

However, of all the characters bearing scars in the Harry Potter series, the first-place award winner undoubtedly goes to Auror and part-time professor Alastor "Mad-Eye" Moody. He serves with distinction during the first wizarding conflict, acquiring a significant reputation, as well as losing an eye and other body parts. Indeed, his physical appearance becomes so extremely distorted from fighting the dark arts that Hogwart students are alarmed by his numerous scars — and those are just his external wounds!

Harry notes in *The Goblet of Fire* that the professor comes into the great hall "looking as though his face was carved from wood by an untalented person." Due to injuries from his long career as an Auror, his visage is covered with scars, and a chunk of his nose is missing. He has dark grey, grizzled hair, speaks with a growling voice, and ambles about on a wooden leg. His eyes, however, are his most shocking feature: one is small and dark, while the other is a vivid, electric blue, magical eye which moves around independently from his 'normal' eye. Due to his magical eye, he can see through objects, Invisibility Cloaks, and even the back of his own head. His eccentric eyes alone earn him his kooky nickname.

Moody's multitude of scarring is symbolic of his highly repeated catchphrase to his students: "Constant vigilance," meaning to be on watch endlessly and always guard against threats.

The wise headmaster is correct: "Scars can come in handy." Indeed, Harry, Ron, Hermione, and Moody indisputably agree with Dumbledore's statement, for their own battle marks are obtained while fighting evil and will always be symbolically linked to their honor, integrity, and the goodness they diligently defended.

Perhaps the most poignant scar in *Dracula* was Mina Harker's. Stoker's classic suggests that vampires are damned beings and do not belong on earth — that the 'undead' were 'unclean,' as are those who have taken 'the Vampire's baptism of blood,' even before they have become one of the undead. Thus, it is tragically ironic that the purest of all, Wilhelmina Murray Harker, finds herself scarred and 'unclean' in Chapter 22. Indeed, by placing the 'piece of Sacred Wafer' on Mina's forehead, Stoker symbolically implies that the undead are damned while simultaneously relying deeply on religion and the power of goodness to abolish immorality:

"Jonathan Harker's Journal.

3 October. — [Professor Van Helsing speaking] "It may be that you may have to bear that mark till God himself see fit, as He most surely shall, on the Judgement Day, to redress all wrongs of the earth and of His children that He has placed thereon. And oh, Madam Mina, my dear, my dear, may we who love you be there to see, when that red scar, the sign of God's knowledge of what has been, shall pass away, and leave your forehead as pure as the heart we know. For so surely as we live, that scar shall pass away when God sees right to lift the burden that is hard upon us. Till then we bear our Cross, as His Son did in obedience to His Will. It may be that we are chosen instruments of His good pleasure, and that we ascend to His bidding as that other through stripes and shame. Through tears and blood. Through doubts and fear, and all that makes the difference between God and man."

There was hope in his words and comfort. And they made for resignation. Mina and I both felt so, and simultaneously we each took one of the old man's hands and bent over and kissed it. Then without a word we all knelt down together, and all holding hands, swore to be true to each other. We men pledged ourselves to raise the veil of sorrow from the head of her whom, each in his own way, we loved. And we prayed for help and guidance in the terrible task which lay before us. It was then time to start. So I said farewell to Mina, a parting which neither of us shall forget to our dying day, and we set out."

Mina is terrified because "she with all her goodness and purity [is] outcast from God" and damned through no fault of her own. After the Eucharist symbol burns a blemish into her forehead, she wails, "Unclean! Unclean! Even the Almighty shuns my polluted flesh! I must bear this mark of shame upon my forehead until Judgment Day."

In this context, Stoker's vision of the undead is that they were damned, no matter if "God is merciful and just." In other words, the vampire is a creature that God shuns… period. A being can only be damned through religion, and Stoker implies that religion is the almighty force to use against the undead.

These critical points illustrate the direst and saddest case — the most scarred of all the characters in *Dracula*. The fact that it is a holy object that actually sears into her skin makes the scar even more symbolic as it produces a 'scarlet letter' effect: A Godly woman is being marked and shamed. Yet Jonathan Harker's journal alludes to the fact that perhaps Mina herself is responsible for the unprecedented ostracism.

This sentiment and understanding fuel the sub-plot of the book. Not only are the men working nonstop to rid the world of a monster, they all take it as their personal mission to save the wonderful and pure Madame Mina. And they do. The scar disappears just as Dracula crumbles to dust.

The lightning bolt on Harry Potter's forehead is likewise the most relevant scar in Rowling's seven novels. Just as Mina and her band of men charge full steam ahead while being recalled and motivated daily by the unsightly and sometimes painful reminder on Mina's forehead, Harry, Ron, and Hermione also lead their own crusade amidst often searing and throbbing forehead mementos at Potter's expense. Just as Mina carries a psychic connection with Count Dracula, Harry connects spiritually with Lord Voldemort. The famous lightning bolt scar doubles and triples as a portal, rune, and Horcrux to the very end of the seventh and final book. In fact, the scars of both Mina and Harry are so crucial to their respective stories that they mutually end with references to each.

Though Mina's scar vanishes an instant before Quincey P. Morris' untimely death, Harry's remains for all to see. Nevertheless, "All was well." However, it is worth mentioning that the original last sentence of the series would have made it even more closely aligned with the ending of *Dracula*.

Prior to publication, J.K. Rowling stated in interviews that the final word of *Harry Potter and the Deathly Hallows* was to be 'scar.' After publication, she revealed what the last sentence would have been. Therefore, with due respect to the lady author and 'Potterheads' (not to mention the subject of this chapter), this writer finds it appropriate to end this chapter — and this book for that matter — with the closing line that might have been:

"Only those whom he loved could see the lightning scar."

Conclusion

Few could argue the far-reaching, momentous impact Bram Stoker and J.K. Rowling have created in the world of literary and pop culture. There has been no shortage of interest on the vampire front one hundred and twenty years after *Dracula's* initial publication. Six months ago, I read a long-lost Icelandic version of *Dracula* titled *Makt Myrkranna* (or *Powers of Darkness*.) The story goes that in 1901, Icelandic publisher and writer Valdimar Asmundsson embarked on a mission to translate Bram Stoker's masterpiece with the author's knowledge and collaboration. However, this Icelandic version was remarkably unnoticed outside of Iceland until 1986, when researchers discovered Stoker's original preface to the book. In 2014 scholar Hans Corneel de Roos realized that Asmundsson did more than translate *Dracula*: he had authored a completely new-fangled adaptation of the story with many new characters and an alternate plot. Like many other interested Stoker and *Dracula* enthusiasts that read it, the last forty-six pages seemed rushed and incomplete compared to the rest of the narrative. On Halloween 2017, I had the great privilege to attend a lecture given by a friend and great-grandnephew of Bram Stoker, Dacre Stoker, who explained that the great interest in the Icelandic version kicked off further investigations. Now a Swedish literary scholar has unearthed an earlier adaption of *Dracula*, which was serialized in the newspaper *Dagen* in 1899. Apparently, it too was never noticed outside of Sweden — that is, until now. Per a recent article in the *Iceland Monitor*, "[The] Swedish version bore an identical title. *Mörkrets makter*, as is the title of the Swedish serialization, means the same as *Makt myrkranna: Powers of Darkness*. That is how he made the link between the Swedish and the Icelandic version. First, he assumed that *Makt myrkranna* would be a straight translation of the Swedish publication, but then he found out that the Swedish text was more complete and contained scenes neither described in *Dracula* nor *Makt myrkranna*. And the madman Renfield was still in the story, among others.

Indeed, the preface to the Icelandic version, written by Bram Stoker himself, was absent from the 1897 version. This preface is probably the most interesting of all, for Stoker wrote from the viewpoint that the narrative was completely true, that the characters were actual friends of his, and that it was written under their "solemn duty to present it to the eyes of the public." This perspective and revelation have become a sort of a muse as it has fueled the imagination and creative literary interest to spawn at least two *Dracula* prequels, one of which has already been purchased by Paramount Pictures to be turned into a movie.

More than ever before, today, there is only increasing interest in the man who wrote *Dracula*. Currently, one can count the number of Bram Stoker biographies on two hands. However, the striking point in this fact is that all but one was written after 1975, with the majority being published within the past ten years. Of them all, David J. Skal's six-hundred-plus-page 'tour-de-force' *Something in the Blood: The Untold Story of Bram Stoker the Man Who Wrote Dracula* (2016) is the most thorough, enlightening, compelling, and entertaining.

While writing this conclusion, I went to the mailbox and opened up the latest issue of *Entertainment Weekly* magazine. In the back of my mind, I was actively thinking about how to bring this ending full circle to the Harry Potter universe. The publication 'magically' fell to page twenty titled: *First Look: Fantastic Revelations...in an exclusive interview, Fantastic Beasts: The Crimes of Grindelwald producer David Heyman shares the movie secrets you can't see in this first cast photo.* By James Hibberd. And then, flipping to page 42 *Holiday Gift Guide for the Movie Enthusiast*, I noticed that I could purchase a Golden Snitch clock for $49. Indeed, the Harry Potter phenomenon is far from over. Though the seventh book was published over ten years ago, J.K. Rowling has collaborated on a script called *Harry Potter and the Cursed Child*, billed as the eighth Harry Potter story. According to publisher Little, Brown, it was published in August 2016 and immediately broke records—selling an astonishing 680,000 copies in its first three days on sale. The play, which officially premiered at the Palace Theatre in London on July 30, 2016, earned no less than twenty prestigious awards and opened on Broadway on April 22, 2018, at the Lyric Theatre in New York.

The Wizarding World of Harry Potter, which recently expanded its coverage to include Diagon Alley and a high thrill-seeking ride Harry Potter and the Escape from Gringotts, continues to entice thousands of obsessed fans of all ages to make the ultimate Potterhead pilgrimage to Universal's Orlando theme park.

J.K. Rowling's Pottermore website, which was launched in 2012, continues to recruit new members every day as the site is updated regularly with new features, facts, stories, and information. Personally, I have found Pottermore to be the ultimate 'go-to' location while researching this book, as the author has carried on writing and elaborating upon even the most mundane person, place, or thing that was even briefly mentioned in the series. Naturally, while I was there, I was sorted into the Hufflepuff House, got chosen by my Redwood wand (9 ¾ inches, Phoenix feather core, and with slightly yielding flexibility), and discovered my Tonkinese Cat Patronus.

As Hogwarts' supplemental books used in the saga have been published, Newt Scamander's *Fantastic Beasts and Where to Find Them*, first published in March 2001 by J.K. Rowling, has and continues to gain the most attention. Indeed, Warner Brothers and Potter director David Yates have agreed to five movies, with the second *The Crimes of Grindelwald* released on November 16, 2018.

"Listeners, that brings us to the end of another Potterwatch. We don't know when it will be possible to broadcast again, but you can be sure we shall be back. Keep twiddling those dials: the next password will be 'Mad-Eye.' Keep each other safe. Keep faith. Good night."

— Lee Jordan concludes a 1998 broadcast of Potterwatch

Appendix

Across Land and Water

As previously noted, the use of locations — regardless of whether real or imaginative driven — play an important element in the thread of any effective storytelling: they assist in making the tale authentic to the reader; they aid in defining the narrative; and, if done successfully, the use of copious settings can create an entire world for the reader to marvel at. For example, J.R.R. Tolkien fashioned a wide, complex Middle-Earth fantastical world that was so well thought out that he even illustrated his books with detailed maps for fans to follow. Likewise, it is apparent that Bram Stoker and J.K. Rowling devoted plenty of quality, methodical thought to their respective creations, crossing numerous treacherous grounds and raging seas to teach us longstanding lessons.

Since Chapter Seven of this book was devoted solely to the United Kingdom, this section will focus on other essential settings outside the British Union. For organizational purposes, these remaining points of reference will appear in chronological order as presented in the novels *Dracula* and the Harry Potter series.

Section One: Dracula

To read *Dracula* (while jotting down each place mentioned in the text) from cover to cover is to be taught one massive, worldwide geography lesson. Indeed, there are over fifty settings described in the narrative. From Texas to China to the United Kingdom to Southeast Europe, having a map or globe around could be beneficial to maximize the literary experience.

Chapter 1:

Munich, Germany. *Dracula* begins with Munich being a stopover point for Johnathan Harker en route for his trip to Count Dracula's castle in Transylvania, leaving the city at 8:35 P.M. on May 3rd. Munich is the capital and the most populated city in the German state of Bavaria, located on the banks of River Isar north of the Bavarian Alps. Munich is the third-largest city in Germany, after Berlin and Hamburg, and the twelfth biggest city in the European Union, with a population of around 1.5 million. The Munich Metropolitan Region is home to 6 million people. At the time *Dracula* was being written, King Ludwig II was dethroned after a team of experts led by psychiatrist Bernhard von Gudden declared him insane. Ludwig was found dead the next day, his passing occurring under mysterious circumstances. Ludwig II's younger brother, Otto, became king but never reigned due to severe mental illness. Not surprisingly, mental illness and mysterious deaths are critical factors in Bram Stoker's masterpiece.

Vienna, Austria. The start of *Dracula* continues with Vienna, the capital of Austria, being mentioned as another stopover point for main character Jonathan Harker's trip to Castle Dracula in Transylvania. He arrives in Vienna early on May 2 at 7.46 (an hour late). Today, Vienna is the capital and largest city of Austria and one of its nine states. Vienna is also Austria's primary city, with a population of about 1.8 million (2.6 million within the metropolitan area, nearly one-third of Austria's population) and its cultural, economic, and political center. When Stoker was researching *Dracula*, Sigmund Freud, the Austrian neurologist and founder of psychoanalysis, had set up shop in Vienna, causing it to be known as 'The City of Dreams.' Freud's debatable, radical, and controversial studies were well known to Stoker, and Freudian themes appear throughout his novel (i.e., hunger, mortality, sexuality, dreams, mental illness, entrapment, paranoia, and hallucinations). These thematic threads are particularly sewn during conversations between Doctor Seward and Professor Van Helsing.

Budapest, Hungary. Spelled as Buda-Pesth at the beginning of the novel and named after the two towns on each side of the river, Budapest is yet another layover destination during Jonathan Harker's trip to Transylvania. He does not have much time to explore the city but is impressed by it as a transition from West to East while referring to it as a "wonderful place." After his encounter with Dracula, Harker is found raving and delusional and becomes a patient at the Hospital of St. Joseph and Ste. Mary in the town. Sister Agatha writes Mina on August 12, and Mina comes to rescue him, arriving in Budapest on August 24. Budapest is the capital and most populous city of

Hungary and one of the largest cities in the European Union. With an estimated 2016 population of 1,759,407 distributed over a land area of about 525 square kilometers (203 square miles), Budapest is also one of the most densely populated major cities in the European Union. In Bram Stoker's time, Count Szecheny, beginning in 1854, had a great bridge constructed over the Danube, linking Buda with Pest. It took almost twenty years to build and was considered an absolute marvel at the time. When the permanent structure was opened in 1873, Buda and Pest were officially merged with the third part, Óbuda (Ancient Buda), thus creating the new metropolis of Budapest. Jonathan Harker referred to this bridge in his journal:

"Jonathan Harker's Journal — (kept in shorthand.)

3 May. Bistritz. — Left Munich at 8:35 P.M., on 1st May, arriving at Vienna early next morning; should have arrived at 6:46, but train was an hour late. Buda-Pesth seems a wonderful place, from the glimpse which I got of it from the train and the little I could walk through the streets. I feared to go very far from the station, as we arrived late and would start as near the correct time as possible. The impression I had was that we were leaving the West and entering the East; the most Western of splendid bridges over the Danube, which is here of noble width and depth, took us among the traditions of Turkish rule".

Cluj-Napoca, Romania. In Stoker's narrative, the city is referred to by its German name, Klausenburg. This locale serves as another stop Jonathan Harker visits briefly during his trip to Transylvania. The text mentioned he arrives after nightfall on May 2 and stays at the Hotel Royale, where he dines on a chicken goulash dish known locally as paprika hendl. Cluj-Napoca is considered to be the unofficial capital of the historical province of Transylvania and is commonly known as Cluj, the third-most populous city in Romania after Bucharest, the national capital of the country, and Iaşi. Geographically, it is located in the Someşul Mic River valley and roughly equidistant from Bucharest (201 mi), Budapest (218 mi)) and Belgrade (200 mi). While Bram Stoker was researching *Dracula*, he read Emily Gerard's *The Land Beyond the Forest: Facts, Figures, and Fancies from Transylvania* (1888). Her familiarity with Transylvanian folklore came about due to her husband being stationed in the city from 1883 to 1885. Founded in 1932, the Cluj-Napoca International Airport became the common starting point for most Transylvanian tourism.

"Jonathan Harker's Journal — (kept in shorthand.)

3 May. Bistritz. [—] We left in pretty good time, and came after nightfall to Klausenburgh. Here I stopped for the night at the Hotel Royale. I had for dinner, or rather supper, a chicken done up some way with red pepper, which was very good but thirsty. (Mem. get recipe for Mina.) I asked the waiter, and he said it was called "paprika hendl" and that, as it was a national dish, I should be able to get it anywhere along the Carpathians."

Bistriţa, Romania. Main character Jonathan Harker enjoys a brief layover in Bistriţa on his way to Castle Dracula, having arrived on the "dark side of twilight" on May 2. At Count Dracula's suggestion, he lodges at the Golden Krone Hotel. No such hotel existed when the novel was written; however, a hotel of the same name has since been built. Harker leaves the town on May 5, St. George's Day. Bistriţa is the capital city of Bistriţa-Năsăud County, in northern Transylvania, Romania. The city is positioned on the Bistriţa River and has a population of approximately 70,000 inhabitants, dwelling in six villages: Ghinda, Sărata, Sigmir, Slătiniţa, Unirea, and Viişoara.

"Jonathan Harker's Journal — (kept in shorthand.)

3 May. Bistritz. [—] It was on the dark side of twilight when we got to Bistritz, which is a very interesting old place. Being practically on the frontier — for the Borgo Pass leads from it into Bukovina — it has had a very stormy existence, and it certainly shows marks of it. Fifty years ago a series of great fires took place, which made terrible havoc on five separate occasions. At the very beginning of the seventeenth century, it underwent a siege of three weeks and lost 13,000 people, the casualties of war proper being assisted by famine and disease. Count Dracula had directed me to go to the Golden Krone Hotel, which I found, to my great delight, to be thoroughly old-fashioned, for of course I wanted to see all I could of the ways of the country."

Bucovina, Romania. Today, Bukovina (Bucovina in Romanian) is a region in the Carpathian Mountains, split between Romania and Ukraine. Historically part of Moldavia, the land which became known as Bukovina was an administrative division of the Habsburg Monarchy, the Austrian Empire, and Austria-Hungary from 1774 to 1918. After World War I, Romania established control over Bukovina; and in 1940, the northern half of Bukovina was annexed by the Soviet Union, presently a part of Ukraine. Jonathan Harker treks from Bistritz to Bukovina via the notorious Borgo

Pass and arrives at Castle Dracula on May 5. The Borgo Pass, known in Romanian as the Tihuța Pass, is a high mountain passage in the Romanian Bârgău Mountains or Eastern Carpathian Mountains connecting Bistrița, Transylvania, with Vatra Dornei or Bukovina, Moldavia. It is interesting to point out that Stoker made this route famous when he termed it the 'Borgo Pass' (in Hungarian), where he made it the gateway to the realm of his iconic vampire Count. The ever-growing popularity of the novel and the corridor to the fictitious castle resulted in the Hotel 'Castel Dracula' being opened on the road in 1974, located at an elevation of 1,116 m (3,661 ft). Today the hotel has become a magnet to fans of the novel and tourism in general due to its medieval villa architectural style and breathtaking view.

"Jonathan Harker's Journal — (kept in shorthand.)

5 May. The Castle. [—] When it grew dark there seemed to be some excitement amongst the passengers, and they kept speaking to him, one after the other, as though urging him to further speed. He lashed the horses unmercifully with his long whip, and with wild cries of encouragement urged them on to further exertions. Then through the darkness I could see a sort of patch of grey light ahead of us, as though there were a cleft in the hills. The excitement of the passengers grew greater. The crazy coach rocked on its great leather springs and swayed like a boat tossed on a stormy sea. I had to hold on. The road grew more level, and we appeared to fly along. Then the mountains seemed to come nearer to us on each side and to frown down upon us. We were entering on the Borgo Pass. One by one several of the passengers offered me gifts, which they pressed upon me with an earnestness which would take no denial. These were certainly of an odd and varied kind, but each was given in simple good faith, with a kindly word, and a blessing, and that same strange mixture of fear-meaning movements which I had seen outside the hotel at Bistritz — the sign of the cross and the guard against the evil eye. Then, as we flew along, the driver leaned forward, and on each side the passengers, craning over the edge of the coach, peered eagerly into the darkness. It was evident that something very exciting was either happening or expected, but though I asked each passenger, no one would give me the slightest explanation. This state of excitement kept on for some little time. And at last we saw before us the Pass opening out on the eastern side. There were dark, rolling clouds overhead, and in the air the heavy, oppressive sense of thunder. It seemed as though the mountain range had separated two atmospheres, and that now we had got into the thunderous one."

Chapter 9:

Hamburg, Germany. After finally receiving news that her fiancé has been institution-alized with 'brain fever' for several weeks, Mina Murray sails from Kingston-Upon-Hull, England, to Hamburg, Germany, in order to reach Jonathan in Budapest, so she can bring him home again to England. She travels from Hamburg to Budapest by train.

Officially referred to as the Free and Hanseatic City of Hamburg, or Freie und Hansestadt Hamburg in German, the flourishing port city is the second-largest state in Germany, with a population of over 1.7 million people. Hamburg is on the south-ern point of the Jutland Peninsula, between Continental Europe to the south and Scandinavia to the north, with the North Sea to the west and the Baltic Sea to the north-east. It is on the River Elbe at its confluence with the Alster and Bille. The name Hamburg derived from the first permanent building on the site, a castle that Emperor Charlemagne ordered constructed in AD 808. It rose on rocky terrain in a marsh be-tween the River Alster and the River Elbe as a defense against Slavic incursion and acquired the name Hammaburg, burg meaning castle or fort. In 1842, just five years before Bram Stoker was born, about a quarter of the inner city was destroyed in the 'Great Fire.' The fire started on the night of 4 May and was not extinguished until 8 May. It destroyed three churches, the town hall, and many other buildings, killing 51 people and leaving an estimated 20,000 homeless. Reconstruction took more than 40 years. A major outbreak of cholera in 1892 was badly handled by the city government, which retained an unusual degree of independence for a German city. About 8,600 died in the largest German epidemic of the late 19th century and the last major cholera epidemic in a major city in the Western world. Castles, fires, and cholera all wove their way into Bram Stoker's life experiences. Indeed, part of *Dracula* was written in Cruden Bay, Scotland, in a hotel near Slains Castle; a fire broke out on February 18, 1898, at the Lyceum Theatre's storage facility, destroying countless theatrical effects (Stoker was employed as Business Manager of the theatre and actor Sir Henry Irving from 1878 — 1898). Bram's mother told Stoker many horror stories of the great cholera epidemic, fueling his imagination for the absurd.

"Letter from Mina Harker to Lucy Westenra.

"Buda-Pesth, 24 August.

"My dearest Lucy, —

"I know you will be anxious to hear all that has happened since we parted at the railway station at Whitby. Well, my dear, I got to Hull all right, and caught the boat to Hamburg, and then the train on here. I feel that I can hardly recall anything of the journey, except that I knew I was coming to Jonathan, and, that as I should have to do some nursing, I had better get all the sleep I could…I found my dear one, oh, so thin and pale and weak-looking. All the resolution has gone out of his dear eyes, and that quiet dignity which I told you was in his face has vanished. He is only a wreck of himself, and he does not remember anything that has happened to him for a long time past. At least, he wants me to believe so, and I shall never ask. He has had some terrible shock, and I fear it might tax his poor brain if he were to try to recall it. Sister Agatha, who is a good creature and a born nurse, tells me that he raved of dreadful things whilst he was off his head. [—]"

Amsterdam, Netherlands. Professor Abraham Van Helsing of Amsterdam, Dr. John Seward's mentor and friend, unearths the cause of Lucy and Mina's ailment and summons the intestinal fortitude to stamp out Dracula from the face of the earth. Amsterdam is the capital and most heavily populated metropolis of the Kingdom of the Netherlands. Its rank as the capital is mandated by the Constitution of the Netherlands; however, it is not the seat of the government, which is The Hague. Amsterdam has a population of 851,373 within the city proper, 1,351,587 in the urban area, and 2,410,960 in the Amsterdam metropolitan area. The city is located in the province of North Holland in the west of the country. The metropolitan area comprises much of the northern part of the Randstad, one of the larger conurbations in Europe, with a population of approximately 7 million. During the end of the 19th century, and in Stoker's day, these years were referred to as Amsterdam's second Golden Age: new museums, a railway station, and the Concertgebouw were built; at the same time, the Industrial Revolution reached the city. The Amsterdam–Rhine Canal was dug to give Amsterdam a direct connection to the Rhine, and the North Sea Canal was dug to provide the port with a shorter link to the North Sea. Both projects dramatically improved commerce with the rest of Europe and the world. There is little information to fully support why the author decided to give his famous vampire killer a Dutch origin, but there has been speculation over the years. Some Stoker scholars believe the Irishman modeled Van Helsing after himself, but since the first name 'Bram' (short for Abraham) is of Dutch ancestry, Stoker made his meta-physician from the Netherlands. Other *Dracula* experts have speculated Amsterdam was chosen because Van Helsing had an exotic imagination and a worldly open-minded aptitude for knowledge. And then, there is a theory that Stoker was influenced by a Dutch doctor named A. Van Renterghem.

"Letter from Dr. Seward to Arthur Holmwood

"2 September.

"My dear old fellow, —

[—] I am in doubt, and so have done the best thing I know of; I have written to my old friend and master, Professor Van Helsing, of Amsterdam, who knows as much about obscure diseases as anyone in the world. I have asked him to come over, and as you told me that all things were to be at your charge, I have mentioned to him who you are and your relations to Miss Westenra. [—]"

Chapter 10:

Haarlem, Netherlands. Professor Abraham Van Helsing orders garlic to be sent to him in London from his friend Vanderpool, who lives in Haarlem and raises herbs in his greenhouses year-round. In addition to being a city, Haarlem is a municipality in the Netherlands and the capital of the province of North Holland, positioned at the northern edge of the Randstad, one of the greatest occupied municipalities in Europe. In 2017, Haarlem, which is only a 15-minute train ride from Amsterdam, had a population of 155,758. Many of its residents commute to the country's capital for work. Haarlem became the provincial capital of Noord-Holland province in the early 19th century. In Stoker's lifetime, the city's economy slowly started to improve: new factories were opened, and many large industrial companies were founded in Haarlem, such as cotton mills, train and tram operations, and waterworks.

"Dr. Seward's Diary.

11 September. [—] Come with me, friend John, and you shall help me deck the room with my garlic, which is all the way from Haarlem, where my friend Vanderpool raise herb in his glasshouses all the year. I had to telegraph yesterday, or they would not have been here."

Chapter 18:

Sibiu, Romania (also known as Hermannstadt). Dracula studies his wicked craft at the fabled school of the Scholomance, located "amongst the mountains over Lake Hermannstadt" near Sibiu (known in the novel by its German name Hermannstadt). A city in Transylvania, Romania, with a population of 147,245, Sibiu is located some 134 miles northwest of Bucharest and straddles the Cibin River, a tributary of the river Olt. Presently known as the capital of Sibiu County, between 1692 and 1791 and 1849–1865, Sibiu was the capital of the Principality of Transylvania. Until 1920 Sibiu belonged to the Kingdom of Hungary. The Scholomance, the mythical, legendary school of black magic run by Satan, was supposedly located near an unnamed lake in the mountains south of the city of Hermannstadt (or Nagyszeben in Hungarian, or Sibiu in Romanian) in Transylvania. Stoker used Emily Gerard's research on the subject which read: "As I am on the subject of thunderstorms, I may as well here mention the Scholomance, or school supposed to exist somewhere in the heart of the mountains, and where all the secrets of nature, the language of animals, and all imaginable magic spells and charms are taught by the devil in person. Only ten scholars are admitted at a time, and when the course of learning has expired and nine of them are released to return to their homes, the tenth scholar is detained by the devil as payment, and mounted upon a zmeju (dragon) he becomes henceforward the devil's aide-de-camp, and assists him in 'making the weather,' that is, in preparing thunderbolts. [—] a small lake, immeasurably deep, and lying high up in the mountains to the south of Hermannstadt, is supposed to be the cauldron where is brewed the thunder, under whose water the dragon lies sleeping in fair weather. Roumanian peasants anxiously warn the traveller to beware of throwing a stone into this lake, lest it should wake the dragon and provoke a thunderstorm."

Gerard also suggested that the inhabitants of Hermannstadt are reputed to be the descendants of those children who followed the Pied Piper as he took his revenge against the pinchpenny burghers of Hamelin.

It is interesting to point out that Gerard did not mention a 'Lake Hermannstadt' but rather 'a small lake.' From what is known, there never was a Lake Hermannstadt. It is believed that Stoker misread this research material, thus referring to the small lake using the city name. The part of the Carpathians near Hermannstadt holds two bodies of water: Păltiniș Lake and Bâlea Lake — both hosting popular resorts today for the people of the surrounding area.

"Mina Harker's Journal.

30 September. [—] If it be so, then was he no common man; for in that time, and for centuries after, he was spoken of as the cleverest and the most cunning, as well as the bravest of the sons of the 'land beyond the forest.' That mighty brain and that iron resolution went with him to his grave and are even now

arrayed against us. The Draculas were, says Arminus, a great and noble race, though now and again were scions who were held by their coevals to have had dealings with the Evil One. They learned his secrets in the Scholomance, amongst the mountains over Lake Hermannstadt, where the devil claims the tenth scholar as his due. In the records are such words as 'stregoica' — witch, 'ordog,' and 'pokol' — Satan and hell; and in one manuscript this very Dracula is spoken of as 'wampyr,' which we all understand too well." (Professor Abraham Van Helsing speaking)

Chapter 24:

The Black Sea. The Count travels by boat on the Black Sea, a body of water and marginal sea of the Atlantic Ocean between Eastern Europe and Western Asia, bounded by Abkhazia, Bulgaria, Georgia, Romania, Russia, Turkey, and Ukraine. It is supplied by a number of major rivers, such as the Danube, Dnieper, Rioni, Southern Bug, and the Dniester. The Black Sea has an area of 436,400 km (168,500 sq mi) (not including the Sea of Azov), a maximum depth of 2,212 m (7,257 ft), and a volume of 547,000 km (131,000 cubic mi). It is constrained by the Pontic Mountains to the south and the Caucasus Mountains to the east and features a wide shelf to the northwest. The longest east-west extent is about 1,175 km (730 mi). It is known that Bram Stoker was very interested in maps, traveled frequently, and paid close attention to the extensive research that went into his most celebrated work. At the time the novel was written — and almost two decades before the first commercial plane flight — one could not have avoided the Black Sea if traveling the most direct path to Transylvania. Finally, it probably goes without saying that the name of the body of water is also a direct reflection of the condition of the notorious Count's immortal soul.

"Mina Harker's Journal.

5 October 5 p.m. [—] Dr. Van Helsing described what steps were taken during the day to discover on what boat and whither bound Count Dracula made his escape: —

"As I know that he wanted to get back to Transylvania, I felt sure that he must go by the Danube mouth; or by somewhere in the Black Sea, since by that way he come. It was a dreary blank that was before us. Omne ignotum pro magnifico; and so with heavy hearts we start to find what ships leave for the Black Sea last night. He was in a sailing ship, since Madam Mina tell of sails being set. These not so important as to go in your list of the shipping in the Times, as so we go, by suggestion of Lord Godalming, to your Lloyd's where are note of all ships that sail, however so small. There we find that only on Black-Sea-bound ship go out with the tide."

Varna, Bulgaria. Count Dracula is shipped from Varna to Whitby on The Demeter, and it appears that he will return to Varna from London's Doolittle Wharf on The Czarina Catherine, sailing on October 4.

Chapter 25:

Orient Express, Gare de l'Est, Paris. Van Helsing's journey to obliterate Dracula arrives in Paris on the night of October 12, seemingly crossing over the English Channel from Dover to Calais. While the intrepid pursuers are in Paris, they board the Orient Express, which runs from Paris' Gare de l'Est (Eastern Station) to Varna. Paris is the capital and most populous city of France. During Stoker's life, Paris was — and remains — the major rail hub. Paris was the setting for French-born Victor Hugo's famous gothic romance novel *The Hunchback of Notre Dame* (1831). Calais is a town and major ferry port in northern France which overlooks the Strait of Dover, the narrowest point in the English Channel, which is only 34 km (21 mi) wide and is the closest French town to England. The white cliffs of Dover can easily be seen on a clear day from Calais. During Stoker's lifetime, Calais was a major port for ferries between France and England, as the Channel Tunnel was not yet built, linking Coquelles to Folkestone by rail. The Orient Express was a long-distance passenger train service created in 1883 and was considered a high-class vehicle of lavishness and security at a time when traveling was deemed to be rugged and precarious. The original route, which first ran on October 4, 1883, was from Paris, Gare de l'Est, to Giurgiu in Romania via Munich and Vienna. At Giurgiu, passengers were ferried across the Danube to Ruse, Bulgaria, to pick up another train to Varna. Again, Stoker did his homework very well when maneuvering characters in his novel from one point to another and connecting all the dots along the way. On December 14, 2009, the Orient Express ceased to operate due to the increasing competition from high-speed trains and cut-rate airlines. However, by this time, the name has been ever linked to mystery, murder, suspense, and intrigue through the means of numerous literary, film, and television references, including the famous *Murder on the Orient Express* (1934) by Agatha Christie.

"Jonathan Harker's Journal.

15 October. Varna. — We left Charing Cross on the morning of the 12th, got to Paris the same night, and took the places secured for us in the Orient Express."

The Dardanelles. The Dardanelles is a narrow strait that connects the Aegean Sea to the Sea of Marmara. The strategized protagonists request timely notice as soon as Dracula's ship passes the Dardanelles. It is an estimated 24 hours sail from the Dardanelles to Varna, where they secretly await Dracula. The Dardanelles is distinctive in several respects, for the very restricted and snaky shape of the strait is more similar to that of a river, considering it one of the most dangerous, heaving, grim, and potentially hazardous waterways in the world. Indeed, the lethal undercurrents bent by the tidal action in the Black Sea and the Sea of Marmara are such that ships under sail must await at anchorage for the precise conditions afore entering the Dardanelles. Need we assume Count Dracula will go anywhere without some degree of threat or peril?

"Telegram, October 24th.
Rufus Smith, Lloyd's, London, To Lord Godalming,
Care Of H.B.M.10 Vice-Consul, Varna.

"Czarina Catherine reported this morning from Dardanelles."

"Dr. Seward's Diary.

25 October. [—] It is only about 24 hours' sail from the Dardanelles to here, at the rate the Czarina Catherine has come from London. She should therefore arrive sometime in the morning; but as she cannot possibly get in before then, we are all about to retire early. We shall get up at one o'clock, so as to be ready."

Galați, Romania. While using his mind control on a transitioning Mina Harker, Count Dracula decides to thwart his pursuers by having his ship arrive in Galatz, Romania (Galați in Romanian) on October 28 instead of in Varna. Upon receiving word of this unexpected obstruction, the Van Helsing expedition hurriedly travels to Galați by train. Dracula's coffin is removed from the ship by Immanuel Hildesheim, who, in turn, delivers it to Petrof Skinsky, "who dealt with the Slovaks down the river." Galați, the capital City of Galați County, is a port town on the banks of the Danube River in the historical region of Moldavia, eastern Romania. Consisting of around 249,432 residents, it was the 8th most populous Romanian city in 2011, and the economic center consisted of a naval shipyard and steel plant. During Stoker's lifetime, the city had a stormy existence with many wars and periods of unrest. Galați was declared a free port in 1837 and developed based on trade, especially grain exports; however, this was revoked in 1882. The Danube, which was once a long-standing frontier of the Roman Empire, today flows through 10 countries, more than any other river in the world.

"28 October. — Telegram, Rufus Smith, Lloyd's, London, to Lord Godalming, care of H.B.M.10 Vice-Consul, Varna.

"Czarina Catherine reported entering Galatz at one o'clock today."

Chapter 26:

The Bosporus Channel. Dracula's getaway ship, the Czarina Catherine, transports him in his 'earth box' traveling through the Dardanelles, the Sea of Marmora, the Bosporus, and across the Black Sea to Galati, Romania. The Bosporus is a slender, natural strait and a major international waterway located in northwestern Turkey, which forms part of the continental boundary between Europe and Asia, separating Asian Turkey from European Turkey. Known as the world's narrowest strait used for international navigation, the Bosporus connects the Black Sea with the Sea of Marmara and, by extension, via the Dardanelles, the Aegean, and Mediterranean Seas. Most of the shores of the strait are heavily settled, straddled by the city of Istanbul's metropolitan population of 17 million inhabitants extending inland from both coasts. Together with the Dardanelles, the Bosporus forms the Turkish Straits.

"Jonathan Harker's Journal.

30 October. [—] "When we got past the Bosphorus the men began to grumble; some o' them, the Roumanians, came and asked me to heave overboard a big box which had been put on board by a queer lookin' old man just before we had started frae London. I had seen them speer at the felow, and put out their two fingers when they saw him, to guard against the evil eye." (The Scottish Captain Donelson speaking).

Verești, Romania. Mina Harker and Van Helsing leave Galați on the night of October 30 at 11:40 and take a train to Verești on the Suceava River, where they get a carriage to drive to the Borgo Pass. They arrive at Verești at noon the next day. Verești is a community located in Suceava County, Romania, composed of four villages: Bur-suceni, Corocăieşti, Hancea and Vereşti. The Suceava is a river located in the north-east of Romania (Suceava County) and western Ukraine (Chernivtsi Oblast). It is a right tributary of the river Siret. During Stoker's time, Vereşti was known for its rail-way system, medieval fortifications, markets, and lumber. When *Dracula* was written, it was the ideal place to cross the country between the river and the Carpathians. A carriage ride from Vereşti to the Borgo Pass would have meant traveling over around ninety miles of rough terrain.

"Mina Harker's Journal. — continued

Later. [—] Van Helsing and I are to leave by the 11:40 train to-night for Vereşti, where we are to get a carriage to drive to the Borgo Pass"

The Siret River. During the latter part of the Van Helsing expedition to destroy Count Dracula, Jonathan Harker and Lord Godalming sail up the Siret River — known in the novel as the Sereth — from Galaţi in pursuit of catching up with Dracula's boat. The Siret is a river that rises from the Carpathians in the Northern Bukovina region of Ukraine and flows southward into Romania before it joins the Danube.

"Jonathan Harker's Journal.

October 30. Night. [—] Regarding our plans, we finally decided that Mina's guess was correct, and that if any waterway was chosen for the Count's escape back to his Castle, the Sereth and then the Bistritza at its junction would be the one. We took it, that somewhere about the 47th degree, north latitude, would be the place chosen for crossing the country between the river and the Carpa-thians."

The Bistriţa River. The Siret River connects to the Bistritza (Bistriţa in Romanian) River near Bacău, Romania. Jonathan Harker and Lord Goldaming continue up the Bistritza at the junction of the two rivers on November 1. Sometimes referred to as Bistriţa Moldoveană, the Bistritza is a river in the Romanian regions of Maramureş, Bukovina, and Moldavia — the latter being most of its length. It is a right tributary of the river Siret, where it enters near Bacău. The Bistritza's source is in the Rodna Mountains, at the foot of the Gârgalău peak. It flows through the counties Bistriţa-Năsăud, Suceava, Neamţ and Bacău.

"Jonathan Harker's Journal.

1 November, evening. — October 30. Night. [—] We have now passed into the Bistritza; and if we are wrong in our surmise our chance is gone. We have overhauled every boat, big and little. Early this morning, one crew took us for a Government boat, and treated us accordingly. We saw in this a way of smoothing matters, so at Fundu, where the Bistritza runs into the Sereth, we got a Roumanian flag which we now fly conspicuously."

The Borgo Pass. The Borgo Pass is en route from Bistrița to Bukovina. Van Helsing and Mina arrive at Borgo Pass just after sunrise on the morning of November 3.

"Memorandum By Abraham Van Helsing.

4 November. [—] We got to the Borgo Pass just after sunrise yesterday morning."

Section Two: The Harry Potter Series

Like *Dracula*, there are over fifty settings described in the series — including eight dwellings, seven schools, seventeen businesses in Diagon Alley, eleven businesses in Hogsmeade, and six government locations. Though the majority of J.K. Rowling's settings are fantasy, as mentioned in a previous chapter, many were inspired by real places. Real or unreal; nevertheless, Rowling's storytelling was so wonderfully crafted that every single location is visited personally by every reader, becoming favorite virtual vacation spots.

As with *Dracula*, because Chapter Seven was dedicated exclusively to the United Kingdom, the remainder of this chapter will focus on further vital locales external to the British Union. For structural reasons and consistency sake, the remaining spots of interest shall be listed in sequential order as presented in the Harry Potter series.

Book 1: The Philosopher's Stone

Brazil. In Chapter 2, Harry and the Dursleys visit the London Zoo, where Harry befriends a boa constrictor. Brazil, formally referred to as the Federative Republic of Brazil, is the prevalent country in South America and the Latin American region. Its capital city is Brasília, and according to J.K. Rowling's Pottermore website, Brazil was home to a wizarding community equivalent to that of the United Kingdom. It further suggested that [...] "the Amazon rainforest, along with the municipalities of Caxambu, Manaus, and Teresina, may have significant magical populations, as the Daily Prophet saw fit to include forecasts for them in its international weather section." Also according to the site, the Brazilian Ministry of Magic is the main governing body in the magical community of Brazil. At the beginning of the first novel, Harry sees a sign next to the snake's glass that specifies 'Boa Constrictor, Brazil.' The empathetic Harry proceeds to carry on a conversation with the captive reptile, learning that the snake was bred in the zoo, and shakes its head when Harry asks, "Was it nice there?" When Cousin Dudley's friend, Piers, notices that Harry and the snake are conversing, Harry frees the snake:

> "Piers and Dudley were leaning right up close to the glass, then next, they had leapt back with howls of horror.
>
> Harry sat up and gasped: the glass front of the boa constrictor's tank had vanished. The great snake was uncoiling itself rapidly, slithering out onto the floor. People throughout the reptile house screamed and started running for the exits.
>
> As the snake slid swiftly past him, Harry could have sworn in a low, hissing voice said, "Brazil, here I come…. Thanksss, amigo."

The Black Forest, Germany. The Black Forest is a dense mountainous, evergreen, wooded region in southwest Germany, often associated with the stories by The Brothers Grimm. The largest village is Freiburg, famous for its gothic buildings and picturesque vineyards. In the Harry Potter series, the Black Forest is home to several magical creatures, including bowtruckles, vampires, and Erklings. According to the book *Quidditch Through the Ages*, one of the oldest broomstick manufacturers, Ellerby and Spudmore, is based out of the Black Forest. In Chapter 5, Hagrid explains to Harry why Professor Quirrell trembles and stammers upon meeting him:

> "Is he always that nervous?"
>
> "Oh, yeah. Poor bloke. Brilliant mind. He was fine while he was studyin' outta books but then he took a year off ter get some first-hand experience…They say he met vampires in the Black Forest, and there was a nasty bit o' trouble with a hag — never been the same since. Scared of the students, scared of his own subject —"

The Zombie Trail, North America. In the first film, a page from the *Daily Prophet* is posted in Diagon Alley as Harry and Hagrid are shopping for school supplies. It advertises Terror Tours, located at 59 Diagon Alley. One of the specified tours is for a Zombie Trail. According to Pottermore, the Zombie Trail is a path where hikers can encounter the living dead up close, covering the Southeast part of the United States.

Romania. As in *Dracula*, Romania is brought up in the Harry Potter series numerous times. In Chapter 6, Ron tells Harry about his family. After leaving school, Charlie Weasley relocates to Romania to study dragons at the Romanian Dragon Sanctuary.

"Harry was wondering what a wizard did once he'd finished school.

"Charlie's in Romania studying dragons [...]"

In Chapter 8, several students begin to question the garlic smell in Quirinus Quirrell's classroom while speculating he is attempting to ward off a vampire he met in Romania and feared would come and find him.

The class everyone had really been looking forward to was Defense Against the Dark Arts, but Quirrell's lessons turned out to be a bit of a joke. His classroom smelled strongly of garlic, which everyone said was to ward off a vampire he'd met in Romania and was afraid would be coming back to get him one of these days.

In Chapter 12, Arthur and Molly Weasley visit Charlie in Romania during Christmas break. Not much was stated about their trip, but one cannot help but wonder if the sites of the historical and fictional Dracula were on their sightseeing agenda.

Africa. Africa is a continent in the eastern hemisphere, comprising wizarding nations Benin, Burkina Faso, Chad, Congo, Egypt, Ethiopia, Ivory Coast, Mauritius, Nigeria, Tanzania, Togo, Uganda, and Zaire. In Chapter 6, Ron tells Harry about his family. After graduating from Hogwarts, Bill goes to work for Gringotts Wizarding Bank as a Curse Breaker in Egypt.

"[...] Bill's in Africa doing something for Gringotts," said Ron.

In Chapter 11, the Sahara Desert is referenced when Harry learns about Quidditch:

"Harry learned that there were seven hundred ways of committing a Quidditch foul and that all of them had happened during a World Cup match in 1473; that Seekers were usually the smallest and fastest players, and that most serious Quidditch accidents seemed to happen to them; that although people rarely died playing Quidditch, referees had been known to vanish and turn up months later in the Sahara Desert."

Africa was also home to the Erumpent, a large magical beast that carries a long combustible horn by its nostrils, similar to a rhinoceros. The horn contains a deadly fluid that causes whatever it is injected into to explode. This was highly prized as potion ingredients but also listed as a Class-B Tradeable Material. Xenophilius Lovegood, Luna's father, displays an Erumpent horn in his living room, under the false belief that it was a Crumple-Horned Snorkack. Without heading Hermione's warning, the Lovegood house catches fire when the Death Eaters attack and a spell hits the horn, causing a detonation.

Book 2: The Chamber of Secrets

Sardinia, Italy. Sardinia is a sizable island off the west coast of Italy in the Mediterranean Sea. A sub-committee of sorcerers from this island did something of significance in September of 1289. In Chapter 9, Professor Binns attempts to give more detail on the exact involvement during a lecture on the International Warlock Convention of 1289 to second-year History of Magic students but is interrupted by determined Hermione Granger, who requests an alternate lecture on the Chamber of Secrets.

"Professor Binns blinked.

"My subject is History of Magic," he said in his dry, wheezy voice. "I deal with facts, Miss Granger, not myths and legends." He cleared his throat with a small noise like chalk snapping and continued, "In September of that year, a sub-committee of Sardinian sorcerers —"

He stuttered to a halt. Hermione's hand was waving in the air again.

"Miss Grant?"

"Please, sir, don't legends always have a basis in fact?"

Transylvania, Romania. Transylvania is brought up several times in the Harry Potter series, and as primarily referenced in *Dracula*, J.K. Rowling usually connects this region to some kind of supernatural reference. For example, in Chapter 10, Harry is involuntarily picked to portray a Transylvanian peasant in Professor Lockhart's Defense Against the Dark Arts class.

"Since the disastrous episode of the pixies, Professor Lockhart had not brought live creatures to class. Instead, he read passages from his books to them, and sometimes reenacted some of the more dramatic bits. He usually picked Harry to help him with these reconstructions; so far, Harry had been forced to play a simple Transylvanian villager whom Lockhart had cured of a Babbling Curse, a yeti with a head cold, and a vampire who had been unable to eat anything except lettuce since Lockhart had dealt with him."

Ron Weasley also assumes the identity of Dragomir Despard, a Dark Lord sympathizer from Transylvania, when he, Harry, Hermione, and Griphook sneak into Gringotts in disguise to break into Bellatrix Lestrange's vault. They aim to steal Helga Hufflepuff's small, golden cup, which Lord Voldemort turns into a Horcrux.

The North Sea. Azkaban, a wizarding prison where violators of the British wizarding world laws are sent, is located in the middle of the North Sea. In Chapter 12, Harry and Ron are disguised as Malfoy's cronies Grabbe and Goyle. In the Slytherin common room, they surreptitiously pull information out of Draco about the Chamber of Secrets. The next chapter of this book features Azkaban in great detail.

"Ron was clenching Crabbes's gigantic fists. Feeling that it would be a bit of a giveaway if Ron punched Malfoy, Harry shot him a warning look and said, "D'you know if the person who opened the Chamber last time was caught?"

"Oh, yeah…whoever it was was expelled," said Malfoy.

"They're probably still in Azkaban."

"Azkaban?" said Harry, puzzled.

"Azkaban — the wizard prison, Goyle," said Malfoy, looking at him in disbelief. "Honestly, if you were any slower, you'd be going backward."

In Chapter 14, Hagrid is falsely accused of opening the Chamber of Secrets; and Cornelius Fudge, Minister of Magic, orders the half-giant to be taken to Azkaban until the real culprit behind the Hogwarts attacks is caught in Chapter 18.

Armenia, Eurasia. Armenia is an independent state in the South Caucasus region of Eurasia, located in West Asia on the Armenian Highlands. It is bordered by Turkey to the west, Georgia to the north, the de facto independent Nagorno-Karabakh Republic and Azerbaijan to the east, and Iran and Azerbaijan's exclave of Nakhichevan to the south. In Chapter 16, Professor Lockhart broaches the subject of Armenia with Harry and Ron as he is packing up his belongings to flee the school.

"You mean you're running away?" said Harry disbelievingly. "After all that stuff you did in your books –"

"Books can be misleading," said Lockhart delicately.

"You wrote them!" Harry shouted.

"My dear boy," said Lockhart, straightening up and frowning at Harry. "Do use your common sense. My books wouldn't have sold half as well if people

didn't think I'd done all those things. No one wants to read about some ugly
old Armenian warlock, even if he did save a village from werewolves. He'd look
dreadful on the front cover. No dress sense at all."

Bandon, Thailand. Brandon, also called Surat Thani, is the capital of the Surat Thani
Province in Thailand. A Banshee, who threatens Bandon in the mid-1990s, is defeated
by a courageous witch. This witch recounts her adventure to Gilderoy Lockhart, who
casts a memory charm on her, thus wiping away all details of her heroic event. Afterward, he publishes the tale as his own accomplishment in his book, *Break with a Banshee.* Also in Chapter 16, Professor Lockhart further comments to Harry and Ron the
truth about the Banshee encounter while packing up his office belongings:

> "[…] And the witch who banished the Bandon Banshee had a hairy chin. I
> mean, come on —"

The Forests of Albania. Albania, located on Southeastern Europe's Balkan Peninsula, is
a small country with Adriatic and Ionian coastlines and an interior crossed by the Albanian Alps. Voldemort flees the country and takes refuge in Albania after his spell
backfires on the infant Harry. The Dark Lord returns to Albania when his 'attachment'
to Professor Quirrell ends at the conclusion of Book 1. In Chapter 18, Dumbledore
ponders over He-Who-Must-Not-Be-Named's travels:

> "What interests me most," said Dumbledore gently, "is how Lord Voldemort
> managed to enchant Ginny when my sources tell me he is currently in hiding
> in the forests of Albania."

The Albanian forest is also where Helena Ravenclaw (a.k.a. The Grey Lady and
ghost of Ravenclaw house) hides her mother's stolen diadem. Voldemort finds the
object concealed in a hollow tree and turns it into a Horcrux.

Book 3: Prisoner of Azkaban

Giza, Egypt. Situated near Cairo, Giza is the site of the iconic pyramids and Great
Sphinx, dating to the 26th century BC. In the summer of 1993, the entire Weasley
family embarks on a trip to Egypt after Arthur Weasley wins *The Daily Prophet* Grand
Prize Galleon Draw. In Chapter 1, Harry receives an Owl Post from his best mate
Ron, including a page from the newspaper. It announces his father's winnings and
includes a moving wizarding photograph of all nine Weasleys standing in front of a
'large pyramid' actually known as the Great Pyramid of Giza.

"A delighted Mr. Weasley told the *Daily Prophet*. "We will be spending the gold on a summer holiday in Egypt, where our eldest son, Bill, works as a curse breaker for Gringotts Wizarding Bank.""

Dijon, France. France is a country in western Europe, although it holds territories in other parts of the world. France is bordered by Belgium, Luxembourg, Germany, Switzerland, Italy, Monaco, Andorra, and Spain. In the summer of 1993, Hermione Granger and her parents go on holiday in France, during which they visit the city of Dijon. Dijon is the capital city of the historical Burgundy region in eastern France, one of the country's principal wine-producing areas. It's known for its vineyard tours, autumn gastronomic fair, and building styles ranging from Gothic to art deco. In Chapter 1, Harry receives a letter from Hermione which mentions her vacation and newfound interest in French witchcraft:

"I'm on holiday in France at the moment [...]. There's some interesting local history of witchcraft here, too. I've rewritten my whole History of Magic essay to include some of the things I've found out."

Mongolia. Mongolia is an East Asia country that borders Russia and China. According to Pottermore, Asian countries never embraced Quidditch as European nations because they preferred using flying carpets over broomsticks. In Chapter 9, Severus Snape substitutes for Remus Lupin's Defense Against the Dark Arts class while Lupin is recovering from werewolf sickness. As part of Professor Snape's examination of Lupin's teaching, Snape claims that Kappas are primarily found in Mongolia. The Kappa, a creepy-looking water dweller demon that feeds on human blood, is known for strangling unwitting waders that invade their shallow ponds. The book *Fantastic Beasts and Where to Find Them* states that Kappas are from Japan, a fact Harry Potter makes a note of in his copy of the book.

"[...] Snape prowled up and down the rows of desks, examining the work they had been doing with Professor Lupin.

"Very poorly explained...That is incorrect, the kappa is more commonly found in Mongolia...Professor Lupin gave this eight out of ten? I wouldn't have given it three..."

Book 4: The Goblet of Fire

Unidentified Tropical Location. After Harry Potter and Hermione Granger rescue Sirius Black, he hides somewhere tropical. In Chapter 2, Harry has already received two letters from his godfather delivered by large, tropical birds that barely fit through his window. One could surmise that Black is hiding in a tropical rainforest near the United Kingdom. The most logical answer would be the Amazon due to its great size and wild isolation. The Gambia is also a possibility, but due to its intense tourism and resort-like quality, the likelihood of being caught would be much greater than the seclusion of the Amazon.

> "Harry had received two letters from Sirius since he had been back at Privet Drive. Both had been delivered, not by owls (as was usual with wizards), but by large, brightly colored tropical birds. [...] he hoped that, wherever Sirius was (Sirius never said, in case the letters were intercepted), he was enjoying himself. Somehow, Harry found it hard to imagine dementors surviving for long in bright sunlight; perhaps that was why Sirius had gone south."

Ireland vs. Bulgaria. Ireland is an island in the northern Atlantic Ocean located off the western coast of Great Britain. The majority of the isle is occupied by the Republic of Ireland — also known simply as Ireland — a sovereign nation, while the northeast corner is home to Northern Ireland, which is part of the United Kingdom. The capital city of the Republic of Ireland is Dublin, and the de facto capital of Northern Ireland is the city of Belfast

In 1994, representing Ireland in the Quidditch World Cup is the internationally known Irish National Quidditch team.

Bulgaria is a country in southeastern Europe bordering five countries: Romania, Serbia, Macedonia, Greece, and Turkey. The Black Sea defines the extent of the country to the east. Its capital city is Sofia. The Bulgarian National Quidditch team plays for this nation.

In 1994, the Irish National Quidditch team wins the 422nd Quidditch World Cup, defeating the Bulgarian National Quidditch team in the final match. In Chapter 3, Harry receives a hastily scribbled note from his best friend Ron, which reads:

> "Harry — DAD GOT TICKETS — Ireland versus Bulgaria. Monday night. Mum's writing to the Muggles to ask you to stay. They might already have the letter. I don't know how fast Muggle post is. Thought I'd send this with Pig anyway."

Australia. The Commonwealth of Australia is a country encompassing the mainland of the Australian continent, the isle of Tasmania, and several smaller islands. It is the biggest country in Oceania and the earth's sixth-largest country by overall area. The adjacent countries are Papua New Guinea, Indonesia, and East Timor to the north; the Solomon Islands and Vanuatu to the northeast; and New Zealand to the southeast.

Australia's capital is Canberra, and its largest urban area is Sydney. In Chapter 5, Ludo Bagman pokes fun at the 'hopeless' disappearance of Bertha Jorkins, who supposedly goes missing during her holiday to Albania:

"Mr. Crouch was quite fond of her — but Bagman just keeps laughing and saying she probably misread the map and ended up in Australia instead of Albania."

Australia is also where Hermione sends her parents for protection from Lord Voldemort after modifying their memories.

Uganda and Luxembourg. Uganda, a landlocked nation located in East Africa, has its own National Quidditch team, which beats Wales at the 1994 Quidditch World Cup. Luxembourg, a small European country surrounded by Belgium, France, and Germany, also competes and beats the Scottish National Quidditch team, as explained by Charlie Weasley in Chapter 5:

"[...] And Wales lost to Uganda, and Scotland was slaughtered by Luxembourg."

Mentioned in *The Goblet of Fire* only, Uagadou is the Ugandan wizarding school located atop the Mountains of the Moon in western Uganda. It accepts students from all over Africa and is the largest of the eleven wizarding schools. According to Pottermore, visitors speak of a stunning edifice carved out of the mountainside and shrouded in mist; so that it sometimes appears simply to float in mid-air. Unlike all other wizarding schools, Uagadou pupils do not utilize wands; they instead learn spells through hand gestures. They also specialize in self-transfiguration, leaving countless international wizards threatened by the utter talent that numerous Uagadou students showcase. Uagadou is also the only wizard school to send their invitations through dream messengers.

Norway. Norway — officially known as the Kingdom of Norway — is a self-governing state and unitary dominion whose territory comprises the western portion of the Scandinavian Peninsula plus the remote island of Jan Mayen and the archipelago of Svalbard. At some point after starting his work with the Department of International Magical Co-operation in 1994, Percy Weasley receives some dragon dung in his in-tray, which he excuses during a dinner at The Burrow in Chapter 5 as being merely a 'sample of fertilizer from Norway' and 'nothing personal.'

"It was," Fred whispered to Harry as they got up from the table. "We sent it."

Salem, Massachusetts, U.S.A. The Salem Witches' Institute is a wizarding organization for women, presumably based in Salem, Massachusetts. J.K. Rowling has stated that the Salem Witches' Institute is a play on the Women's Institutes of the United Kingdom, claiming, "These organizations seek to provide women with educational opportunities and to campaign on issues of importance to women and their communities." In Chapter 7, Harry, Ron, and Hermione spot this group of American witches as they find their way across the campsite to fetch some water:

> "Three African wizards sat in serious conversation, all of them wearing long white robes and roasting what looked like a rabbit on a bright purple fire, while a group of middle-aged American witches sat gossiping happily beneath a spangled banner stretched between their tents that read: THE SALEM WITCHES' INSTITUTE."

Brazil. Castelobruxo, the Brazilian wizarding school for the South American continent, is located deep within the Amazon rainforest in northern Brazil. It accepts students from all over South America and is described as a fabulous building — an imposing square edifice of golden rock, often compared to a temple. Both buildings and grounds are protected by the Caipora. In Chapter 7, Ron describes how his brother Bill is pen pals with a student at Castelobruxo, but their relationship deteriorates after Bill is given a cursed hat.

> "Bill had a penfriend at a school in Brazil...this was years and years ago...and he wanted to go on an exchange trip, but Mum and Dad couldn't afford it. His penfriend got all offended when he said he wasn't going and sent him a cursed hat. It made his ears shrivel up."

Pyrenees, France. The Beauxbatons Academy of Magic (French: Académie de Magie Beauxbâtons) is a magical school first introduced by Hermione Granger in Chapter 9.

> "Oh..." The girl who had spoken turned her back on him, and as they walked on, they distinctly heard her say, "'Ogwarts."

> "Beauxbatons," muttered Hermione.

> "Sorry?" said Harry.

> "They must go to Beauxbatons," said Hermione. "You know... Beauxbatons Academy of Magic...I read about it in An Appraisal of Magical Education in Europe."

The Pyrenees is a mountain range in southwest Europe that forms a natural border between France and Spain. According to Pottermore, the glittering palace of Beauxbatons is believed to be located somewhere in the Pyrenees, and its grounds were magically formed from the mountainous landscape. The phrase beaux bâtons means 'beautiful wands' in French. Beauxbatons has a history that goes back at least 700 years when it first began participating in the Triwizard Tournament. In *The Goblet of Fire*, the participants and their half-giant headmistress arrive in a carriage the size of a house flown by horses whose hooves are as big as dinner plates. The school carriage is pale blue and painted with the Beauxbatons' coat of arms: two crossed golden wands, each emitting three stars.

According to student Fleur Delacour, the school serves delicious food, its pupils wear blue and grey silk uniforms, and statues of ice that glitter like diamonds are used at Christmas to flank its halls instead of suits of armor. While only female students of Beauxbatons are included in the Potter film, the book implies that the school is co-ed since Hogwarts students Parvati and Padma Patil are asked to dance by two Beauxbatons boys at the Yule Ball.

Sweden. The Durmstrang Institute, a Scandinavian wizarding school, located in the northernmost region of Sweden, is first mentioned in Chapter 11 when Harry, Ron, and Hermione overhear a conversation Draco Malfoy is having on the Hogwarts Express:

> "...Father actually considered sending me to Durmstrang rather than Hogwarts, you know. He knows the headmaster, you see. Well, you know his opinion of Dumbledore — the man's such a Mudblood-lover — and Durmstrang doesn't admit that sort of riffraff. But Mother didn't like the idea of me going to school so far away. Father says Durmstrang takes a far more sensible line than Hogwarts about the Dark Arts. Durmstrang students actually learn them, not just the defense rubbish we do...."

Durmstrang, like Hogwarts School of Witchcraft and Wizardry, is in a castle, but the building is not quite as big as Hogwarts. According to Pottermore, it is only four stories tall, and fires are only lit for magical purposes. It is described as having very extensive grounds surrounded by lakes and mountains. In addition, the school is deemed 'Unplottable' because it prefers to conceal its whereabouts so the other schools cannot steal its secrets. The Institute is said to be in the northernmost regions of either Sweden or Norway, although it might have been located in the Baltic States or in Karelia, which is in western Russia, and eastern Finland by the Baltic Sea. Indeed, their students' arrival at Hogwarts by ship implies that Durmstrang is located somewhere at the seaside or by some river or major lake.

Having existed since at least 1294, Durmstrang is one of the three schools that competes in the Triwizard Tournament and is willing to accept international students from as far afield as Bulgaria.

Though Durmstrang does not admit Muggle-borns, it is shown that certain students do not necessarily share this prejudice. Indeed, in 1994, Viktor Krum attends the Yule Ball with Hermione Granger, who is Muggle-born and therefore excluded from the campus. In addition, because the school is situated so far north, the students wear fur capes as part of their uniform to combat the cold.

The prestigious school is not the only Potter-related reference to Scandinavia. The Swedish Short-Snout is a species of dragon native to Sweden. According to Pottermore, its scales are silvery blue, and it emits a powerful, brilliant blue flame hot enough to reduce timber and bone to ashes in seconds. Its attractive skin is much sought after for the making of gloves and shields. It prefers to live in wild, uninhabited areas; thus, the breed rarely comes into contact with humans and has a higher survival rate than most dragons. Due to its agile flying ability and extremely hot fire, the Short-Snout is a dangerous species.

In the 1994 Triwizard Tournament, Cedric Diggory of Hogwarts has to face a Short-Snout in the First Task. He transfigures a rock into a dog to distract the dragon and retrieves the Golden egg that it is guarding.

Hungary. As referenced earlier in *Dracula*, Hungary is a landlocked country in Central Europe, bisected by the Danube River. The Hungarian Horntail is a dragon native to Hungary and considered one of the most dangerous breeds. According to Pottermore, it has black scales and is lizard-like in appearance. It also has yellow eyes with vertical pupils like a cat's, bronze horns, and similarly colored spikes that protrude from its nasty long tail, which it uses fiercely in combat. The dragon's roar is a yowling, screeching scream, and its flame can reach fifty feet. Because of its far-shooting flame, the Horntail's breath reaches extremely high temperatures as it makes a stone turn red hot within seconds. Its eggs are cement-colored and particularly hard-shelled. The Horntail's foods of choice include cattle, sheep, goats, and, whenever possible, humans.

"I don't envy the one who gets the Horntail. Vicious thing. Its back end's as dangerous as its front."

— Charlie Weasley about the first challenge
of the Triwizard Tournament.

Known for being one of the most vicious and aggressive dragon breeds, they become even more hostile and ferocious when protecting their young. Along with their viciousness, tail spikes, and fiery breath, Horntails are extremely fast in flight, able to keep up with a Firebolt broomstick — a broom capable of going from 0 to 150 miles per hour in 10 seconds. This is demonstrated in the Triwizard Tournament's First Task when Harry unwillingly picks the Horntail as his dragon to face while seizing its golden egg.

"Oh, don't worry about 'em, Harry, they're seriously misunderstood creatures — [Horntail breathes fires a bit too close to Harry and Hagrid's position] ...Although, I have to admit that Horntail is a right nasty piece of work."

— Hagrid about the Hungarian Horntail

Wales, United Kingdom. Wales is a country in southwest Great Britain recognized for its rocky coastline, mountainous national parks, distinctive Welsh language, and Celtic culture. The United Kingdom has not been brought up as a location in this appendix due to Chapter Seven being devoted strictly to the subject. However, an exception is being made here to discuss the different breeds of dragons used for the Tri-Wizard Tournament. The third breed, the Common Welsh Green dragon or just Welsh Green, is a native of Wales and nests in the higher mountain regions where a reservation is set up. Pottermore explains that this dragon is a comparatively subdued breed (except for the rare instance of the Ilfracombe Incident in 1932, when a rogue Common Welsh Green dragon attacked a group of sunbathers). It prefers to prey mainly on sheep and other small mammals, avoiding human contact altogether. The Welsh Green's roar is somewhat unique and melodious. It issues its fire in narrow jets and lays eggs the color of earthy brown, flecked with green. According to Pottermore, "It is possible that a young Common Welsh Green may have been the actual cause of the Great Fire of London."

Fleur Delacour faces this dragon breed for the First Task of the Triwizard Tournament in 1994, enchanting the creature into a magical slumber to retrieve her golden egg.

Harry: "But there aren't wild dragons in Britain?"

Ron: "Of course there are. Common Welsh Green and Hebridean Blacks. The Ministry of Magic has a job hushing them up, I can tell you. Our lot have to keep putting spells on Muggles who've spotted them, to make them forget."

— Harry Potter and Ronald Weasley

China. China is an especially populated nation in East Asia whose immense landscape is comprised of savannahs, deserts, foothills, lakes, rivers, and more than 14,000 km of shoreline. Beijing, its capital, fuses contemporary architecture with ancient sites like the Forbidden City palace complex and the historic Tiananmen Square. Shanghai is a worldwide economic center of skyscrapers, and the famous Great Wall of China travels east-west across the country's north.

The Chinese Fireball, also known as the Liondragon, is a dragon native to China. The Fireball is crimson and even scaled with an outlying of gilded spikes around its snub-snouted face and dreadfully bulging eyes. According to Rowling, its name originates from the mushroom-shaped blaze that emits from its nostrils when angered, along with the enormous mushroom-shaped flame it shoots from its mouth. The Fireball, which weighs between two and four tons, is aggressive; but unlike other dragons, it is more accepting of its own kind — such as consenting to share its territory with up to two other dragons. The Chinese Fireball generally produces females that are larger than males. They are purported to be very fast and clever, and their eggs — which are prized for use in Chinese wizardry — are vivid scarlet speckled with gold. The Fireball's diet comprises mainly mammals but usually prefers pigs and humans. Like the other dragons previously discussed, a Chinese Fireball is brought to Hogwarts by Charlie Weasley and used as one of the obstacles in the First Task of the Triwizard Tournament in 1994. Viktor Krum faces the dragon in an attempt to retrieve the golden egg it is guarding by utilizing a Conjunctivitis Curse. This spell temporarily blinds the dragon, causing it to crush its own eggs. Points are taken off Krum's score due to retrieving a broken golden egg.

Hagrid: "What breeds you got here, Charlie." But there aren't wild dragons in Britain?"

Charlie: "— and a Chinese Fireball, that's the red."

— Rubius Hagrid and Charlie Weasley

Book 5: The Order of the Phoenix

Tibet. An occupied region of China, Tibet is nicknamed the 'Roof of the World' due to its lofty Tibetan plateau and towering peaks on the northern side of the Himalayas, sharing Mt. Everest with Nepal. Its capital, Lhasa, is the site of hilltop Potala Palace, once the Dalai Lama's winter home, and Jokhang Temple, Tibet's spiritual heart, revered for its golden statue of the young Buddha. Likewise, the yeti were indigenous to the Tibetan mountains. Pottermore claims the creature is frequently sighted by Muggles, and, as a result, Tibet is deemed one of the major offenders of Clause 73 of the International Statute of Wizarding Secrecy. Thus, an International Task Force is permanently stationed in the mountain ranges of Tibet to try to contain the problem. In Chapter 5, Mr. Weasley explains to Harry various activities certain members of the order have been engaged in while Harry is at the Dursley's for the summer months. Because Sirius Black is still being tracked down by the Ministry of Magic, Kingsley Shacklebolt, the Auror leading the investigation and one who recognizes that Sirius is innocent, misleads the officials into believing that Sirius is hiding in Tibet.

"— Kingsley Shacklebolt's been a real asset too. He's in charge of the hunt for Sirius, so he's been feeding the Ministry information that Sirius is in Tibet."

Assyria. Assyria was a main Mesopotamian East Semitic-speaking realm and empire of the ancient Near East and the Levant. It survived as a state as early as the 25th century BC in the form of the Assur city-state until its fall between 612 BC and 599 BC, crossing the Early to Middle Bronze Age through to the late Iron Age. Although in the Muggle world, the region no longer bears this name, it still exists in the wizarding world. Indeed, in Chapter 10, Neville Longbottom explains to Harry that Assyria is where his Uncle Algie got his Mimbulus Mimbletonia, a stunted gray potted cactus covered with boils as opposed to spines and which squirted thick, rancid, manure-smelling 'Stinksap' as its defense mechanism.

"Harry stared at the thing. It was pulsating slightly, giving it the rather sinister look of some diseased internal organ.

"It's really, really rare," said Neville, beaming. "I don't know if there's one in the greenhouse at Hogwarts, even. I can't wait to show it to Professor Sprout. My great-uncle Algie got it for me in Assyria. I'm going to see if I can breed from it."

Asia. Known as Earth's biggest and most populated continent, Asia is located primarily in the Eastern and Northern Hemispheres. It shares the continental landmass of Eurasia with the continent of Europe and the continental landmass of Afro-Eurasia with both Europe and Africa. Libatius Borage's *Asiatic Anti-Venoms* is a textbook about potions. At the beginning of Chapter 16, Harry refers to this manual while he completes some fifth-year Potions homework for Professor Snape. Harry does not seem too occupied with it as he fictitiously scans a page as he ponders Hermione's suggestion to teach Defense Against the Dark Arts to interested students.

"Harry did not answer at once. He pretended to be perusing a page of Asiatic Anti-Venoms, because he did not want to say what was in his mind."

Poland. Officially known as the Republic of Poland, Poland is a country in Central Europe and a unitary state split into 16 administrative subdivisions, covering an area of 312,679 square kilometers (120,726 sq mi) with a primarily temperate climate. Amongst a population of over 38.5 million citizens, Poland is the sixth most populous member state of the European Union. Poland's capital and largest city is Warsaw. It borders Germany, the Czech Republic, Slovakia, Ukraine, Belarus, Lithuania, and Russia. In the wizarding world, magical creatures such as the Doxy, Dugbog, Graphorn, Nogtail, and Troll can all be found in Poland. Grodzisk Goblins are the most popular and best Polish Quidditch team, with arguably the world's most innovative Seeker, Josef Wronski. In Chapter 19, the Gryffindor Quidditch team feels that a save Ron Wesley makes in practice is comparable to an internationally known Keeper against Poland's top Chaser:

> "During one memorable practice, he [Ron Weasley] had hung one-handed from his broom and kicked the Quaffle so hard away from the goal hoop that it soared the length of the pitch and through the center hoop at the other end. The rest of the team felt this save compared favorably with one made recently by Barry Ryan, the Irish International Keeper, against Poland's top Chaser, Ladislaw Zamojski."

In Chapter 20, Hagrid recounts his adventure with Madame Maxime in the northeast mountains inhabited by giants; however, he socializes with Polish trolls along the way:

> "We chanced a bit o' magic after that, and it wasn' a bad journey. Ran inter a couple o' mad trolls on the Polish border…"

Minsk, Belarus. Minsk is Belarus' largest and capital city, situated on the Svislach and the Nyamiha Rivers. It is the administrative capital of the Commonwealth of Independent States (CIS). As the national capital, Minsk has a special administrative status in Belarus and is the administrative center of the Minsk Region and Minsk raion (district). In 2013, it had a population of 2,002,600. In 1995, while journeying from Dijon, France, to the Eastern European mountains to meet with the Giants, Hagrid quarrels with a vampire in Minsk. As Hagrid explains to Harry, Ron, and Hermione in Chapter 20:

> "…an' I had a sligh' disagreement with a vampire in a pub in Minsk, but apart from tha', couldn't' a bin smoother."

The mountains of Northern Europe. Northern Europe is comprised mostly of Fennoscandia, the cape of Jutland, the Baltic delta, located in the east, along with numerous islands that lie offshore from mainland Northern Europe, Greenland, and the main European continent. The area is made up of volcanic islands of the far northwest, notably Iceland and Jan Mayen, the mountainous western seaboard, extending from the steep, rocky areas of Great Britain and Ireland to the Scandinavian mountains peaking in Norway, the central north precipitous hills of Sweden — commonly referred to as the foothills of the Scandinavian mountains — and the large eastern plain, which contains, Lithuania, Latvia, Estonia, and Finland. In Chapter 20, Hagrid provides a detailed account of his trip to the Northern Europe Mountains to visit with the giants to gain their support in building Dumbledore's army to fight against Lord Voldemort. A giant is an extremely huge humanoid that theoretically can mature to roughly twenty-five feet tall and appear to be an oversized, hairy human. Pottermore suggests that some may have bestial features, such as protruding sharp molars. Once a powerful and nearly unstoppable race, giants began to combine themselves into tribes since their numbers have greatly dwindled in recent centuries. Hagrid and Madame Maxime visit a giant tribe in the mountains of northern Europe led by the strongest of the species, beasts known as the 'Gurg.'

> "They're not meant ter live together, giants ... they can't help themselves, they half kill each other every few weeks."
>
> — Rubeus Hagrid [sic]

Book 6: The Half-Blood Prince

The Canary Islands. A self-governing community of Spain, The Canary Islands, is located off the shoreline of northwestern Africa. They are made up of rocky volcanic isles recognized for their black- and white-sand beaches. Pottermore notes that the weather of Tenerife is considered noteworthy by the International section of *The Daily Prophet*, proposing that wizards are living there. In Chapter 4, Horace Slughorn resides in a house in Budleigh Babberton while its Muggle owners are on holiday for the summer in the Canary Islands.

> "I've been on the move for a year. Never stay in one place more than a week. Move from Muggle house to Muggle house — the owners of this place are on holiday in the Canary Islands — it's been very pleasant, I'll be sorry to leave."
>
> — Slughorn to Dumbledore

Book 7: The Deathly Hallows

Greece. A country in southeastern Europe, Greece is made up of thousands of islands all over the Aegean and Ionian seas. Prominent in the ancient world, it is frequently referred to as the cradle of Western civilization. The capital Athens contains remnants of historical landmarks such as the 5th-century B.C. Acropolis citadel with the Parthenon temple. Greece is also popular, from the black sandy beaches of Santorini to the festive resorts of Mykonos. Pottermore states that the country is known for native mythical creatures — such as the Basilisk, Cyclops, and Griffin — and home to powerful wizards, Andros the Invincible, Falco Aesalon, and Herpo the Foul, just to name a few. In Chapter 2, Harry read Albus Dumbledore's obituary written by Elphias Doge, which mentioned he wrote to Albus when he was caring for his younger brother and sister and recounting his travels to Greece.

> "That was the period of our lives when we had least contact. I wrote to Albus, describing, perhaps insensitively, the wonders of my journey, from narrow escapes from chimaeras in Greece to the experiments of the Egyptian alchemists."

North America. The Term 'Native American' is used to signify a member of any of the indigenous peoples of North America. Pottermore informs that the existence of North America was known to witches and wizards long before European explorers founded the continent. Because methods of magical travel — such as brooms and Apparition — have allowed distant magical communities to maintain contact with each other from the Middle Ages onwards, the magical communities of Africa and Europe have been in touch with the Native American magical community before the Pilgrims sailed on the Mayflower. Native American witches and wizards practiced wandless magic and were particularly skilled when it came to animal and plant charms. Pottermore further suggests that their potion-making knowledge is far more advanced than Europe's. Native American witches and wizards were often accepted members of their respective tribes, attaining positions of prominence and respect as medicine men or skilled hunters. However, others were ostracized within their tribes, assuming they were possessed by demons. In Chapter 11, Harry examines a picture of Albus Dumbledore's family and thinks his mother bears a resemblance to Native Americans.

> "The mother, Kendra, had jet-black hair pulled into a high bun. Her face had a carved quality about it. Harry thought of photos of Native Americans he'd seen as he studied her dark eyes, high cheekbones, and straight nose, formally composed above a high-necked silk gown."

Germany or Bulgaria. Nurmengard is a wizarding prison probably near Germany or Bulgaria, as Pottermore proposes. With respect to enchanted fortifications, its exact defensive charms remain unknown; however, it is recognized to have anti-Apparition wards similar to Hogwarts. In Chapter 18, Nurmengard is described as the prison that Gellert Grindelwald builds to detain his enemies and certain Muggles. The entrance is branded with the symbol of the Deathly Hallows along with the legend "For the Greater Good." After Dumbledore beats Grindelwald in their historic duel, the prisoners are freed, and Grindelwald himself is incarcerated in the top-most cell. Nurmengard is depicted in *The Deathly Hallows* when Voldemort arrives at the prison searching for Grindelwald and information about the Elder Wand. When Grindelwald refuses to provide him with any details, Voldemort kills Grindelwald in his own prison.

Hermione: "They say 'For the Greater Good' was even carved over the entrance to Nurmengard."

Harry: "What's Nurmengard?"

Hermione: "The prison Grindelwald had built to hold his opponents. He ended up in there himself, once Dumbledore had caught him."

This chapter shows that it is possible to travel the entire world while reading *Dracula* and *The Harry Potter Series*. However, the extensive geography references have caused many serious fans of both authors to purchase airline tickets to go abroad for the ultimate enthusiast holiday. Indeed, by Googling the phrase 'a Dracula or Harry Potter vacation,' one will find there are pages and pages of itineraries, packages, tours, and ideas or insider tips, tricks, and secrets to take the next giant step for hardcore aficionados.

It is interesting to note how many of the countries featured in each text overlap — the most obvious ones being Romania, England, Hungary, and Bulgaria. Certainly, their rich history lends itself to captivating and colorful storytelling. Although a few vampire and magical references never hurt anyone either!

Acknowledgments

I wish to thank the following individuals who inspired my creativity over the years, helped shape this vision, and ultimately assisted in taking this idea to print:

First and foremost, I would like to recognize my paternal father, Kelly Cherry, for buying me a graphic version of *Dracula* in 1976 and encouraging me along the way to write and rewrite, and my heavenly father for gifting me with this skill which I now believe to be a talent.

I would like to acknowledge my high school English teacher, Marilyn Proffitt, for encouraging, praising, and allowing me to turn in and grade my writing projects that were much, much longer than required.

A distinctive salute goes out to *Dracula* and Bram Stoker scholars Dacre Stoker, John Edgar Browning, David J. Skal, and Elizabeth Miller for their works, friendship, and correspondence which have kept a fire burning in my belly.

Kudos to my son Jacob Cherry who patiently listened to *Dracula* and all seven Potter books in the car to and from school every day.

I tip my hat to the wonderful and extremely talented actor Jim Dale for bringing all seven Potter books to life in a way only he could have amazingly accomplished.

Thank you, Katie Ledbetter Hale, who encouraged me to read the Harry Potter series. You were correct, my dear friend, "they are not just for kids."

My most sincere gratitude and respect to Bram Stoker and J.K. Rowling for blessing and sharing their amazing talents with the world.

And finally, I give my deepest love and appreciation to Kevin Scott Bilbrey, who is almost as big of a *Dracula* and Potter fan as I, and beyond anyone else, made this book possible.

Bibliography

ABC News (2009, Jul 15) *Inside the Magical World of 'Harry Potter'* Author. Retrieved from https://abcnews.go.com/Entertainment/story?id= 8081011&page=1

BBC Radio4 (2005, Dec 10) Living with Harry Potter. Retrieved from http://www.accio-quote.org/articles/2005/1205-bbc-fry.html

Colavito, Jason. (2011) What Was the Scholomance? Retrieved from http://www.jasoncolavito.com/scholomance-the-devils-school.html

FANDOM powered by Wikia (2019, Mar 11) Harry Potter WIKI. Retrieved from https://harrypotter.fandom.com/wiki

Gander, Kashmira. Independent. (2015, Mar 24) J.K. Rowling responds to a fan tweeting she 'can't see' Dumbledore being gay retrieved from https://www.independent.co.uk/news/people/jk-rowling-responds-to-fan-who-tweeted-she-cant-see-dumbledore-being-gay-10131369.html

Gerard, Emily. The Land Beyond the Forest: Facets, Figures, and Fancies From Transylvania. New York: Harper & Brothers, Franklin Square. 1888.

Hearn, Chester G. *Lincoln and McClennan at War*. Louisiana: Louisiana State University Press, 2012

Hogwarts Professor Thoughts for Serious Readers (2007, Oct 21) "I always thought of Dumbledore as gay." [ovation.] Retrieved from http://www.hogwartsprofessor.com/i-always-thought-of-dumbledore-as-gay-ovation/

Holy Bible, New International Version (New York, 1978)

LightWorkers, The (2007, Oct 17) Top 4 Christian Moments in Harry Potter retrieved from https://www.lightworkers.com/harry-potter/

Mbl. is (2017, Mar 6) Icelandic version of *Dracula*, Makt myrkranna, turns out to be Swedish in origin retrieved from https://icelandmonitor.mbl.is/news/culture_and_living/2017/03/06/icelandic_version_of_dracula_makt_myrkranna_turns_o/

Melton, J. Gordon. The Completely Revamped Vampire Book: The Encyclopedia of the Undead. MI: Visible Ink Press. 1999.

Poe, Edgar Allan. *The Fall of the House of Usher*. New York: Octopus Books. 1984.

Potter Cast 130: The One with J.K. Rowling (2007, Dec 18) retrieved from http://www.the-leaky-cauldron.org/2007/12/18/pottercast-130-the-one-with-j-k-rowling/

Ramisetti, Kirthana. *NY Daily News* (2015, Mar 25) J.K. Rowling strikes back at fan questioning Dumbledore's sexuality retrieved from http://www.nydailynews.com/entertainment/rowling-calls-fan-questioning-dumbledore-sexuality-article-1.2161784

Renton, Jennie (2001, Oct 28) *The Story Behind the Potter Legend.* Retrieved from https://www.hp-lexicon.org/source/interviews/smh/

Rowling, J.K. *Harry Potter and the Sorcerer's Stone.* New York: Scholastic, Inc. 1997

Rowling, J.K. *Harry Potter and the Chamber of Secrets.* New York: Scholastic, Inc. 1998

Rowling, J.K. *Harry Potter and the Prisoner of Azkaban.* New York: Scholastic, Inc. 1999

Rowling, J.K. *Harry Potter and the Goblet of Fire.* New York: Scholastic, Inc. 2000

Rowling, J.K. *Harry Potter and the Order of the Phoenix.* New York: Scholastic, Inc. 2003

Rowling, J.K. (2004, Aug 15) J.K. Rowling at the Edinburgh Book Festival. Retrieved from http://www.accio-quote.org/articles/2004/0804-ebf.htm

Rowling, J.K. *Harry Potter and the Half-Blood Prince.* New York: Scholastic, Inc. 2005

Rowling, J.K. *Harry Potter and the Deathly Hallows.* New York: Scholastic, Inc. 2007

Rowling, J.K. (2019, Mar 11) Professor Quirrell By J.K. Rowling. Retrieved from https://www.pottermore.com/writing-by-jk-rowling/professor-quirrell,

Rowling, J.K. (2019, Mar 13) Azkaban By J.K. Rowling. Retrieved from https://www.pottermore.com/writing-by-jk-rowling/azkaban

Silverman, Stephen M. (2006, Jan 10) J.K. Rowling Admits Obsession with Death. Retrieved from https://people.com/celebrity/j-k-rowling-admits-obsession-with-death/

Skal, David J. Something in the Blood: The Untold Story of Bram Stoker, the Man Who Wrote 'Dracula.' New York. Liveright Publishing Corporation. 2016.

Stoker, Bram. *The Essential Dracula.* Edited by Leonard Wolf. New York: Penguin Books, 1993.

Sutherland, John. *Who Is Dracula's Father?* GoogleBooks.com. 2017.

White, James (2009, Jul 15) *The Story Behind Harry Potter.* Retrieved from https://www.gamesradar.com/the-story-behind-harry-potter/

About the Author

CALVIN H. CHERRY is a published author and fantasy and horror scholar. He maintains an author Facebook page and YouTube channel where he posts weekly blogs (written or video), sharing information about the research effort, writing progression, and publication process that went into his debut novel, *STOKER: Evolution of a Vampire* ©2018, along with lectures about Bram Stoker, Dracula, Vlad the Impaler and all things vampires. He has spoken at numerous colleges and bookstores around the southeast and has been interviewed by several radio and news stations about his novel and his passion for literature and writing. He has also participated in many podcasts and writing blogs where he was asked questions about his travels to the actual locations used in Bram Stoker and J.K. Rowling's works. He served a combination of twenty-two years in the US Navy (active and reservist) and has spent thirty years in the insurance industry. He earned his Bachelor of Business Administration from Kennesaw State University and has his Project Management Professional and Six Sigma Green-belt certifications. He is a Georgian native, currently living in Macon — the musically influenced "Heart of Georgia" — with his husband, Kevin, and their feline child Francis.